Fast and Furious

FAST AND FURIOUS
The Story of
American International Pictures

by
Mark Thomas McGee

McFarland & Company, Inc. 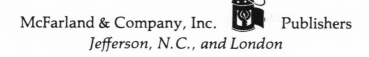 Publishers
Jefferson, N.C., and London

Title page drawing by Mark Thomas McGee

Library of Congress Cataloging in Publication Data

McGee, Mark Thomas, 1947–
Fast and furious.

Includes index.
1. American International Pictures (Firm).
I. Title.
PN1999.A6M35   1984   384'.8'0979494   83-42892

ISBN 0-89950-091-9

Printed in the United States of America

McFarland & Company, Inc., Publishers
Box 611, Jefferson, North Carolina 28640

For Wendy Wright, Danielle Milici,
Bill and Louise McGee,
and Randy Robertson. My little friends.

Acknowledgments

My sincerest thanks to the following people who made this book possible:

Forry Ackerman	Beverly Garland
John Agar	Bert Gordon
William Asher	Jonathan Haze
John Ashley	Albert Kallis
Dick Bakalyan	David Kramarsky
Edward Bernds	Jacques Marquette
Whit Bissell	Ib Melchior
Paul Blaisdell	Dick Miller
Leon Blender	Betty Nicholson
Bob Burns	Wyott Ordung
Robert Clarke	Joe Solomon
Herman Cohen	Herb Strock
Roger Corman	Les Tremayne
Jim Danforth	Martin Varno
Beach Dickerson	Bill Warren

Special thanks to Sam Arkoff, Alex Gordon, Chuck Griffith and Susan (Hart) Hofheinz — and to the late Barry Brown who loaned me his taped interviews with Allison Hayes and Bruno Ve Sota.

Thank you, all.

Table of Contents

Foreword

From July 26 to August 28, 1979, The New York Museum of Modern Art screened 39 American International Pictures — *The Abominable Dr. Phibes, The Amazing Colossal Man, The Amityville Horror, Beach Party, Black Caesar, Bloody Mama, The Bonnie Parker Story, Born Losers, Boxcar Bertha, A Bucket of Blood, Chastity, The Comedy of Terrors, Cooley High, Dementia 13, Dillinger, The Fast and the Furious, Girls in Prison, Heavy Traffic, House of Usher, Invasion of the Saucer-Men, The Island of Dr. Moreau, I Was a Teenage Werewolf, Machine Gun Kelly, Master of the World, A Matter of Time, Night Tide, Panic in Year Zero, Psych-Out, Rolling Thunder, Sisters, Submarine Seahawk, Tales of Terror, Three in the Attic, The Trip, The Unholy Rollers, What's Up Tiger Lily?, The Wild Angels, Wild in the Streets, "X" — The Man with the X-Ray Eyes* — to honor AIP's 25th anniversary.

Samuel Z. Arkoff, the company's surviving cofounder, assured the crowd at a press luncheon that when he and his partner, James H. Nicholson, made the pictures the thought furthest from their minds was that they'd end up in a museum. "We went into business to make money, for ourselves, for franchise distributors and for exhibitors," Sam explained. The Museum's retrospective validated his belief that if you can hang around long enough you'll become respectable.

When Jim and Sam opened shop in 1954 as the American Releasing Corporation the motion picture business was in a turmoil. Half of the nation's theatres weren't breaking even. The Supreme Court's decision to separate exhibition from productions, which took nearly five years to swing into effect, started a war between the studios and the exhibitors. No longer able to enjoy the luxury of guaranteed bookings, the studios began asking for higher percentages of the boxoffice. Television was already cutting into the exhibitors' profits so they began looking for bargains. AIP offered an alternative: black and white double feature programs, tailored to the juvenile trade and for a fraction of what a single feature cost from the majors. How a former exhibitor and a lawyer were able to do this, at a time when two of their competitors (Republic and RKO) went out of business, is what this book is about.

The Museum's program notes pointed out that "a surprising number of AIP films have come to be regarded as classics," although a quick look at the titles chosen for the retrospective reveals nary a classic in the bunch. There may be a cult favorite or two — *A Bucket of Blood, Sisters, What's Up Tiger Lily?* — but a bonafide, enduring classic? Never. Quality was not part of the AIP story. In the early days, films were shot in ten days or less for $100,000 or less. Screenplays were written, often by Sam's brother-in-law, based on the titles that Jim would cook up. The entire advertising campaign for *The Beast with 1,000,000 Eyes* was ready to go before a single frame of the movie had been shot. Directors were selected for their speed, not their artistic abilities, which gave young, inexperienced producers and directors an opportunity to show their stuff. Francis Ford Coppola, Martin Scorsese, Brian De Palma and John Milius all got their start at AIP. You can also catch early performances by Peter Fonda, Jack Nicholson, Sally Kellerman, Charles Bronson, Richard Dreyfuss, Michael "Touch" Connors, Margot Kidder, Richard Pryor, Cher and Bruce Dern.

The Museum's notes went on to explain that "the entire body of work may be seen as a striking reflection of a quarter-century of popular culture. Sociologists may argue that this phenomenon requires some interpretation, but there is no denying the verve, vitality, and creative energy with which AIP set about capturing the period." This is my cue to say that the intention of this book is to interpret the phenomenon, a lie that would be obvious after reading one or two pages. I wrote this book because I love AIP, which is not to say that I love every AIP movie or that I love any of them. I love what the company meant to me when I was a ten-year-old looking for entertainment. In those days millions of dollars weren't poured into the kinds of movies I wanted to see because horror, science fiction and youth-oriented comedies and dramas weren't considered fit properties for respectable producers and directors. The field was left wide open for the maverick low-budget producers to exploit. A child raised on *Star Wars* and *Fast Times at Ridgemont High* would have little patience for something like *The Angry Red Planet* or *Beach Party*. True, we had *Forbidden Planet* and *Rebel without a Cause*, which were terrific in their day but were exceptions to the rule. AIP's juvenile fantasies may have been weak tea (or dishwater) but they were almost the only game in town. Where else but in an AIP movie could you see something as outrageous as a sixty foot tall bald man spear a normal-sized doctor with a gigantic hypodermic needle? Or Marla English, stripped naked and tied to a stake on top of an anthill?* Or John Ashley straddling two

*This scene from Flesh and the Spur was added to the film after the producers saw it depicted in Al Kalis's ad art (completed before he had the opportunity to read the script).

Samuel Zachary Arkoff (left), vice president, and James Harvey Nicholson, president, AIP, in 1970.

speeding hot rods? These moments are still precious to me. I confess that I even applauded during scenes in *Jet Attack* which is a truly awful picture.

Throughout my life I've attempted to connect with AIP. When I was ten I called them. I was surprised when, instead of a secretary, Sam Arkoff answered the phone. I was not unaware of his coarse reputation*

---

*Sam told the authors of Kings of the Bs *that he drove the black car and Jim drove the white car. Jim was the PR man, dressed in white, sporting a big smile. The good cop. Sam was the overweight hatchet man. He was the one who handled the problems. The bad cop. In the later years, when Sam once dropped sixty pounds and Jim porked up to the point that he was the heavier of the two, Sam told a crowd of exhibitors, "From now on, Jim has the black car."*

even then so I was more nervous than I would have normally been which put me second only to the way Don Knotts appeared on the old Steve Allen show. But Sam wasn't coarse nor was he abrupt. He rapped with me a little bit about the movies they were planning to make and told me they were in the process of moving. Sam kept calling me "honey" because my voice hadn't yet changed but I never bothered to correct him. It didn't matter. I was talking to Samuel Arkoff! It was nothing short of sensational.

Two years later I saw Vincent Price at an amusement park. I had just seen *House of Usher* and he asked me if I liked it. "Yes," I said, even though I thought it was a bore. No reason to hurt his feelings. The next week I saw the picture again. And again. And again.

One morning a friend of mine and I lied our way onto the set of *Comedy of Terrors*. Jim Nicholson showed up around noon. Suddenly, the crew got an attack of motivation. I didn't understand what had gotten them until I saw the gaunt man in the white suit. It was the first and last time I ever saw Jim Nicholson. We talked about *Circus of Horrors*. After that, my friend and I chatted with Vincent Price, Peter Lorre and Jacques Tourneur. Basil Rathbone arrived in the late afternoon, strutting with great purpose past my friend who stopped him for an autograph. Making sure my friend realized it was an inconvenience, the actor consented. But when Rathbone saw that issue of *Famous Monsters* magazine, the issue with his likeness on the cover, he screamed, "Oh! No! Not one of those things!" and disappeared into his dressing room. Now and then I'd catch him looking at us and I heard him ask one of the grips, "What are those boys doing here?" We were on our way out when Vince insisted that we meet Basil. I told him that we sort of had on the way in. Vince shook his head. "Well, you simply can't leave without meeting Basil. You wait here." Off he went toward Basil's dressing room. "Basil," we heard him say, "there's a couple of boys out here who would like to meet you." At the top of his lungs Basil screamed, "I don't want to meet them. Take them away."

If that story has any relevance to this book it's because it's the only story related on these pages based on my own experience. And it's had a goodly number of years to be embellished. The other stories were told to me by the people who were there at the time. Their stories too have had a goodly number of years to be embellished. Director Herb Strock told me that when they were filming *How to Make a Monster*, an inebriated effects man set fire to the chamber of horrors set. The director had to race his actors through their lines before the set burned to the ground. (The set was supposed to burn. It's just that the effects man decided to rehearse the gas jets early.) The producer of the film said the incident never happened. There's an old saying: Nothing spoils a good story like an eyewitness.

There's another old saying: When in doubt print the legend. So I compromised and printed all of the stories.

One of my favorite stories (which you'll find a more detailed account of later on in the book) has producer Jerry Wald attacking Jim and Sam at an AIP sponsored luncheon for exhibitors. In front of the crowd, Wald said AIP movies could ruin the industry. That was 1958. Five years later Jim and Sam were hailed as "Producers of the Year" by the Allied States Association of Motion Picture Owners. (That was the year *"X"—The Man with the X-Ray Eyes* won the Silver Globe Award at the First International Science Fiction Film Festival at Trieste, Italy.) In 1964 the Theatre Owners of America called them "Master Showmen of the Decade." They were honored three times by *Motion Picture Exhibitor* for being among the top ten producers. In 1971 they received the Motion Pictures Pioneer's Award.

"I am privileged, as your dinner chairman, to extend to you a warm welcome to the 1971 Motion Picture Pioneers' Reunion," said Mike Frankovich. "It is a special pleasure for me this year because we are honoring two very close friends of mine—Sam Arkoff and Jim Nicholson—two men who have made their mark on the motion picture world and whose spirit and drive typify all that is good and exciting about this wonderful business of ours."

There were letters of congratulations from people like James Carreras of Hammer Films in England, Vincent Price, Jack Valenti (president of the Motion Picture Association) and...

> Dear Sam and Jim:
> It is pleasant to know that the industry to which I owe so much has chosen to honor two of the men to whom it owes so much.
> The state of which I am administrator joins the motion picture community in the pride of their accomplishments. Sam and Jim, the Governor of California congratulates you and wishes you many more years of success, progress and pioneering accomplishment.
>
> Ronald Reagan

Be warned that this book primarily focusses on AIP's first 15 years. A more detailed account of the company's closing days will have to come from another writer. With that out of the way let's get started. Hope you enjoy it.

Mark McGee
La Crescenta, California
Summer 1983

One

Partners

Jim Nicholson was a warm man. He used to come over to our apartment every once in a while for dinner. The place was a dump. After I adopted my daughter and went to work for Jim he said, "Why don't you go find a house?" I told him I needed money. "Find a house," he said. "We'll find the money." And he loaned me the money.

— Leon Blender

No bullshit about Sam Arkoff. (I'm not talking about his speeches in front of public gatherings where he gives all this wisdom about the industry. That's all a crock of shit.) He was very straightforward and had an interesting dry sense of humor.

— Charles Griffith

James Hartford Nicholson sat behind his desk at Realart Pictures, where he worked as a general sales manager for Jack Broder, and thought about making motion pictures. Jim was positive he knew what the folks in the Bible Belt wanted to see. What Jim wanted to do was start his own releasing corporation. And fast. His days with Realart were numbered. The company earned most of its income from reissues of old Universal features. And the Universal library had just about been milked dry.

It was a bad time for the motion picture business. Half of the nation's 19,000 theatres weren't breaking even. Educators blamed the producers for underestimating the intelligence of the audience, advertising their movies like French postcards that talk. Producers blamed exhibitors for not having the sense to keep the butter for their popcorn hot. The exhibitors blamed television. CinemaScope, 3-D and Smell-O-Vision were just a few of the gimmicks used by desperate producers to give their product a "new and improved" look, "bigger and better" than the free entertainment at home. Nothing worked. As TV sales increased theatre attendance dropped. Just as sure as Jim Nicholson was bound and determined to make movies, 3,000 theatres had closed their doors.

1

While he was in grade school Jim converted the family basement into a theatre. Jim ran the projector. The films were rented from the local camera store or home-made. Jim's sister, Betty, sold tickets for a penny apiece and ran the concession stand, which usually consisted of lemonade.

During the Depression it was necessary for Percival and Esther Nicholson to part company and move in with their respective parents. Jim moved to Florida with his father. Betty went with Mom to Washington. Jim didn't get along well his his Grandmother. At 16 he took a bus to San Francisco where he'd been promised a job as an usher at the El Rey Theatre. The promise had come during his days as class president at Aptos Junior High. He often made arrangements to have special screenings at the theatre to raise money for the Red Cross. (Throughout his life, Jim Nicholson continued to use motion pictures as a means of raising money for charitable causes.)

Jim did a little of everything at the El Rey. He tore tickets, worked the snack bar, operated the elevator and eventually became projectionist. It wasn't exactly the aspect of the business he wanted to be in but it was closer than selling newspapers. Like the man in the circus who cleaned up after the elephants said to the real estate broker who offered him a job in real estate: "What? And quit show business?"

It was sinus trouble that forced Jim to seek a warmer climate. He moved out of his basement apartment in San Francisco and came to Los Angeles. He came down with scarlet fever and made tracks for Omaha. Percival and Esther were there, reunited. They'd help him get his strength back.

While in Omaha, Jim went to work for the Goldberg chain. He managed their Avenue and Arbor theatres. It was during his collections that Jim was shot.

He'd collected receipts from his own two theatres and the Military Theatre when Jim stopped at his home on 2906 T Avenue to pick up the Military's manager, James Schlatter. Schlatter rode with Jim to the Winn Theatre. They were headed downtown to pick up the receipts from the Town and State theatres when a car passed them on Hamilton Street. Neither Jim or Schlatter thought anything about it until that same car suddenly appeared in front of them, from the blackness of particularly poorly lit strip along Oregon trail. That's when Jim remembered that he'd seen the car before. Following him home one night from the theatre.

All at once someone was on Jim's running board. "Don't you know how to drive?" the man snarled.

Jim threw the car into reverse. The man on the running board pounded the window with the butt of his gun.

"Open the door," the man screamed. Then he gave up trying to

Dorothy Malone and John Ireland in "The Fast and the Furious" (1954), AIP's very first feature.

shatter the glass and fired a bullet through it instead. Jim felt the fire in his chest.

"Get the hell out of there," the man ordered, pointing his gun.

The two Jims were more than eager to comply. The gunman slid behind the wheel and fumbled with the button gearshift but he couldn't figure it out. He scooped up the bags of money and carried them to his own car instead and sped off into the night.

Schlatter watched from behind a bush, hoping to give the police the most accurate description possible. He and Jim raced toward the nearest house. It belonged to Ray Koontz. Mr. Koontz let them use his phone.

A police doctor treated Jim's wound which was minor. The bullet had only grazed his chest.

The bandits, and there were three according to Jim Schlatter, made off with $1,500.

It was during Jim's round that he met Sylvia Svoboda. She was employed by the Goldberg chain as an usherette. Six weeks later they became engaged and married in Iowa.

After his theatre went bust Jim and Sylvia came to Los Angeles. Jim worked as a spot man in a burlesque house for a while then found employment in radio. Just as he had as an usher, Jim did a number of things in radio. He wrote, acted and announced.

With the help of Joseph Moritz, Jim was able to buy a chain of theatres. He is credited with being one of the first to present TV on the theatre screen by showing the 1949 Rose Bowl game. His primary source of income, however, came from his coupling of the old classics like *Casablanca* and *The Maltese Falcon*, a practice that has since become quite popular. But in the late 40s Jim Nicholson was just about the only one doing it. His theatres were called the Academy of Proven Hits. And he usually played to packed houses. Seeing the success Jim was having convinced others to get in on the action. The market was soon cornered which left Jim with nothing to play. Business got so bad that he and his family took up residence in one of the theatres, the Markel on Hollywood Boulevard (which has since become a porno house). Jim was the projectionist. Sylvia sold the tickets. They both worked the snack bar.

Jim became ill. His lung collapsed. Leon Blender, a branch manager for Realart, took up a collection to send Jim to the hospital. Leon and Jim had become friends during Leon's days as a booker at 20th Century–Fox. When Jim was well, Leon was one of the first people he talked to about starting a distribution company. But Jim needed $2,500 and Leon didn't have it.

It was during his visit to the 1933 Chicago World's Fair that Samuel Zachary Arkoff, then only 15 years old, saw his first copy of *Variety*, a publication devoted to news about the motion picture industry. Sam was fascinated by the show-biz jargon. He'd always been a movie fan but then he believed everybody in America was a movie fan. Sam saw a lot of movies. Growing up in Fort Dodge, Iowa, there wasn't a lot to do except go the movies. Or the pool hall. But there was always a risk involved with the pool hall. His father, Louis, didn't think it was any place for a nice Jewish boy. If he caught Sam there he'd chase him out.

Sam continued to read *Variety*. He ordered it every week from the man who ran the pool hall. He paid his 15¢, took the magazine home and read it in secret, never daring to tell anyone about his plan to become a movie mogul. People might think he was nuts. They might laugh at him.

Certainly his father wouldn't care for the idea. To the owner of a small clothing store in a farm town during the Depression Hollywood was a fantasy. Something for others. Not Louis Arkoff and his children.

Louis had come from Russia, a Jew in a country not too fond of Jews. During the Russian-Japanese War Louis was drafted into the military, destined for Siberia. Like many young men at the time he deserted and came to America. He stayed with some relatives in New York. There, at the age of nineteen, he became an apprentice goldsmith. Next he worked for a jeweler in Chicago, later moved to Iowa where he met his bride-to-be, Helen Lurie, and opened the Louis Clothing Company.

Louis Arkoff was an intelligent man, although he had had little in the way of formal education. He devoured books, the only Jew in town who could read Hebrew books. He often sat in the back of his store and read any sort of book he could lay his hands on. Anyone dropping by might think the place deserted. A kind, intelligent man, Louis Arkoff was a lousy merchant.

In August of 1942 Sam Arkoff entered the Air Force. Overweight, his high blood pressure would have made him ineligible had not some friends given him some pills to lower it. He passed the physical and became a cryptographer. It was during this time that he met Hilda Rusoff, the woman he would eventually marry (in December of 1945), on a blind date. By that time Sam decided to become a lawyer and let Uncle Sam pay for his schooling. He hoped the profession would somehow lead him into the motion picture business. If not, it would at least be a dignified profession to be in. Something he could fall back on. Actually, even after Sam became a producer he never stopped being a lawyer. He simply became his own client.

Loyola, closed during the war, opened an accelerated course for veterans which Sam attended. After graduating he took up residency in the Lawyer's Building on Selma Avenue, between Hollywood and Sunset, one block east of Vine, a place owned by Abe Levin. Levin's place was full of lawyers, all of whom were involved in the entertainment business one way or another. Sam worked part-time for one of the attorneys to help pay for his office space, an arrangement that netted him the use of a secretary.

Many of Sam's clients were referred by Hilda's relatives who would never have thought asking Sam for legal assistance. He didn't have enough experience. Sam's other clients were would-be movie makers who never had any money. He became the patron saint of one-lung producers. Hank McCune was one of these clients, a tall, thin fellow with big ears who had been in the Air Force with Sam. Hank and Sam formed Video Associates and sold Hank's idea for a 30 minute sit-com to NBC. At a time when most everything on TV was live, *The Hank McCune Show* was on 16mm film for $5,500 an episode. It aired on Saturday night at 7:00 on September 9, 1950. *Variety* made note of an innovation in the soundtrack:

> Although the show is lensed on film without a studio audience, there are chuckles and yocks dubbed in. Whether this induces a jovial mood in home viewers is still to be determined, but the practice may have unlimited possibilities if it's spread to include canned peals of hilarity, thunderous ovations and gasps of sympathy.

Another of Sam's early clients was London-born Alex Gordon. Alex wrote for movie fan magazines when he was a boy. He and his brother, Richard, published *The Westerner*. He served in the British Army from 1942 to 1946 then joined Renown Pictures as a publicity director. A year later he came to the U.S. and worked as an assistant booker to Jack Harris, Walter Reade Theatres Circuit from 1948 to 1950. After that he was Gene Autry's public relations man. Wanting to be a producer he got involved in the production of an extremely low budget western, *The Outlaw Marshal*, put together by Johnny Carpenter, a stuntman turned actor. Edward D. Wood Jr., was the associate producer and the production manager. He made a breakdown and a budget which turned out to be completely inaccurate because Eddie was working from a second unit type of budget which nobody realized at the time. There were many things that Eddie didn't take into consideration as well. *The Outlaw Marshal* mushroomed from a $20,000 feature to a $57,000 feature. There were labor claims and lab liens against the picture. No withholding tax had been paid, which was and is a fairly common practice in the motion picture business. Every penny is used to keep the machinery rolling but it still upsets the government and they do put people in jail for it.

The investors were a group of Mormons, one of them in construction in Compton. His wife was the leading lady. A Mormon bishop had arranged for some financing. They wanted to know when they were going to be paid.

"It got to such a state that I needed a lawyer," Alex recalled. "Carpenter had once been involved with Sam Arkoff on something else so Carpenter said, 'I know a lawyer named Sam Arkoff.' So that's how I first met Arkoff. I walked into his office and I told him what my problem was and that I had no money and he agreed to take the thing on on a contingency basis. He wanted to get into production and he saw in me a way towards production and distribution because I'd been involved with my brother in British productions and things like that.

"It took two years to get that picture out. The backers attached the picture so it couldn't leave the lab. Although Arkoff and I managed to get a release deal, first with Lippert then Jack Broder, the backers would not

Producer Alex Gordon (right) and Director Edward L. Cahn.

lift the attachment. They insisted on being paid. We argued from ten o'clock in the morning till one a.m. We were standing in a small room with all of these investors and Arkoff was talking to them and trying to explain to them that the only way they were going to get their money back was to let us release the picture. You can imagine without coffee or food or anything, a highly emotional crowd of burly guys screaming and shouting. It was like England and Argentina. Finally they agreed and United Artists took the picture on."

Incidentally, the production manager, Ed Wood, went on to direct some of the most notoriously awful films of the 1950s — *Glen or Glenda?*, *Bride of the Monster, The Sinister Urge, Plan 9 from Outer Space* — most of which he wrote and produced. He was said to have been a transvestite and often wore women's clothing on the set. The tale is told that he wore a bra and panties beneath his Marine uniform the day his unit hit the beach at Okinawa. If such is true then good for Eddie.

Sam and Alex started making plans. Their first idea was to put together a picture with Bela Lugosi who was Alex's friend. Bela had recently starred in British-made comedy titled *Vampire Over London*. It featured a character called Old Mother Riley brought to life by Arthur Lucan who played the character in a series of films. Alex and Sam wanted to remove all the footage with Old Mother Riley, leaving only scenes of Bela and his robot. New footage with the actor would be added to make it feature length. Alex penned another tale for Bela, *The Atomic Monster*. Ed Wood whipped it into screenplay form. Alex took it to Jack Broder at Realart Pictures.

"What do you want to do out here?" Broder asked.

"I'd like to produce low budget pictures," Alex softly replied.

"But you haven't made any pictures before," Broder reminded him.

"I'm quite willing to have someone with your experience act as an executive producer," Alex said, mentally keeping his fingers crossed. Hal Roach had, in fact, already agreed to lend his name to the project.

"Well," Broder said, "let me read the script and I'll think about it."

The script was rejected but its title turned up on a re-issue of an old Lon Chaney horror film.

"We don't really have a case," Sam told Alex. "But I'll see what I can do."

Together they drove to Realart. They found a thin looking fellow in the office. Sam and Alex introduced themselves, said they had business with Jack Broder, and while Alex waited out front, Jim Nicholson ushered Sam into Broder's office.

"Jim here is the one who came up with the title," Broder said. "Do you remember a script called *The Atomic Monster*? It came into this office a short time ago."

Jim said he didn't remember it.

"It may just be one of those things, Jack," Sam said. "A coincidence. But the fact of the matter is you did have access to my client's script. We could go to court and you might win but it's going to cost you some money no matter how you look at it." Sam was bluffing. He counted on Broder's reputation for hating courtrooms and lawyers.

Sam finally emerged with a check for $500.

"Leave me your card," Jim said. He knew his boss was an impossible man to separate from a dollar. "There are an awful lot of people in this town who could use you."

Jim and Sam got to talking and decided to become partners. They wanted to form their own distribution company. Sam knew something about production and Jim knew about exhibition. They set up shop in Sam's office.

Now all they needed was a film to distribute.

Two

Cock 'n' Bull

At that point I had quite a lot of influence with Roger about actors and writers and all that because he didn't know anything. I was responsible for getting a lot of the people started — Bob Campbell, Chuck Griffith, Dick Miller, Mel Welles, Bruno Ve Sota — who became part of his stock company.

— Jonathan Haze

On the Monster from the Ocean Floor *Roger drove his own trucks until the teamsters told him he couldn't do that.*

— David Kramarsky

*[*Monster from the Ocean Floor*] was the only picture I saw made without any direction at all.*

— Floyd Crosby

Roger Corman was born in Detroit on April 5, 1926. He came to California when his father, William, retired from his job as an engineer and moved his family to Beverly Hills. For a short time Roger intended to follow in his father's footsteps. He attended Stanford University to study engineering but it bored the hell out of him. He sold a few articles, technical pieces, and considered writing as a vocation. But no jobs came his way so after graduating he took a job as an engineer at U.S. Electric Motors. He held that job until he could stand it no longer and quit ... after four days. He was a stagehand at KLAC-TV and later went to work for 20th Century–Fox as a messenger boy. He worked his way up the ladder to the story department where he became a story analyst, a fancy name for a reader. The whopping $32.50 a week he earned hardly impressed William and Ann Corman who felt their son's schooling at Stanford warranted better. Roger spent his three years in the Navy as a teacher in the college Officer Training Program at the University of Colorado. He used his G.I. Bill to study literature at Oxford then returned to Hollywood to once again try his hand at writing. He got a job with the Dick Irving Hyland Agency from which he was fired when he used the position

9

Roger Corman, 1960

to peddle one of his own scripts, *The House by the Sea*, to Allied Artists. The money Roger made on the deal, $3000, wasn't much but he also wrangled an associate producer's credit which he hoped would make it easier for him to borrow the money necessary to finance his own picture. Allied Artists released *The House by the Sea* as *Highway Dragnet*, a title designed to capitalize on *Dragnet*, a popular TV show at the time.

At General Services Studio, Roger met a writer named Wyott Ordung who was washing dishes and hauling garbage at Alfonso's Restaurant to help pay the bills. Born in Shanghai, China, Wyott had been interested in motion pictures since he was three years old. But after appearing in about 30 pictures as an actor (his first was *Fixed Bayonets* in 1951) he still had yet to establish himself. So Roger introduced him to Jack Broder who was looking for a war script. Wyott wrote something called *Combat Squad* which eventually starred Lon McCallister and John Ireland and was released in 1953.

Roger and Wyott decided to make a movie together. They needed an office but had no money between them so they rented the reception room of someone else's office (a fellow who was going bankrupt) above the Cock 'n' Bull Restaurant on the Sunset Strip near Doheny. Roger saw a picture in the newspaper of a one-man submarine that the Aerojet-General Company had made. He asked Aerojet if they would let him use it in a motion picture. They said yes after Roger convinced them it would garner them a good deal of free publicity. *The Flaming Sea*, a science fiction story, was written to include the one-man sub. Wyott raised

$15,000 by hocking his life insurance and his home in Sun Valley, a two-bedroom chicken coop. Roger borrowed $2,000 from his parents. After that, Wyott and Roger went searching for their cast and crew.

Wyott already knew where he'd find one actor ... at a gas station on Santa Monica Boulevard. A fellow named Jonathan Haze. He had the night shift so he'd be able to go out on interviews during the day.

Jonathan Haze did a season of summer stock in Connecticut before drifting to New York to take acting classes. He felt there were only two ways that a young fellow like himself could make a lot of money. Either as an athlete or an actor. His father wanted him to be a jockey but Jonathan had grown too tall for that. So he tried his hand at boxing for a while in Pittsburgh but there were professionals who were being paid as little as $50 a fight. It didn't seem too promising.

Wyott drove to the gas station and found Jonathan by the pumps.

"We're gonna do it," Wyott said. "We're finally gonna make the movie. Come on. I want you to meet the producer."

At the Cock 'n' Bull Restaurant Jonathan Haze was introduced to Roger Corman. By this time the title of the movie had been changed to *It Stalked the Ocean Floor.*

"There's a part for you," Roger told Jonathan. "A Mexican. But you'll have to grow a mustache. You'll also have to bring your own costumes, do your own stunts, and you won't be paid overtime. You still want it?"

Of course Jonathan did.

They filmed for six days at the beach. Wyott was allergic to seagulls. Everytime one flew by he wanted to throw up. The finished product was sneak previewed at the California Theatre which has since become a church. When the monster appeared one of the people in the audience, in a voice loud enough for everyone to hear, exclaimed: "It looks like my wife's diaphragm." Everyone laughed. Everyone but Roger and Wyott who immediately went looking for someone to build them another monster. They hired a marionette maker, Bob Baker, who constructed both the monster and a miniature underwater set. Baker was asked to paint glycerine on the vegetation in the hope that everything would *look* like it was underwater. Baker's monster looked like a one-eyed octopus instead of the giant amoeba described by the film's actors. As a result, most people (including the critics at the time) thought it *was* a giant one-eyed octopus. Oh, well, better that than a giant diaphragm.

Wyott heard that Jim Nicholson, a fellow he'd met at Realart, was looking for a movie to start his own releasing company, American Releasing Corporation. Wyott arranged for a meeting with Jim and his wife, Sylvia, and Roger. The four of them sat in the Cock 'n' Bull, eating spareribs, while Jim outlined his plan. He wanted to fly around the

Leon Blender

country and show *It Stalked the Ocean Floor* to the sub-distributors, many of whom Jim had met while working for Jack Broder. He thought he could make a deal whereby the sub-distributors would not only buy the film at a profit, but advance enough money to make another picture. (It was a method of film distribution, developed for companies financially unable to own and operate their own string of film exchanges, called states' rights.)

But Roger wanted a quicker return on his investment and sold the picture to Robert Lippert for $110,000 profit. It was released as *Monster from the Ocean Floor*, Lippert's way of making sure everyone knew it was a science fiction picture. Science fiction had become a popular genre, although its appeal was to a limited audience. That was the reason the major studios stayed clear of the genre. The market was left wide open for low-budget filmmakers to pick up the scraps. If a movie could be made cheaply enough and found a distributor it was almost guaranteed a profit. Today this has changed. Young producers and directors, with state-of-the-art technology and inflated budgets at their disposal, have given A treatments to B movies, giving the kinds of movies they enjoyed as kids the energy, craftsmanship and attention to detail the filmmakers that inspired them almost never did. In doing so they have turned science fiction–horror–fantasy films into an extremely profitable field of endeavor, making it increasingly difficult for their less talented predecessors to stay in business.

Lippert's sales manager, Leon Blender, received a call from Fred Stein, the buyer for United Artists Theatres.

"What do you got?" Fred asked.

"*Monster from the Ocean Floor*," Leon replied.

"I want to book it next week."

"You want to play it," Leon said, knowing the picture was a dog, "be my guest."

To help promote the ticket sales Leon set up a projector on top of the box office at one of the theatres and ran the film's trailer on a continuous loop. It grossed $850,000. Wyott Ordung collected a check for 26 years for which he thanks Leon Blender. Wyott did not, however, get the initial 20% of the picture as promised. When it came time to divide the money Roger claimed that an error had been made.

"I sold 120% of the picture," Roger said in a panic. "I can only give you 15%."

According to Wyott, by the time everyone else's shares were whittled, Roger owned 60% of the picture. That money was immediately put into another production.

Three

A James H. Nicholson–
Samuel Z. Arkoff Production

*I'd never directed a film before. I enjoyed the hustle and the
spontaneity of it. I remember one scene with Dorothy Malone
and myself running from one set to the other, making up dialogue as we went along. When we got to the next set I said:
"Okay. That's it." And she said: "Can't we rehearse?" And I
said: "We just did."*

—John Ireland

*Dorothy Malone was working for ZIV at the time. Roger
would pick her up at noon, during lunch, and tell them that he
just needed her for a few drive-bys. He brought her back after
four.*

—David Kramarsky

In *The Films of Roger Corman* published by Arco, author Ed Naha
relates an amusing anecdote about *The Fast and the Furious* (1954), the
movie Roger produced after *Monster from the Ocean Floor*. The script
called for a sequence in which the hero, while driving in a race, is passed
by the villain. After a few tense moments the hero manages to overtake
the villain and win the race. Roger is quoted as saying that there wasn't
enough money to hire actual race car drivers so people like Jonathan Haze
had to fill in. Roger himself drove the vehicle that the film's hero was supposed to pass. However, when the time came for the hero to race ahead,
Roger pressed his pedal to the metal and won the race which, naturally,
ruined the shot. Roger told author Naha that although he wouldn't admit
it at the time, he wasn't about to come in second just because the script
said so.

When *The Fast and the Furious* was in the can, Republic offered to
distribute it. (Some sources say that Columbia also showed an interest.)
But Roger was reluctant to enter a deal that would tie up his money for six
or eight months. He wanted a fast return on his $66,000 investment so he

14

could get to work on another picture. So Roger gave Jim Nicholson 30 days to get him a better deal with the subdistributors.

Jim needed traveling expenses. He went to his old friend, Joe Moritz (who was either in the shoe business or the bakery business or neither of those things, I never could find out) and borrowed anywhere from $2,500 to $3,500, the most often quoted sum being $3,000. He* went all over the country on a bus, taking Roger's film with him. It wasn't long before ARC had deals with the following subdistributors:

George Waldman, Buffalo	W.R. Richardson, Atlanta
Joe Levine, Boston	Bob Pinson, Charlotte
Max Roth, Chicago	Selma & Jay Blachslager, Cincinnati
Irwin Pollard, Cleveland	"Chick" Lloyd, Denver
Helen Bohn, Indianapolis	Bob Herrell, Kansas City
"Red" Jacobs, Los Angeles	Fred Myers, Memphis
Bill Benjamin, Milwaukee	Don Swartz, Minneapolis
Milton Dureau, New Orleans	Myer Stern, Omaha & Des Moines
Sam Brunk, Oklahoma City	John Scheaffer, Philadelphia
Milton Brauman, Pittsburgh	George Phillips, St. Louis
Fred Paloski, Salt Lake City	Fred Sandy, Washington, D.C.
E.V. Atkinson, Montreal	Nat Cohen, England

Sylvia Nicholson was ARC's secretary. Alex Gordon wrote press-book copy, was the casting director and executive producer. Sam's brother-in-law, Lou Rusoff (who had had some minor successes as a novelist and as a teleplay writer), was their resident writer. Bartlett A. Carré, who had worked in films since the year one, was their production supervisor. (It was his job to make certain no film went one dime over budget, a job he did very well.) Joe Moritz became their treasurer. And, on occasion, Aggie McCulloch, Jack Broder's secretary, did a little moonlighting and balanced the company's books.

Everyone worked for practically nothing. Sam collected nothing for approximately 1½ years. He lived off his legal fees. Alex had some money he had saved working as a publicist for Gene Autry. And Jim and Sylvia ... nobody knew what they were living on. Leon Blender, their sales manager, lived on $115 a week when the money did start coming in. He and Jim and Sam would go to the exhibitor conventions and all stay in the same room at the Astor Hotel. Jim and Sam got the twin beds. Leon slept on a cot.

Alex Gordon and Roger Corman went with him to some of these places. In New Orleans Roger made a deal of his own with a couple of brothers who owned a string of drive-ins. They financed Swamp Women *(1955).*

"The first few pictures were not great pictures," Leon admitted. "The exhibitors wouldn't look at them because if they looked at them they wouldn't buy them. They would look at Jim's ad campaigns and press sheets instead."

An exhibitor's magazine called *Motion Picture Herald*, November 6, 1954 issue, had this to say about *The Fast and the Furious*:

> With names as good as John Ireland and Dorothy Malone for top billing, and with sportscar racing a rising interest of today's young folks, this Palo Alto production ... has a good deal of exploitability in its favor.... Sportscar enthusiasts may get more satisfaction than other people out of the principal novelty in the picture — escape of a fugitive who smuggles himself into an international road-race that takes him into Mexico — and exploitation pointed toward that segment of the public might yield good results.

The review also mentioned the fact that the picture was the first of four productions to be distributed by the newly formed American Releasing Corporation. It also negatively pointed out that the movie was nothing more than a protracted chase story, indistinguishable from hundreds of others like it. Speed of movement did not make for speed in the story.

Shortly after the release of Roger's movie Jim Nicholson announced ARC's plans to release eight features in 1955, four in color and one or more in Vistarama, an anamorphic process.

"We are not interested in Academy awards," Jim told the press, "only in pictures which the exhibitor can play with the assurance that he will make a profit.

"It is the opinion of many exhibitors that in the days when they could buy a year's supply of product that were considerably better off. As the method of runs and clearances has developed in the past few years, however, this is not now a practical plan for every situation. ARC will operate in both ways. Exhibitors may buy picture-by-picture, or they can contract for our entire line-up."

First of the eight features was *Five Guns West*, originally sold to the exhibitors as *Johnny Big Gun*. *King Robot*, Alex and Sam's project, was next in line, to be followed by *The Day the World Ended* in color and Vistarama.

The decision to make a western was logical. Westerns had been a mainstay in Hollywood since the silent days, when real outlaws and marshals took part in misrepresenting frontier life. Until the 1960s there was an old saying in Hollywood: If you want to make money, make a western. It didn't matter who was in it or what it was about, just so long as it had horses and blazing guns. Westerns provided limitless possibilities

Jonathan Haze and Dorothy Malone in "Five Guns West" (1955).

for action and violence. Plus they were fairly easy for audiences to relate to. As late as the 1930s there were still horse and cattle drives through Topanga Canyon. Lynchings in the San Fernando Valley were commonplace. Outdoor settings for westerns could be found at nearby Hemet, Victorville, Chatsworth, Vasquez Rocks, Corriganville and Iverson's Ranch.

The cast of Roger's western included John Lund, an ex-Paramount contract player, Dorothy Malone, Jonathan Haze in a role written especially for him by his friend, Bobby Campbell (listed in the credits as R. Wright Campbell) who also wrote a part for himself, Touch Connors* and Paul Birch. It was a landmark picture for Roger, his first as a director. Since what he knew about directing wouldn't have supplied enough material for a three minute oral report, Roger sat with his eyes glued to the script the whole time the performers played out their scenes. Bobby Campbell had to tell him to forget about the script and watch what the people were doing.

Roger was understandably frightened. It was his first time at bat. He couldn't relax. During the lunch breaks he sat away from the others with his eyes closed, trying to second-guess any future problems. When it started to rain on the first day of shooting, Roger pulled his car to the side of the road and threw up.

*Touch later dropped his old football nickname and became Mike Connors. His real name was Kreker Ohanian.

The picture was finished in two weeks, on schedule, and reviewed in the April 23, 1955 edition of *Motion Picture Herald*:

> Acutely critical areas can be expected to point out possible anachronisms and the bookishly inclined may be counted on to argue that R. Wright Campbell started out with a better basic idea than he wound up with ... but these are not the areas for which the picture is designed. The broader, plainer audience that has been the mainstay of the western melodrama ever since Bronco Billy Anderson rode the range is quite likely to give this attraction substantial support.... Floyd Crosby's photography is an outstanding plus....

Showman's Trade Review said it had a "reasonably good story, with a sufficient enough twist to give it some fine individual characterizations" and had violence that was "suspensefully presented via the capable cast and Roger Corman's able direction."

The agreement that Roger had with ARC was that if he spent more than the allotted budget, the additional money would come out of his own pocket. *Five Guns West* went over budget. There was only $33,000 left to make the next picture. For that amount there was no way Roger could afford a union crew. Which meant that he couldn't direct because he was a union member. He gave the money and a script — "The Unseen," by Tom Filer — to his production assistant, David Kramarsky. A small cast was assembled which consisted of Paul Birch, Lorna Thayer (who years later played the waitress who wouldn't give Jack Nicholson a piece of toast in *5 Easy Pieces*), Dona Cole, Chester Conklin and Richard Sergeant. Lou Place was told to direct it (he had been Roger's assistant director on the previous picture) on location in the desert.

Meanwhile Jim Nicholson was cooking up an advertising campaign for the picture. He changed the title to *Beast with 1,000,000 Eyes* (1955), a metaphoric reference to the invisible force in Filer's script that takes control of animals and humans. The slaves become the creature's "eyes," ergo the title. But the illustration on the poster that Jim mailed to the subdistributors — a beautiful young woman in a bathing suit menaced by a multi-orbed, tentacled creature with a mouthful of razor-sharp teeth — was a gross misrepresentation.

"We do our planning backwards," Jim told a reporter from the *Los Angeles Times*. "We get what sounds like a title that will arouse interest, then a monster or gimmick, then figure out what our advertising is going to consist of. Then we bring in a writer to provide a script to fit the title and concept." This horse-in-front-of-the-cart approach to filmmaking was nothing new, even back in 1955. During the 40's Edgar Ulmer, Leon Fromkess and Sigmund Neufeld used to sit around Producers Releasing Corporation and dream up titles like *Girls in Chains*, *Isle of Forgotten Sins* and *Jive Junction* and worried about the plots later.

Jim Nicholson mailed this poster art for "The Beast with 1,000,000 Eyes" (1955) to the exhibitors before shooting began; the initial print had no beast at all.

Jim Nicholson felt right at home with a science fiction picture. Ever since his high school days, when he lived in a modest bungalow on Luando Way, he saw every science fiction movie he could, always more intrigued with the scientific elements of the fiction. He joined a science fiction club when he was in high school, a club run by Forrest Ackerman, who later became the editor of *Famous Monsters of Filmland* magazine. Jim introduced Forry to a printing process called hectography. The two immediately produced a short-lived fanzine devoted to SF and horror.

Nine days into production, with only one day left of location shooting, Dave Kramarsky received a frantic call from Roger Corman.

"The union is on my back," Roger exclaimed. "They're threatening to shut us down."

"What are we going to do?" Dave asked.

"Calm them down," Roger told him. "We're going to have you join the union. Come on in tomorrow."

The remaining 48 pages of interiors were shot in two days at a little studio Lou Place rented on La Cienega. Wanting to finish in a hurry Roger stepped in to direct. He replaced Everette Baker, a professor from UCLA's cinema department, with Floyd Crosby.

"I don't care whether the mike is in the shot or not," Roger told Floyd. "Let's just finish this thing."

The picture was screened for the subdistributors at Pathe Lab. When the lights came on everyone was in shock. The unspeakable horror promised on the poster was apparently also unseeable. The closest thing the film offered in the way of a special effect was a spaceship which was actually a round tank, half buried in the sand, with a propeller spinning around its top. One reviewer would later describe it as an over-sexed tea kettle. Sam Arkoff was quoted as saying that it *was* a tea kettle.

Joe Levine, ARC's distributor in Boston, reached into his coat pocket and withdrew his checkbook.

"I'll give you $100,000 right now," Levine said, "if you'll keep the title and the advertising but burn this thing. Make a new picture." He offered twice the amount for a color picture.

Jim Nicholson believed it could still be salvaged. He took the last reel into the editing room and with a pair of scissors scratched the emulsion on the scenes of the spaceship. He filled in the jagged white scratches with ink from his fountain pen. Projected again, the tank now looked as if it were discharging dangerous rays.

Still no go. As far as the exhibitors were concerned, ARC was trying to sell a hamburger with no meat. The film had to have a Beast.

Roger telephoned Forry Ackerman, Jim's high school chum. Forry was an agent for various science fiction writers and himself collected books and movie memorabilia pertaining to the subject. Forry suggested

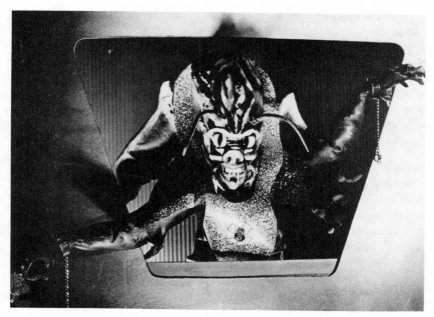

Paul Blaisdell's realization of "The Beast with 1,000,000 Eyes" (1955).

that Roger contact Ray Harryhausen, who had done most of the animation on *Mighty Joe Young*, an Oscar winner for special effects. Ray had done some incredible work in *The Beast from 20,000 Fathoms* and *It Came from Beneath the Sea*. There wasn't another effects specialist that could touch him.

"Are you kidding?" Roger screeched. "He charges $10,000 a tentacle!" He was referring to Ray's then most recent movie about a giant octopus.

"Well," Forry drawled, "there's a chap named Jacques Fresco that might be more in your price range. Do you want his number?"

Not long after Roger was back on the phone to Forry.

"He wanted a thousand dollars!"

Forry asked Roger what sort of money he was talking about.

"Two hundred. That ought to cover it. All I want is a little hand puppet or something."

Forry explained that $200 wouldn't pay for the cost of the materials. After some dickering Roger agreed to pay $200 for the labor plus the cost of materials. There was a young artist working as an art director for *Spaceway* magazine. Paul Blaisdell. He'd illustrated one of Forry's short stories.

The son of Harry and Ruth Blaisdell, Paul was born in Newport,

R.I., on July 21, 1927. It was during his three years at the New England School of Art and Design that he met Jackie, his wife-to-be. She was there to paint. He'd come to learn about cartooning.

Once Roger paid for the Beast he also expected Paul to build a miniature spaceship, crater, and ray-gun for the alien to wave. Years later, in his own monster magazine, Paul tried to explain why the monster he made was missing 999,998 eyes: "In the film the monster that appears with the hypnotic spiral superimposed over him is actually the slave of the beast with a million eyes. The true 'Beast' is never shown."

One afternoon, in Lou Place's studio, Paul and Lou wired the spaceship to blast off to the accompaniment of smoke and fire. By the time they were ready the studio was covered with wires. It looked as if a mad tarantula had been at play. That was when Lou's assistant, John Milani, returned from lunch. Paul and Lou tried to warn him. They yelled and screamed. But John kept on coming until he tripped over one of the wires. The rocket went flying, and it was still on the ceiling that night when they went home.

"We called the slave of the Beast 'Little Hercules' because he was built to about the scale of King Kong, about eighteen inches tall," explained Paul. "He was everybody's pet and everybody thought he was the greatest along with the mock-up of the spaceship I made that the propmen created from a pile of junk out in the desert in Indio. Herky and the spaceship worked fine. The only trouble was when it came time to shoot everybody and his brother wanted to get in on the act, to get into the set, and they crowded me to the point where I could hardly work the controls. Herky could do just about anything including picking up a ray gun and trying to shoot Paul Birch with it before Paul could kill him with a thirty-thirty Winchester. However, the road to Hell is still paved with good intentions and I'm afraid everybody loused that up. I don't know what's left of the scene in the picture of little Herky but perhaps most of it ended up on the cutting room floor. Which is okay with me. He was pretty badly photographed anyway."

Dave Kramarsky was shocked when he saw the effects sequences. The miniatures had looked fine at the studio. On film they looked terrible. He asked the lab to print the scenes darker but they didn't. Cards were dispensed asking for the opinions of the audience at the sneak preview.

"Television is better," was written on one of the cards; "Fumigate the theatre," on another.

Lou Place asked that his name be removed from the credits. Dave Kramarsky took the director's credit.

The next project on ARC's agenda was *King Robot* but it had to be scrapped. Bela Lugosi's continuous bouts with drugs had drastically altered his appearance since he'd been to England filming *Vampire Over*

Roger Corman (lower left, with notebook) directs Joan Taylor and Lloyd Bridges, Paul Birch aims rifle (bottom right), in "Apache Woman" (1955).

London. There was no way new scenes of the actor would match the old. As a consolation Alex Gordon was made executive producer on a color western *Apache Woman* (1955). Roger Corman was to produce and direct it. Alex's main function was as a casting director. Placing some of the ARC regulars in the supporting roles Alex looked elsewhere for the leads.

Lloyd Bridges had scored some minor successes with the critics in pictures like *Home of the Brave* and *High Noon.* Later he would become familiar to TV watchers as Mike Nelson on "Sea Hunt." But when he was asked to play Rex Moffet, a government agent sent to a small Arizona town to catch the perpetrators of the raids and murders there, Bridges' career was pretty much at a standstill.

Joan Taylor had been a member of Paramount's "Golden Circle." She appeared in a string of westerns — *Fighting Man of the Plains, The Savage, War Paint, Fort Yuma* — mostly as Indians. Not one to break tradition, Alex cast her as Anne Libeau, a half-breed living on a reservation close to the troubled Arizona town.

Lance Fuller played Joan's college-educated brother, Armand, the leader of the outlaw band of Indians committing all the crimes. Alex had seen Lance in Republic's *Cattle Queen of Montana.*

Other members of the cast included Morgan Jones, Paul Birch, Jonathan Haze, Paul Dubov, Lou Place, Gene Marlowe, Chester Conklin, Jean Howell and Dick Miller. Alex had nothing to do with hiring Dick Miller. Dick was a friend of Jonathan Haze. They'd been drinking buddies in New York. Dick had come to Hollywood to try his hand at writing. But it was actors that Roger needed, not writers, so Jonathan introduced Dick as an actor.

"You're timing is good," Roger said. "We're getting ready to do a picture. Would you like to play an Indian?"

"Sure," Dick replied. Why not?

After one week as an Indian, Roger asked Dick if he would like to play a cowboy.

"Are you making another picture already?" Dick asked innocently.

"No," Roger said. "It's the same picture. You can be one of the people in the town. Put a hat on and nobody'll know the difference."

Roger was right and Dick went happily back to work, playing cowboys and Indians. Just like when he was a kid. Only now somebody was paying him for it. A problem arose, however, when Roger wanted him to join the posse gathered to hunt the band of renegade Indians that Dick had been a part of the week before.

"Wait a second," he told Roger. "That means I'll wind up in the last scene of the picture. I could conceivably shoot myself."

"That's right," Roger said. "We can't do that."

Too bad. It could have been a classic moment.

The review of the picture that appeared in *Showman's Trade Review* was only mildly favorable: "there are enough exciting western ingredients ... to satisfy the customers in the action market ... picture also carried good performances by Lloyd Bridges, Lance Fuller and Joan Taylor, with the action sufficiently fast to hold attention, despite some dialogue-heavy spots."

While Roger was at work on *Apache Woman*, Jim and Sam were able to pick up another western from Johnny Carpenter. It was titled *Outlaw Treasure* (1955) and starred Glenn Langan and Adele Jergens. About the same time ARC released *Operation Malaya* (1955), a British documentary that combined staged sequences with newsreel clips of the work being done by the British government to wipe out communist terrorists in Malaya, a film made with full cooperation from the British forces and the local police. One reviewer complimented director David MacDonald for giving the picture a feeling of authenticity and said there was "sufficient reality and suspense" to make it "a suitable second feature in the smaller houses."

The month *Apache Woman* went into release the following article appeared in *The Film Daily*, a New York trade magazine:

American Releasing Corp., by mid-1956 will increase its rate of release to one a month, according to James H. Nicholson, president. ARC in its first year has delivered seven pictures, with the output to be nearly doubled next year.

Essentially a releasing organization, ARC is embarking on a program of signing talent, including actors, writers and technical personnel, for multiple picture deals. These are turned over to the various units supplying features for ARC release.

ARC presently has three units supplying product: Palo Alto Prods., Golden State Prods., and Milner Bros. Prods. In December, two more units American Prods. and National Prods., will be added to the company lineup.

In contrast to optimism expressed in the article, ARC was headed toward disaster. Their pictures were being relegated to the bottom half of double bills, supporting bigger films from the majors, the way B pictures had done during the 30s and 40s. *Apache Woman* opened in Los Angeles with *To Hell and Back*. *The Fast and the Furious* played second fiddle to *Rock 'n' Roll Jamboree* in New York's chain of RKO theatres. Essentially ARC was a B-picture company but nobody could stay in business any longer making B pictures because B pictures got flat rentals. To stay alive, ARC needed to get a percentage of the boxoffice.

If Jim and Sam didn't think of something fast they'd go broke.

Four

Combinations

*While we were organizing, two major companies went out of
business. We started with no capital. Basically, our success has
to be in the fact that a majority of our pictures are financial
winners. This is not true of the major companies. As far as sub-
jects are concerned, we've stuck with a type that was really a
backbone of the industry for so many years. These were visual,
action pictures. And they appeal to the age level of the greatest
number of potential moviegoers. The majors have been aiming
at an audience that is there but it's an infrequent audience.
They've forgotten the people who like to go to a show every
week. All the other companies are reliving the sordid realities
of life and they're even inventing some. They want to gross $10
million on every picture. We wouldn't object but our aim is to
gross $1 or $2 million a picture.*

—James Nicholson

If ARC films couldn't command a percentage of the boxoffice as
single attractions, then the only other alternative was to send them out in
pairs. The first combination program from ARC, modestly touted as "the
top shock show of all time!" was *The Day the World Ended* and *The
Phantom from 10,000 Leagues* (1956). Both pictures were scripted by Lou
Rusoff who fashioned scenarios that exploited the public's fear of nuclear
power, a fear that had been growing ever since 1945, when the first atomic
bomb was exploded. Each test had produced a new tale of distress. New
York City's dust was said to have become radioactive. Some thought the
nation's water supply was being poisoned. Film fogging was reported in
Boston. Radioactivity became as much a threat as the bomb itself.
Newspapers reported that exposure to the invisible and odorless sub-
stance could cause changes in somatic cells, possibly resulting in cancer.
Many of the Hiroshima survivors suffered from leukemia. Attempting to
duplicate the effect of H-bomb radiation, the U.S. Navy experimented
with large doses of x-rays. One of the test animals, a rat, grew an extra set
of teeth after being exposed. Rusoff took that piece of information,

26

embellished it a bit, and created a mutated sea turtle that became "The Phantom" and a three-eyed, four-armed mutated human that menaced the characters in *The Day the World Ended*.

> SEE!   *The World Ended by Atomic Fury!*
> SEE!   *The Horrible Mutant Who Seeks a Mate!*
> SEE!   *The Terrifying Beast on the Ocean Floor!*
> SEE!   *The Battle for Life at the Bottom of the Sea!*
> SEE!   *Fantastic World of Death and Horror!*

Alex Gordon, acting as executive producer and casting director, chose Richard Denning and Lori Nelson for the leads in *The Day the World Ended*. Denning, in films since 1937, had recently costarred with Richard Carlson and Julia Adams in U-I's successful SF programmer, *The Creature from the Black Lagoon*. Nelson, a U-I contract player since 1952, starred opposite John Agar in the studio's follow-up, *Revenge of the Creature*. It was hoped that the two performers, having appeared in higher quality productions, would lend an air of respectability to the project. Adele Jergens, Touch Connors, Paul Birch, Jonathan Haze, Paul Dubov and Ray Hatton were in the supporting roles. Alex liked to hire old-timers like Ray Hatton, in spite of protests from Jim and Sam who feared the exhibitors, seeing the old names, would think ARC was trying to palm off old pictures on them. Alex argued that established players like Hatton had name value, though it is doubtful that Ray's name sold any tickets. Alex believed that as long as there were younger performers in the leads, a few old-timers in the background couldn't hurt. Beside all of that, the fact of the matter was that Alex liked to sit and chat with these people about the old days in Hollywood. His wife would one day remark that the only reason he wanted to be a producer in the first place was so he could hire the old performers.

They filmed for a day in Griffith Park, a day at the pond at the Sportsman's Lodge in the San Fernando Valley and a day at Bronson Canyon. That was all of the location days Bart Carré allowed. The budget breakdown was as follows:

DEPARTMENT	AMOUNT
Story	$ 3,053.77
Staff	12,952.21
Cast	15,402.63
Bits & Extras	4,048.48
Set Construction	5,855.46
Set Operations	1,830.53
Set Dressing	2,937.61
Wardrobe	1,983,35

Left to right, Lori Nelson, Paul Dubov, Richard Denning, Lou Place, Touch Connors, Alex Gordon, Adele Jergens, a guest, Raymond Hatton, from "The Day the World Ended" (1956).

Production Office	959.06
Lighting	1,972,50
Camera	3,937.29
Sound	4,982,99
Music	3,478.75
Special Equipment	1,472.78
Transportation	2,149.79
Location	1,993.40
Studio Rental	6,000,00
Editing	6,449.34
Film	1,490.52
Laboratory	5,192.31
S.S. Benefits	4,026.14
Titles, Etc.	1,021.06
Insurance	755.63
Miscellaneous	1,288.89
	$96,234.49
Plus: Alex Gordon (executive producer)	2,500 deferred
Samuel Z. Arkoff	2,500 deferred

Paul Blaisdell's original mutant design (right); Paul (in rubber suit) and Lori Nelson, left, in "The Day the World Ended."

(ARC kept their lab costs low because Sam made a deal with Pathé whereby the company agreed to defer the cost of the prints plus advance $30,000 per feature.)

During the three location days, Paul Blaisdell almost broke his leg and nearly drowned. He was inside his rubber monster suit both times. There was always some concern about Paul playing his own monsters. Most monsters were tall. Jim Arness, the actor who played *The Thing* in 1951, stood six foot four and still wore lifts to play the part. Paul stood five foot two. He put a stop to the complaints by simply building the costume to fit his frame only. His eyes were level with the monster's mouth. The afternoon he was supposed to carry Lori Nelson down a small incline he stepped in a gopher hole.

"I gotta take a fall," he told her. "I'm going over on my back. You can land on my rubber chest so let's not worry about it—let's just dooooooooooooiiiiiitttttt!"

Paul hit the ground, Lori hit his chest. She started to giggle which made her bounce which made Paul laugh which made her bounce even higher.

One league being three miles, "The Phantom from 10,000 Leagues" (1956) must be from outer space.

He was not laughing during the mutant's big death scene.

Being the product of contamination, the mutant cannot tolerate non-contaminated rain water. Sprinklers were plugged into the park's water system and Paul was soaked. He waved his arms dramatically and staggered a bit before he fell against a tree and collapsed.

It was a hot, September afternoon, 110° in the shade, as Paul recalled, only he couldn't recall any shade. And it was hotter still inside his rubber costume. So when the water started seeping into the suit, Paul thought it best to lay back and enjoy it.

"Okay, Paul," Roger called out. "That's a take."

Paul didn't move. It was the first time he'd felt cool all day. It was only when the water rose above his ears that he figured he ought to get on with it. If he stayed there much longer the water'd be over his nose. To his horror he found he couldn't sit up. The rubber had absorbed too much water. He suddenly knew what a turtle on its back felt like. He tried to roll over, first to the left and then to the right, but it was hopeless. My God! Paul thought. What a silly way to die. He began waving his claws frantically, and although his screams were muffled, they were audible. Two fellows came to his rescue. It took a little effort but after some pushing and pulling they were able to get the beleaguered monster-maker on his feet again. The water shot out of the costume in dozens of little streams. Paul looked much like a fire hydrant that had been sprayed with buckshot.

According to Bill Warren's *Keep Watching the Skies!* (McFarland, 1982) Richard Denning was signed for a proposed sequel but it never materialized.

Unable to finance a second feature, Jim and Sam contracted with two film editors, Jack and Dan Milner, to produce *The Phantom from 10,000 Leagues*. Since one league is equal to three miles, "The Phantom" must actually live 20,000 some odd miles in outer space, another fact pointed out in Warren's book.

"In describing a situation as this hodgepodge draws to a merciful close," wrote the reviewer in *Boxoffice*, "a character intones: 'What a mess.' If it weren't for the fact that a prescribed amount of space has to be filled, that line of dialogue could aptly serve as the beginning and the end of a critique of the offering." The reviewer went on to say that perhaps a sardonic laugh or two might be possible although when I saw the picture in 1958, in a theatre crammed full of children, laughter was in short supply. The kids gave up about halfway through and started playing chase.

Boxoffice closed its review by saying that the best the picture could hope for was "perfunctory attention on the lower half of the most inconsequential tandem" bill.

A bad review from a trade publication, predisposed to supporting the industry and its filmmakers, was not a good sign. Nor was the fact that when the combination opened in Detroit, the newspapers were on strike and there was a blizzard, hardly an auspicious debut.

Five

Success

They had to make money. We literally could not afford failure.
— Samuel Arkoff

In Day the World Ended *they stumbled upon this one human skull that's been cannibalized. It had some skin still left on it. That was the chicken left over from somebody's lunch.*
— Bob Burns

Some people come up with brilliant reasons for their success. I wish I could say there was some strange formula such as I don't drink water — but I don't have any. Maybe it was just being at right place at the right time.
— James Nicholson

The Detroit opening may have been a bust but when ARC's first combination was held over for four weeks at the Los Angeles Hollywood Theatre, there were lines around the block. They'd struck paydirt at last.

Jim and Sam flew to New York with Pathé's West Coast vice president, Duke Murray, to meet with James Wolcott and David Melamed, Pathé's top executives. They discussed the financing arrangements for ARC's 1956–57 line-up. Later, Jim met with the eastern circuit heads to outline production plans. He was feeling a little more confident now. He and Sam had a couple of hits on their hands.

The next double bill from ARC consisted of *Female Jungle* and *Oklahoma Woman* (both 1956). The first picture was a pick-up that had been turned down by Paramount and Allied Artists. The backer, Burt Keiser, was anxious to unload it so Jim and Sam got a bargain. Especially when you consider that the film's leading lady was Jayne Mansfield.

Jayne was hired for a secondary role. She got the part because she was one of two ladies that auditioned for the role and her agent asked for $50 less than the other lady's agent. Kathleen Crowley was the actress signed for the lead. But one afternoon, on her way into downtown Los Angeles where they were shooting, she was raped by a couple of blacks. It

33

Touch (Michael) Connors in "Oklahoma Woman" (1956; top) and "Suicide Battalion" (1958). The women (Peggie Castle and Jewell Lain) and the guns are interchangeable.

rained that afternoon so everyone had gone to Keiser's house to shoot some interiors instead. Dave Kramarsky stayed behind to wait for Kathy who was three hours late.

At Keiser's house, the hairdresser couldn't get enough of the juicy details from Kathy. Dave was downstairs in the kitchen, fixing dinner for everyone, when he heard Kathy scream. "She's giving one hell of a performance," he thought. Except that the cameras weren't rolling.

They called her agent who came and took her away. There was half a picture left to shoot. The script was quickly rewritten to exclude Kathy's character. The emphasis was switched to Jayne's character.

There were only two scenes of Kathy they needed to bridge some other scenes already shot. They hired a double and shot her from behind. It's unfortunate that they chose to shoot her from behind instead of at a distance because the lady had to wear a swimsuit. She had about twenty pounds on Kathy and it was all in her ass.

Roger hired Peggy Castle for the title role of *Oklahoma Woman*. She was a pretty good catch. Her name was familiar to B movie fans. But, like Cathy Downs who had already been signed as the film's heroine, she expected top billing. A compromise was reached. Peggy's name would appear first but in no larger typeface. And Cathy would get the lead in another ARC feature.

Richard Denning was back as the hero. Dick Miller played a bartender. Touch Connors was the villain.

Gunslinger (1956) was Roger's last western. Brother Gene told him not to do it. There were too many problems with westerns. You had horses to contend with. Too much outdoor filming; you were at the mercy of the weather. Too many hassles. Roger went ahead with it anyway. He took a writer named Charles Byron Griffith II to a Randolph Scott western. When it was over Roger told him to write the same picture but make the sheriff a girl. "But he's already a girl," Chuck told him.

It was going to be a six day picture. Three days at Ingram's Ranch in Topanga Canyon and three more at Iverson's Ranch near Chatsworth. Before he wrote the script, Chuck paid Ingram's a visit and decided he could write all of the exteriors to fit the one locale. He wrote down the names painted on the windows and signs of the town and used them as characters in the story. That saved them from having to paint them over. Roger was delighted.

The picture was scheduled to begin in March. Then word reached Roger that the unions were about to shorten the six day workweek to five with no decrease in salary. He hurried into production in February.

It rained the first day. Some of the people I talked to said it never stopped raining. Equipment trucks drove into the mushy ground and sank

The woman marshal is Beverly Garland; the man is John Ireland. He's in love with
Bev. He's also been hired to kill her. From "Gunslinger" (1956).

axle deep. The cameraman couldn't find a decent exposure. The second
female lead broke her arm.

    "That was in the beginning days of Roger Corman when his
promise to himself was he would be a millionaire by the time he was 36 or
37. So he was shooting a gun off on the other side of the camera instead of
paying to have it dubbed in. It spooked the horses. This was in rehearsal.
John Ireland told him not to shoot the gun and Roger said okay. We did
the shot. Sure enough, he shot it off. My horse went up in the air and off I
went. He never even called to ask how I was."

The above was from a taped interview that actor Barry Brown did with Allison Hayes, the film's villainess. Beverly Garland, in the Randolph Scott role, remembered things differently. She was sitting on her horse between scenes and happened to watch Allison casually slide out of her saddle and hit the ground. Later, after her arm was in a sling and nobody else was around, Bev asked her why she had done it. She was tired of working was her reply.

"With Roger you always worked," Bev said. "I mean, you could have one eye hanging and he'd just shoot you from another angle. You really had to be a trooper. But he was a brilliant man. When you went on location with Roger you knew that if the director died, and the script got lost, and the cameraman broke his neck, the picture would still get made cause Roger knew how to do everything. And he did it well."

Bev's foot became so swollen one afternoon they had to slice her boot off. They had a doctor look at her but she suspected he was a horse doctor or something.

Dick Miller played a Pony Express rider. In his own words, he couldn't ride for shit but he was asked to ride into town at full gallop and execute a change of mounts, which the actual couriers did every dozen miles or so. Each time Dick tried to halt the animal it slid about thirty feet because the street was made of asphalt with barely two inches of dirt to cover it. Bets were placed on whether he would fall off the horse or not which was the real reason he was asked to repeat the action so many times.

Reviewed in the August 11, 1956 edition of *Motion Picture Herald*, the film was said to have "stirring moments, despite the obviously-limited budget." Roger's direction was "competent enough" and the story proved to be a "delaying force for the action."

Advertising for the picture was set in the hands of Albert Kallis who took the job with one stipulation, that once he and Roger came to an agreement on concept, he would be left alone to bring that concept to fruition. Jim Nicholson liked his work so much that he asked him to do all of the company's campaigns. He did it for 17 years. He and Jim worked well together. They shared a belief that motion picture advertising had to create a must see feeling in the buyer. A sense of urgency. Because the product offered no refund and it was something the buyer couldn't touch, feel, smell or taste. In the beginning, Al watched the movies for inspiration. After about three years of that he decided he would be better off dipping into his own fantasies. Once in a while he read a script. Then there were times when he created a campaign for a picture that didn't exist. The artwork was sent to the exhibitors to get their reaction. If they liked it they made the picture.

Six

Edward L. Cahn

Eddie Cahn was the kind of a fella, especially on a small show, that wanted to show them how fast he could go. So he'd start a scene and then step in front of the camera and yell, "Cut!" and then point to the next place where the next set-up was going. He was a nice guy but he got carried away.

—John Agar

Eddie was an old pro. I remember there was one day when we shot 56 set-ups. But I think Eddie had reached the point in his life where he knew these pot-boilers that he was knocking out weren't going to get him established.

—John Ashley

Sitting in his chair, waving his pipe, he came on like Roosevelt with a cape. He was the first one who gave me a cold chill of what it must be like to be a has-been. He was a real puff-ball. A blow-hard. But I liked him anyway.

—Chuck Griffith

The Day the World Ended made for $65,000 earned $400,000 after only two months in release. By that time Roger Corman had been responsible in one way or another for eight motion pictures. The *Daily Variety* saluted his energy. Roger had only been in business for a little over a year. It came to be said of him that he could produce a film in a phone booth for the price of a call to New York and complete the shooting before his three minutes were up. Roger was fast. There was no argument about that. But even he couldn't supply ARC with enough product to meet the demand.

Over lunch one afternoon Jim Nicholson introduced Alex Gordon to Edward L. Cahn. He was someone Alex had admired ever since he'd seen *Law and Order,* one of the first (and some say one of the finest) films Eddie ever made.

He worked as a night cutter at Universal during his days as a student at the University of California. When the studio ordered the deletion of all the scenes featuring Zasu Pitts from *All Quiet on the*

On location in Chatsworth filming "Girls in Prison" (1956). Alex Gordon (center) sits with performers, including leading ladies Joan Taylor (at his right) and Adele Jergens (at Joan's right). Bert Carré passes in the background in the skipper's cap.

Western Front, to be replaced with scenes of Beryl Mercer, Eddie was the one who cut the film together on the train from Los Angeles to New York so the movie would be ready for its premiere showing the day the train pulled into the station.

Eddie was a big man. Always smoked a pipe and usually had it in his mouth, which often made it difficult, if not impossible, to understand what he was saying. Alex remembered him as being extremely creative, good with actors, conscientious and kind. And, like Alex, he loved the old-timers. Eddie would insist on interviewing everyone that came in for casting, but Alex was always able to persuade him to hire the old-timers.

The first film Eddie and Alex made together was *Girls in Prison* (1956). Because of Eddie's support, Alex had little trouble with the casting for a change. He selected Richard Denning, Joan Taylor, and Adele Jergens for the leads. And Lance Fuller, but mostly because Jim and Sam thought Lance Fuller and Touch Connors were going to make it big. Sam kept asking Alex, "Do you think one of 'em might be worth placing under contract? Which one do you think?"

Richard Denning and Joan Taylor rehearse (top) and Alex Gordon relaxes at day's end: "Girls in Prison."

Touch wouldn't sign. He was waiting to be discovered and didn't want to be tied down in case his big break came along. Eventually, as Mike Connors, he found a home in television, first as the lead in "Tightrope" and later as Joe "Mannix." So they signed Lance Fuller, who needed 11 takes to say "We'll take them from the hills" in *Apache Woman*, to a three picture contract.

They were on location in Chatsworth, Eddie and his crew, filming a scene where two ladies were wrestling around in the mud, when a minor tornado threatened to close them down. The winds were fierce. There was sand in the camera, in the equipment and in everyone's eyes. But Eddie knew it was the one and only day they could shoot there, Bart Carré wouldn't give them another, so he kept his people working. "It'll add to the realism," he told them all. It was advertised as "the shocking story of one man against 1000 women!"

ARC took up new residence at 8255 Sunset Boulevard on November 30, 1955. Four months later the company's name was changed to American International Pictures. It was apparent that AIP was growing. Everyone could feel the tremble beneath their feet. Still, if they were to continue it was imperative that each picture be a success. There was no margin for error, no cushion for Jim and Sam to fall back on should one of their films flop.

"We were in a business," Sam said. "It was a business we liked and enjoyed. But at the same time we had to get a return on our investment. Unless we did, we were going to go bankrupt. Unlike the Michelangelos, we had no Medicis or Popes or government subsidies or anything else. So it's always been a first rule that when you're in a business, like any other businessman, you must get your money back, make a profit, and continue on. Always more important to continue on than it was to go out on a limb and make some arty farty picture which might very well never get its money back, do you no good, and end your existence."

To help guarantee a profit, more emphasis was placed on the advertising campaigns and the titles of the pictures than the pictures themselves. AIP always went for the throat.

"What must a good girl say to 'belong'?" asked the ad for one of AIP's juvenile delinquency dramas. "Crazy kids ... living to a wild rock 'n' roll beat!" proclaimed another. "Kids living to the deadly thrill of jump and kill!" and "No fury like four girls trapped behind enemy lines!" were tag lines for two of their war movie ads. The titles usually came from Jim Nicholson. But not always.

Jim and Alex Gordon were at the annual Christmas party thrown by Red Jacobs, AIP's sub-distributor in the eleven western states. Red operated a company called Favorite Films which later became Crown International, one of AIP's rivals. Jim and Alex were having a conversation with one of the exhibitors when the man mentioned that he had thought of a great title. "You should make a picture called *The She-Creature*," the fellow said proudly. "I don't have a story but I thought it was a great title."

Later, away from the others, Jim asked Alex if he could come up with the $40,000 necessary to make *The She-Creature*. Alex had a friend at Viking Films in New York, Israel M. Burman, who was dying to break away from the educational films he'd been making and get into feature production. Alex telephoned him. Izzie Burman became the associate producer.

Casting *The She-Creature* (1956) became the biggest headache. Eddie Cahn persuaded Edward Arnold to be in the picture. $3,000 for one week. (The actor had worked with Cahn on *Mainstreet After Dark* at MGM back in '44.) Alex thought it would be a great idea to reunite Arnold with Peter Lorre since they'd been so great together in *Crime and Punishment*. Arnold died two days before they were scheduled to go into production. And that's when Lorre decided to read the script. He refused to do it. His agent reminded the actor that he'd already been committed. Lorre fired the agent and told AIP to find another boy.

John Carradine also refused the picture. He was through with horror pictures. He was going to concentrate on Shakespearean roles. Eventually Chester Morris, Tom Conway, Lance Fuller and Ron Randel were signed for the male leads but it was touch and go right up to the last moment.

Lou Rusoff based his scenario on the reincarnation theme that had swept the nation since Doubleday had published *The Search for Bridey Murphy*, written by a young businessman named Morey Bernstein who claimed to have hypnotized a young woman and regressed her to a time prior to her birth. The woman, Ruth Simmons, under hypnosis said she was someone called Bridey Murphy. Mrs. Simmons was said to have chronicled her previous life as a spirited, saucy-tongued girl of late 1700's Ireland. The book sold over 170,000 copies and for several months reincarnation became the subject of songs, nightclub acts, conversation and motion pictures. One Oklahoma boy committed suicide and left a note explaining that he was so "curious about the Bridey Murphy story" that he decided "to investigate the theory in person."

Lou took the concept to its illogical extreme and penned a tale about a hypnotist in love with the future incarnation of a prehistoric monster. This lunatic is able to materialize the woman's previous self and send the creature on various missions of murder. Lou never clarified why the hypnotist wanted to take credit for materializing the monster since to do so would have made him an accessory to murder.

The script was submitted to the Johnston office and the content

Paul Blaisdell and friend.

was approved but Jim and Sam were cautioned to be certain that in their depiction of the female monstrosity, they were careful not to display too much cleavage. Jim and Sam assured them that the monster would have plenty of seaweed draped across her chest and be ugly to boot.

Everyone had their own ideas about what the She-Creature should look like. Someone suggested that its face should look like a cat while another thought it should swim out of the water like an amphibian. Eddie Cahn wanted it to have a long tail and a large set of scaly breasts. After the Blaisdells put all of those suggestions together, their finished product was more bizarre than anyone could have imagined: a big-breasted thing with whiskers and horns and armor plating, long stalks for ears, lobster-like claws, and something that looked like hair combed back on its head.

Paul made his own casts. He didn't have foam rubber to work with because he couldn't afford it. So the She-Creature was made out of block foam, put together like a jigsaw puzzle. The face was molded but it was built up with rubber pieces. He was given about a month to do it.

Between scenes one afternoon, Eddie noticed six large teeth built

into the monster's abdomen, diagonally arranged like a mouth on its side.

"What are those?" Eddie asked.

"I call them lunch hooks," Paul said.

"Do they work?"

"Sure," Paul said proudly, and began operating the teeth by exercising his stomach muscles. The horrorific possibilities were immediately apparent. The monster could puncture someone to death during an embrace.

"Forget it," Eddie said, shaking his head. "We can't use it. *Too* horrible."

There were some other things Paul's creation could do that weren't too horrible, like pluck a playing card from someone's hand, slap its tail, eat... Lots of things. But it was not designed to go into the water which was, of course, the one thing Eddie wanted it to do.

They were shooting at Paradise Cove in Malibu when Eddie, with his pipe in his mouth, told Paul to walk out into the breakers.

The costume became about a hundred pounds heavier as it soaked up the water. Each time Paul tried to step forward the tide pulled him backward. It was not the most fearsome moment in motion picture history.

And there was that business with the door.

Lou had written a scene where the monster smashed through a door to get to one of its victims. Eddie decided to photograph the scene from two angles, one from inside of the room (the victim's point of view) and the other scene from outside of the room.

Paul did his best to be ferocious during the first take, from inside the room, but his efforts were sort of negated when he tripped on a piece of the balsa wood door that he had splintered. He took two or three steps and fell flat on his face. It was a bit of an embarrassment, not to mention that the end of the take was worthless.

For the second take, an angle outside of the room, Paul promised himself there would be no mistakes. He was grimly determined not to make a mess of it. The last thought in his mind, as he made a mighty lunge at the door, was that he wasn't going to trip again. That was just before he bounced off the door and landed flat on his back. The prop department had run out of balsa wood. The new door was made out of solid pine.

Paul was exhausted by the time everyone was ready to photograph the scene where the monster meets its alter ego, the lovely Marla English,

Opposite, left: Marla English, the tormented Andrea, posing for poster illustration; and right: her prehistoric alter-ego, "The She-Creature" (1956).

The title, "It Conquered the World" (1956), was a slight exaggeration. In truth, the visitor from Venus couldn't hold Beechwood for 24 hours. Beverly Garland meets Beulah, the "It," in a studio shot.

AIP's answer to Elizabeth Taylor. Paul was told to hold his standing position while the crew moved the lights into place. Marla lay comfortably on a couch.

"How come you always have it so easy?" Paul grumbled inside the costume.

"What do you mean?" Marla asked.

"Why is it that I always have to stand while you get to lie on your back?"

Marla chuckled. "You sound like some of my boyfriends."

The review of the film in *Motion Picture Herald* called it "awkward" and "pedestrian at times clamoring for supercharged action." Alex and Eddie pressed on.

Runaway Daughters (1956) was the result of Jim and Sam's coming to grips with the fact that 70 percent of the movie audience consisted of people between the ages of 12 and 20. Parents stayed home to watch TV.

Alex wasn't too happy about being assigned to produce a movie about juvenile delinquents. The genre demanded young performers in the dominant roles. Ergo no old-timers.

Marla English was the number one choice for one of the three runaway daughters. Mary Ellen Kaye copped the second lead because Alex enjoyed her work in some films she'd made for Republic and United Artists. For the third daughter Alex and Eddie auditioned more than 100 young ladies. They were on their way home one evening, it was after six, when they saw a young lady sitting in the corner of the reception room on the couch.

"I'm determined to get this part," she said. "Can I read for you?"

Without realizing Gloria Castello had already proven herself in *The Night of the Hunter*, Alex and Eddie signed her.

To find someone suitable to play the role of Marla's mother, Alex went to one of the smaller, independent agencies. Unlike the larger firms, leary of low-budget productions, the smaller agents were anxious to get their clients some exposure.

Alex was sitting in the office of Wallace Middleton, an actor turned agent, looking through Middleton's book of clients, when he came across a photograph of Anna Sten, an actress Sam Goldwyn had imported from Russia back in 1933, believing she would be another Greta Garbo. But Anna Sten had never clicked with American audiences.

"My God, Wally!" Alex did a double take. "You mean to tell me you're representing Anna Sten?"

"Yeah," Wally said dully. "She's kind of semi-retired. Doesn't need to work. She's married to Eugene Frenke, you know. But she told me if I ever found her anything suitable..."

In other words, the lady wanted to work.

Anna Sten and John Litel, in "Runaway Daughters" (1956).

"I don't think we could afford her," Alex said. "I mean, I'd love to have her in this picture..."

"Why don't you let me show her the script?" Wally quickly inserted.

There was a pregnant pause before Alex asked: "What do you think she'll charge?"

But Wally insisted on the playing the game out.

"Let me show her the script," repeated the agent in the same tone he had used before. "If she likes it I'm sure we can work something out."

"But, Wally, I don't want to insult the woman. I mean, we've only got a thousand dollars for a week's work."

Again Wally asked that he be allowed to show the actress the script.

When Alex told Jim and Sam that Anna Sten might be in the picture they were horror struck.

"Are you crazy?" Jim said and then, without waiting for an answer, added, "You're not Sam Goldwyn. And this isn't Goldwyn studios."

Sam agreed. This was no time to play a big shot producer. The company was just starting to move forward.

"You know it'll mean good publicity," Alex told them, which was something he knew a little bit about. He had, after all, been a publicity man for Gene Autry for more years than Jim and Sam had been movie moguls. "Hedda Hopper will do a headline story in her syndicated column. I know I can swing that. I can probably get Louella Parsons to give us some space too. And Lydia Lane, the one who does the beauty column for the *Times.* ... She'll do a special interview."

True to his word, Hedda made a big-to-do about Anna Sten's return to the screen, giving *Runaway Daughters* top coverage in her column.

Anna Sten arrived at the studio AIP had rented, on the corner of Western and Sunset, in her limousine. She entered the building carrying the makings of a caviar sandwich and walked to her dressing room which her husband had filled with flowers. Not long after, Bart Carré was doing the best he could not to explode in Alex's ears.

"Alex. I'm used to making pictures with cowboys and horses. I like cowboys and horses cause they never give me any trouble. You gotta talk to her. She's impossible. She found out she had to share her dressing room with Adele. She wants her own dressing room. That's why you don't make movies with women and kids. Or any other animal other than a horse. You talk to her, Alex."

"Did you try to explain to her that this was a low-budget picture?" Alex asked calmly. "Does she realize that *everybody* is sharing?"

"She thinks she's still with Goldwyn, for crissakes," Bart said with exasperation dripping from his mouth. "I can't deal with her. I just can't."

Alex heaved a sigh.

"All right. I'll talk to her."

Anna had some caviar on rye when Alex entered her dressing room after politely knocking. He timidly watched for a moment as the woman's make-up was applied. Finally he could wait no longer.

"Miss Sten." It was difficult to talk with a mouth as dry as sanpaper. "The production manager asked me to explain this business about the dressing rooms. This is kind of a small studio we're renting here. And, unfortunately, we just don't have the room or money to supply everyone with their own dressing rooms. So we'd be grateful to you if you'd share your dressing room with Adele Jergens."

"If only he had explained," Anna said graciously. "Why, of course. Adele and I will get along just fine."

There weren't any more problems ... with Anna Sten.

Two days later, at three o'clock in the morning, Alex was awakened by a phone call from Tom Conway's agent. He was the actor playing Anna's husband. He had suffered a hemorrhage.

Alex was suddenly alert. "That's horrible. Thank you for calling me. Keep me posted, will you please?"

The agent said that he would.

Alex hung up and wondered what the hell he was going to do about another actor. It wasn't just a question of *replacing* Tom Conway. The actor Alex chose would have to be immediately available for work and willing to work for the same salary Conway had been given and all without first reading the script. He searched the *Player's Directory*.

John Litel!

Of course. He'd worked in films since 1929. An old pro. And plenty of experience in low budget films. He'd worked with Eddie on *Two Dollar Better*. And his agent was Wally Middleton, same as Conway's.

"Wally? Alex. Do you think you could get John Litel to take over for Tom?"

"I'll give him a call," Wally said. "He's out in Chatsworth someplace. I'll call you right back."

It was a long fifteen minutes.

"Litel's in his car right now," said the voice from the phone. "He'll meet you in front of the studio at ten thirty."

Alex was waiting, at the studio on Sunset near Western, with script in hand when Litel pulled his car to a stop in front of him. Before they were finished shaking hands the actor asked to see the script.

"Just give me twenty minutes," Litel said and stepped inside one of the dressing rooms. Twenty minutes later he emerged with his make-up on and went through the whole day without once fluffing a line. Combined with Eddie's rapid fire takes (they didn't call him "fast Eddie" for nothing), Alex was able to finish the picture on the ninth day as scheduled, running only two and a half hours overtime.

The companion feature for *Girls in Prison* was *Shake, Rattle and Rock*, a title Jim lifted from "Shake, Rattle and Roll," a rock 'n' roll record made popular by Big Joe Turner who was in the picture with Fats Domino, a black singer who'd placed several hit rhythm and blues records on the chart. Fats was under contract to Imperial Records. The owner, Lou Chud, agreed to a low figure ($1,500) AIP offered because he wanted Fats to get some exposure. "But you'll have to talk to him," Chud said. "He has the last word."

Alex and Eddie, who were also producing and directing this picture, respectively, drove to Ontario to catch Fats in a little nightclub there. The place was packed, alive with people clapping their hands and stomping their feet. Fats was at the piano, pounding the keys, singing songs like "Blueberry Hill" and "Ain't That a Shame," draining glasses of beer between numbers. Four mugs sat on top of the piano, constantly kept full.

"We can film all your scenes in one afternoon," Alex explained. "We'll shoot the rest of the picture later."

"Sounds good," Fats said. "I got a free day in two weeks. We can do it then."

(Roger Corman had a similar arrangement with the Platters when he did *Rock All Night*. The four singers agreed to make a movie for AIP contingent upon the company's ability to use them before they went on tour. Roger quickly purchased a half hour TV drama called "The Little Guy" which he had seen with Dane Clark and Lee Marvin on Jane Wyman's series. He hired Chuck Griffith to make it feature-length with the focus on the Platters. Later Chuck was told he had 24 hours to rewrite the script, shifting the spotlight away from the Platters. A change in the group's schedule shortened their availability to one day, and much earlier than anticipated. Roger needed a new script so he could start shooting the next day. Chuck cut his original script into sections which he taped to the new material. The movie was filmed on a set left over from another movie.)

Lou Chud called five days prior to the day Fats was to go before the cameras to say that the deal was off: 20th Century–Fox had offered the singer $25,000 for *one* song in one of their movies.

"I've got your letter of agreement, Lou," Sam reminded him. "I'll use it to get an injunction. I'll stop him from working for Fox. I mean it."

It didn't take too much more persuasion before the deal was back on.

On the morning of the shoot, Alex drove to the Roosevelt Hotel to chauffeur Fats to the studio.

"We have no one by that name registered here," the clerk told him.

A cold panic enveloped Alex. "But there must be."

The man behind the counter regarded him with indifference and said, "Well, there isn't." He started to go about his business then stopped. "Wait a minute. He's probably over at the other Roosevelt Hotel."

Alex felt the ground return beneath his feet again.

"I didn't know there was another one."

"Yeah. In the Negro section. On Adams."

It was fortunate for Alex that he made it a habit to be an hour early wherever he went. At the hotel on Adams he asked the clerk for Fats's room number. All at once two black men were at his side.

"Mister Domino is asleep," one of them said. "He's not seeing anyone just now."

Alex realized they must be Fats's bodyguards. His heart started to pound all the way up into his throat. "He's supposed to be on the set of my picture at nine," he explained.

"The man is sleeping."

"But this is the only day he's available. If we don't get him now, there won't be any picture. We've adjusted our schedules and everything."

Their expressions showed their apathy.

Alex mustered his courage and said, "I'm sorry, gentlemen, but I'm desperate. I've got to go up." With that, he started for the stairs, hoping he'd be too little for them to assault. He marched up the steps to the singer's room and gently knocked on the door at first, then pounded when there was no reply. He checked the knob and found it open. He went on in. Fats was, as the men downstairs had said, asleep. "Mister Domino."

Fats awoke with a start.

"I'm very sorry to disturb you, Mr. Domino. Do you remember me?"

Fats looked at him with no recognition.

My God, Alex thought. He doesn't know who I am. "I'm Alex Gordon. We met at the club in Ontario. I was with Eddie Cahn. You said I should pick you up this morning. We're going to make a movie. Remember?"

Fats smiled. "Oh. Yeah. Today's the day."

"Yes," Alex said, relieved. "Today's the day."

"Right. Right." He yawned. "Just give me a few minutes."

Fats did his two numbers in one take, went home, and the rest of the movie was shot a few weeks later. And Alex still managed to employ a lot of his old-timers into what was supposed to be a movie about young people: Margaret Dumont, Sterling Holloway, and Ray Hatton.

For their next feature, *Dragstrip Girl* (1957), Eddie and Alex wanted someone dark and brooding to play the villain. Lou Rusoff found what they were looking for, sitting in AIP's reception room.

"Are you waiting to audition?" Lou asked the young man.

"No. I'm waiting for a friend. She's auditioning for a part."

"What's your name?"

"John Ashley."

"Are you an actor?"

"Sure," John said. Why not?

He read for the part, threw in an imitation of Elvis Presley for good measure (which he thought at the time was dynamite; it can be seen in the picture) and was hired on the spot. His lady friend wasn't as fortunate. Ashley made such a hit in the picture that Alex, Lou and Eddie held up production of *Motorcycle Gang* (1957) until John could finish his basic training at Fort Ord. John felt like Tony Curtis or James Dean or some other important star so he fought like hell to hold onto his hair. Army skin-heads wasn't what kids wanted to see in a J.D. film. John found a sympathetic second lieutenant who let him start growing his hair after the initial induction cut. But there was a dick of a drill sergeant who was determined to see a military look on John's head and used a full field inspection as an excuse to insist on it. John joined a small squad of soldiers ordered to march to the barber shop. He strategically planted himself at the rear hoping to discover a way out. He spotted a young fellow delivering newspapers and signalled to him.

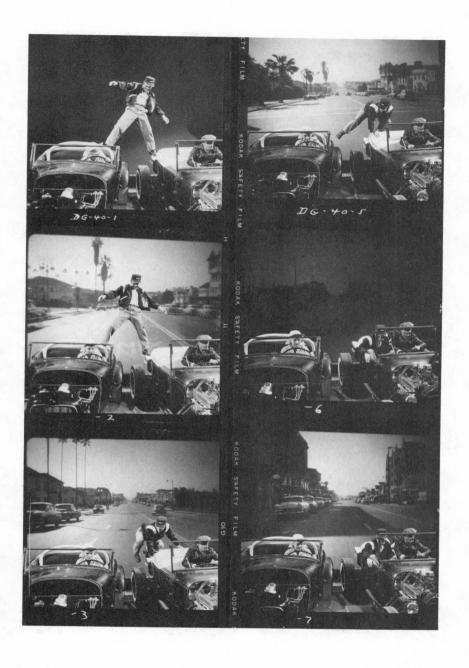

John Ashley straddles the hot rods 'driven' by Fay Spain and Steve Terrell, in "Dragstrip Girl" (1957) — all in a studio, with rear projection.

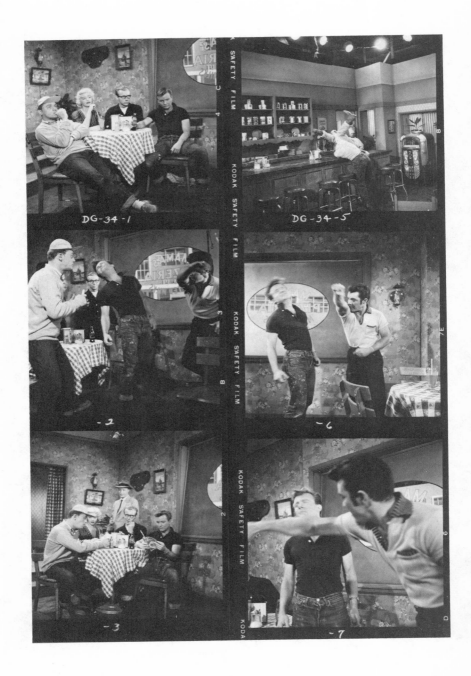

This page and opposite: the fight sequence between John Ashley and Steve Terrell, in "Dragstrip Girl": 'Steve and I were two healthy young guys,' said Ashley, 'and they brought in these two old cockers, old enough to be our fathers, to

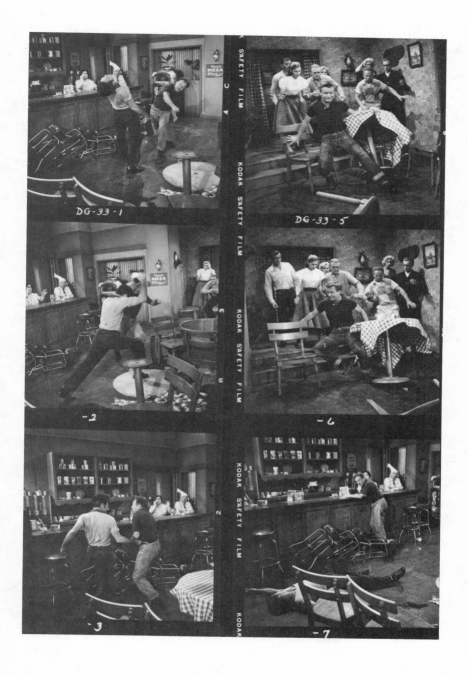

double for us.' Sequences at left show Ashley and Terrell going through the motions for the closer shots; sequences at right show stuntmen filling in.

"I'll give you ten bucks if you'll trade jackets with me and take my place," John whispered, keeping his eye on the drill sergeant.

The young man took John's ten spot, the two men traded fatigue jackets and when the group executed a column right, John did an exceptional left flank.

The picture was shot during his two week furlough.

John Ashley had come to California from Oklahoma to finish college. He loved movies. Sometimes he saw as many as five or six a day. But he never had aspirations of becoming an actor. Never took a drama course. He continued to work for AIP into the 70's.

Having persuaded a group of Armenians to back him in a film, Touch Connors and Charles J. Lyons Jr. acted as executive producers of *Flesh and the Spur* (1957). The script, originally titled *Dead Man's Gun*, was written by Chuck Griffith and Mark Hanna. Touch gave himself the part of the villain, John Agar was hired to play the hero and Marla English was given the lead, primarily because she liked westerns, although she enjoyed watching them more than being in them. Acting was something Marla was doing because her mother wanted her to. Marla retired shortly after the picture went into release and married someone living in San Diego.

At the sneak preview, Touch approached Chuck in the lobby and asked him how he liked it. "Better luck next time," Chuck replied.

Working for Robert Gurney Jr., who often strutted around the set looking through a density glass, Eddie Cahn directed *Invasion of the Saucer-Men* (1957). It was an attempt to tap the flying saucer paranoia that had begun 10 years earlier when a civilian airplane pilot named Kenneth Arnold reported disk-like objects in the vicinity of Mt. Rainier, Washington. They were round, Ken said, the way a saucer might look skimmed across water. Unwittingly he gave birth to the term "flying saucer."

In a separate, unrelated incident an Air Force captain, Thomas Mantell, radioed a UFO report before crashing during his pursuit of the flying object. People went wild. The government had to at least pretend they were looking into the matter. Their findings were negative but not everyone was convinced. There was always the possibility the government might try to conceal something, for security reasons they would say if caught, but who the hell really knew? Enterprising producers exploited the fear with a series of 70 minute nightmares about ugly creatures from other planets, more intelligent and physically stronger than us, possessing weapons that made our nuclear weapons look as effective as squirt guns. *Invasion of the Saucer-Men* was just one such offering. It has the distinction of actually bringing to life one of the most popular cliché phrases of the 50's: little green men from Mars.

Preparing to shoot the drag race between Ashley and Terrell, in "Dragstrip Girl."

Be careful of the little green men from Mars! They were at least two days into production before somebody realized they'd be laughed off the screen. Script changes were made. Gurney ordered Paul Blaisdell to alter the appearance of the bug-eyed Martians. Instead of the big-brains look that he'd asked for, the producer wanted smaller heads. Paul cut a pie-shaped wedge out of the heads, turning the Martians into cabbage heads. Ronald Stein was asked to compose a humorous score. The announcer laughed while reading his copy for the film's trailers. But the newspaper advertisements played it straight.

> *CREEPING HORROR...From the Depths of Time and Space!*
> *SEE Teenagers Vs. the Saucer-Men!*
> *SEE the Night the World Nearly Ended!*
> *SEE the Disembodied Hand That Crawls!*

Oddly enough, the story on which Gurney and Al Martin based their scenario, "The Cosmic Frame" by Paul W. Fairman, was a comedy.

Eddie was back with Alex to make *Voodoo Woman* (1957) in six days for $65,000. Paul Blaisdell was in the middle of his sketch of the

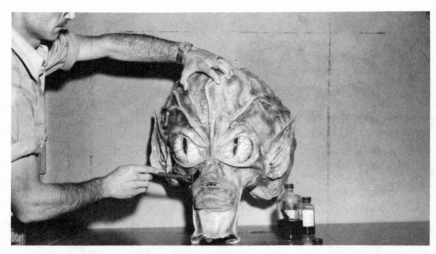

Top: Paul Blaisdell constructs the big-brained Martian invader. Bottom: The Saucer-Man becomes a cabbage head after producer Robert Gurney decided the heads were too big—"Invasion of the Saucer-Men" (1957).

female monster when he was told that there wouldn't be enough money to build a new monster. What he was aked to do was strip the fins and horns of the She-Creature. Harry Thomas had made a new head for it which was nothing but a rubber skull mask with a couple of plastic bug-eyes stuck in it. Shortly before they were to film a shot of the mad doctor pouring acid on the monster to prove its indestructible nature, Paul spied something that he thought looked suspiciously like a sulphuric acid

Top: Jackie Blaisdell, Paul Blaisdell, and Bob Burns on the set of "Voodoo Woman" (1957). Bottom: Al Kallis strikes again.

mixture he and his friends used to make with their chemistry sets. Concerned, he asked the prop man about it.

"It's something new. Brett Smoke. It's harmless."

The stuff ate right through the suit and Paul's leg.

At one point in the story, Marla English pulled a gun on Touch Connors. When they were shooting the scene the parking ticket dangling from the barrel of the gun did nothing to enhance Marla's ruthless image.

The picture was sneaked at the Cornell Theatre in Burbank. Alex took his fiancée, Ruth Succop. They'd met at one of Red Jacob's Christmas parties. Alex wanted to impress her by showing her his latest epic. After the show he took her to the Smoke House for a cup of coffee. That was where she returned the engagement ring. "If that's the kind of picture you make," Ruth told him, "I don't think this marriage is going to work out."

Alex was able to convince Ruth that there was absolutely no way to make a film like *The Red Shoes* with six days and $65,000.

The next and last time Alex and Eddie Cahn joined forces was for *Jet Attack* (1958), which was "The most amazing jet story to ever blast the screen!" The story of three bland jet jockeys who parachute into Korea to rescue an American scientist. They do this with the help of Audrey Totter, who played an American spy working as a nurse for the Korean Ar-Army.

Audrey Totter was an actress that Alex had always wanted to work with. But he'd never been able to afford her before. When he heard she had changed agents, Alex took a chance and called.

"How long do you want her?" the agent asked.

"One week."

"Three thousand dollars."

A bargain! Alex thought. Then he checked with the exhibitors and they all agreed that Audrey Totter was a good name to have on the poster. AIP's sales manager thought so too. But Sam Arkoff didn't. "Anybody *but* Audrey Totter," Sam said. But Sam had not been the one to bring Izzie Burman's money to the project. Alex had. So Alex exercised his privilege as producer and casting director and signed Audrey Totter.

They were coming back from the Ivanhoe Restaurant — Alex, Sam, Jim and Eddie — when Sam asked Alex what was happening with the picture. Bracing himself Alex told him that he had signed Audrey Totter. Furious, Sam pushed him to the ground. Alex was more shocked than he was hurt. Without saying a word he ran to his office. Eddie poked his head in a few minutes later and asked if he was okay. "I never dreamed he would do anything like that." Sam came in to apologize. "I know I shouldn't have hit you," he said. "But sometimes you make me so goddamn mad."

"But, Sam," Alex said, "over Audrey Totter!"

Touch Connors, Marla English, Eddie Cahn, John Agar, Ray Hatton discuss a
scene from "Flesh and the Spur" (1956).

(Sam has said this story is bullshit.)

Not long after, Alex was planning to get married and since he'd
been working for deferred salaries he figured it was a good time to ask for
his money. "We'll *advance* you the money," Sam told him and gave him
$2,000.

At this time AIP had moved into the old Chaplin Studios on the
corner of La Brea and Sunset, which has since become the home of Herb
Alpert's A&M Records. Jim and Sam had been able to take a master lease
on the place, taking advantage of losses suffered by the Kling outfit.

When Alex returned from his honeymoon he realized his affair
with the company had come to an end.

"The problem was," as Sam saw it, "Alex got to taking himself
seriously. And I suppose it was aided and abetted by his wife who kept
saying, 'You should be more important. You should go in and stand up
and tell them.' And ultimately, he came in in his own gentle way. He said,
'If I can't call the tune then I'd like to sell out my share.' I tried to prevail
on him not to do it. I told him that he was being useful, that he was handling things and that the amount of money he was going to get wasn't
going to be an overwhelming amount because none of the pictures had
gone to TV and so on and so forth. I told him I thought he was going to
regret it. So we bought him out. And it's too bad because I liked Alex.
(Jim couldn't stand him.) He could have fitted in. You can always use
somebody that can fawn on actors."

The problem, as Alex saw it, was that profits from his films were
being diverted from his Golden State Productions to companies like Sunset, Carmel and Malibu in which he had no interest.

"We would determine what production company we would use by

the state of the profit and loss division," Sam explained. "In other words, whenever a picture would get into a certain kind of profit, or it would begin to pay off profits, then you had to pay taxes above the minimum level of taxes. Then we'd dump another picture to be made in that corporation. So we'd get a new write-off coming very quickly because we made the picture so fast and got 'em out so fast. This is how the thing would work, in essence, like revolving companies."

Alex was not convinced and sold his interest in the pictures he had made with the stipulation that he make three more pictures for AIP (which Sam has also said is not true). Whatever, Alex made one more film for the company, *Submarine Seahawk* (1958), advertised as "The biggest war spectacle of the year!" The spectacle was cribbed from two Warner Brothers movies, *Air Force* and *Destination Tokyo*. Alex's brother, Richard, purchased the battle sequences and sound effects tracks from Seven Arts who owned the rights. One critic gave the film an approving nod for making such fine use of the Battle of the Coral Sea newsreel footage.

Seven

Herman Cohen

They were potboilers, you know. Cooked-up things. They were fun pictures to make but nobody ever pretended that they were great art. If you didn't flub a line it was a take. Teenage Frankenstein was the better of the two, if I remember. It's been so long. It wasn't very good really. It was done in a hurry, which is pretty obvious when you see it. If you're an actor you take the part and you're glad to get it. It's nice to be working. It's one of those things is all. You've done it and you can't very well say you didn't do it. You're caught with your pants down, so to speak.

— Whit Bissell

Our films concerned teenagers who had doubts about their parents, their teachers or what-have-you. That these doubts influence a teenager to go bad. I felt this would appeal to a teenage audience, which it did.

— Herman Cohen

At the time of its release, *I Was a Teenage Werewolf* (1957) was AIP's most notorious film. It was condemned by all sorts of angry folks, most of whom admitted to never having seen it. Much of the outrage stemmed from the fear that juvenile delinquency depicted on the screen provoked similar behavior on the streets.

Estes Kefauver, a senator from Tennessee who had made a name for himself when his investigations into organized crime were televised at the beginning of the decade, was put in charge of a senate subcommittee which investigated the causes of juvenile delinquency. Kefauver and his men did their best to prove that there was a link between *reel* and *real* violence. After grilling a number of Hollywood big wigs Kefauver's committee published a 122 page report of their findings, which were inconclusive.

Alex Gordon appeared on a local TV program, "Confidential File," to defend his participation in the making of American International Pictures. The show's host, Paul Coates, accused Alex of making inflam-

Above: AIP cleverly merged juvenile delinquency, SF and horror genres in its ad art. Opposite, top: Michael Landon seeks help from psychiatrist Whit Bissell. Bottom: The result. From "I Was a Teenage Werewolf" (1957).

matory pictures. Coates based his complaints on the advertising campaigns. He had not seen any of the movies. During his investigations, Senator Kefauver had registered a similar complaint. Most advertisements, Kefauver said, were "nothing but purplish prose, keyed to feverish tempo to celebrate the naturalness of seduction, the condonability of adultery, and the spontaneity of adolescent relations."

"The advertising is the most provocative thing about the pictures," Alex told Coates. "The pictures are actually quite moral. It's just the old come-on."

But neither Coates nor many of the people who watched his program were convinced. At a luncheon in Miami for exhibitors, sponsored by AIP, producer Jerry Wald blasted his hosts for making what he called irresponsible motion pictures. Wald rattled off a list of titles and said: "These are not the sort of pictures on which we can build a market for the future. While they may make a few dollars today they will destroy us tomorrow." He begged Nicholson and Arkoff to "lift their horizons." Jim waited patiently for Wald to finish then politely reminded the producer that *Peyton Place*, a Jerry Wald production, contained incest, rape and murder. "I'd rather my own children see one of our pictures than something like, say, *God's Little Acre*," Jim remarked. "Our monsters don't drink, smoke or lust." And none of them had ever been condemned by the Legion of Decency.

Most of the exhibitors were on Jim's side. "Before they came along," declared the owner of a San Fernando Valley Drive-In "we were thinking of shutting down to three nights a week. They saved us."

In retrospect, divorced from the prevailing climate, it is difficult, perhaps impossible to understand what all the fuss was about.

John Ashley claimed he was one of the two young men considered for the part of the teenage werewolf. Herman Cohen, the producer of the film, said it was between Michael Landon and Scott Marlowe. Landon won out and some sources claim his appearance in the picture led to his being cast in TV's "Bonanza," although he appeared in a few more pictures prior to that happening.

Roger Corman was said to have turned the picture down, refusing to do something with such a ridiculous title. Herman Cohen said only Sherman Rose and Gene Fowler Jr. were under consideration and it was Fowler that he ultimately chose.

"To take first things first," wrote the reviewer for the *L.A. Examiner*, "the title is a magnificent piece of composition. It had a haunting quality about it, and I ought to caution you that if you let it pierce your consciousness it will echo in your brain in a constant refrain."

In a newspaper article written shortly after the film's release, the title was credited to Jim Nicholson's daughter who was repeating

On location in Hawaii filming "Naked Paradise" (1956): from left, Jonathan Haze, Leslie Bradley, Beverly Garland, Dick Miller.

something cooked up by one of her classmates. Alex Gordon is convinced the title came out of a meeting with himself and Jim and Sam. The three were playing a game, trying to see which of them could remember the longest film title. *I Was a Prisoner on Devil's Island* and *I Was a Communist for the F.B.I.* led to the inspiration: *I Was a Teenage Werewolf.* Herman Cohen said only the front part of the title was Nicholson's. (Sam would call all of this concern over who did what "little minds at work.") Whatever, it's a great title, a beautiful blend of monsters and teenagers, sounding as if it were ripped from the pages of *True Confessions* magazine. Made for $125,000 in seven days, the picture grossed $2,000,000 in less than a year's time and established Herman as a bankable producer.

All things considered, it was not a remarkable film, but then it was better than one might have expected. Why, after all this time, is it still remembered? My guess would be the title, that beautiful, kinky, campy title.

When he was writing the screenplay with Aben Kandel, a friend made Herman think twice about putting his name on it. For a while he wondered if he should take producer's credit. He was just getting started and didn't need a blemish to hold him back. Then people from *Time*,

Director Sherman Rose (left) and Producer Herman Cohen and their robot from "Target Earth."

Newsweek and *Life* began calling, asking for the film's producer. Not wanting to miss the publicity, Herman took credit as producer and used a phony name as writer.

Herman was bitten by the movie bug at twelve. He worked as an usher in Detroit and was arrested twice by the labor board for being underage. He was in the Marines for a while, stationed at Camp Pendleton in Oceanside, a few hours drive from Hollywood. He was with Columbia for a while, first in Michigan and later in Hollywood, working in the publicity department. He was an executive producer at Realart, which was where he and Jim first met. Jim had been the one who gave Herman a copy of a short story called "Deadly City," the basis for Herman's *Target*

Earth which he shot in seven days for $75,000. *Crime of Passion*, which he contracted to do for United Artists,* was his biggest production at that time, featuring such names as Barbara Stanwyck and Sterling Hayden. But the picture passed through town like a dose of salts. Herman decided to tour the country to see what was going on. He discovered what Jim and Sam already knew. The kids were buying all of the movie tickets.

I Was a Teenage Frankenstein and *Blood of Dracula* (both 1957) resulted from a conversation Jim and Sam had with R.J. O'Donnell, the King of Texas Interstate. They were having lunch, talking business, when O'Donnell started bitching about the amount of money the studios wanted for their pictures. "I hate to give those bastards Thanksgiving week."

Sam seized the opportunity. Thanksgiving week was traditionally one of the most profitable weeks of the year. "What if *we* could make two pictures?" he asked.

Knowing he could get two AIP pictures for a fraction of what a major studio production would cost, O'Donnell agreed to book a teenage horror combination into his chain of theatres.

For *How to Make a Monster* (1958), the teenage werewolf and the teenage Frankenstein were stuffed into the same package. During the course of the film, which proported to be a behind-the-scenes look at AIP, a guide mentioned to a group of tourists that the studio was busy at work on *Horrors of the Black Museum* which was actually Herman's next film. He moved his base of operations to England where a Scotland Yard inspector inadvertently gave him the idea to make the picture by ushering Herman through the Yard's Black Museum, a collection of 100 years' worth of murder weapons. One item that especially fascinated the producer was a pair of binoculars. The slightest pressure on the focus released two spikes from the eye-pieces. It had been a gift to an unsuspecting woman from the lunatic stable boy she had jilted. The binoculars, as well as several other weapons from the museum, found their way into the story.

The picture was made as a 50/50 deal between AIP and Nat Cohen's Anglo-Amalgamated in England, each taking their profits from their respective countries. It was made in England because at the time it could be done for less money. It was the first AIP production in color and scope. And though it cost twice as much as *Teenage Werewolf* it earned $1,000,000 more in profits.

"The plot might deserve detailed consideration as a serious comment on violence," wrote David Pirie in his book, *A Heritage of Horror*, "if it were not executed quite so titillatingly.... [It is] unashamedly blatant, lingering over the prosecution of each crime with maximum enjoyment and making the most out of every sexual innuendo."

---

*This deal with UA forced Herman to reject Jim's offer of partnership in ARC.

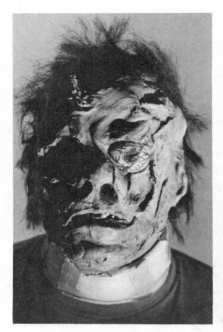

Jim Nicholson thought of a way to help sell the picture to American audiences. His advertisements promised a new screen process called Hypno-Vista which was supposed to cause the viewer to actually feel and experience the events in the movie. It was, of course, just another con.

Once legitimate gimmicks like CinemaScope and 3-D proved to be successful in attracting customers, if only for a short time, bogus gimmicks sprang up like weeds. One producer flashed subliminal images throughout his picture and called it Psychorama. It was outlawed when some theatre owners used it to stimulate interest in the snack bar. A producer named William Castle, the acknowledged king of gimmicks, allegedly once wired theatre seats to shock certain members of the audience during one of his pictures. For *Macabre*, a dull mystery with its title ripped-off from a then popular French film, the producer persuaded Lloyds of London to insure anyone who saw the film for $1,000 against death by fright. "Of course it would be an awful thing if somebody actually did die in the theatre," the producer remarked. Then he added shamelessly, "but the publicity would be terrific."

HypnoVista was a ten or twelve minute prologue, attached to the beginning of the U.S. prints of *Black Museum*, in which a psychologist named Emile Franchell talks about the power of hypnosis. The doctor first introduced himself as a psychologist specializing in hypnosis, then proceeded to lecture the audience, taking a break to demonstrate his hypnotic powers by poking a woman's arm with long needles. The woman smiled and said she didn't feel a thing. Franchelle babbled on and then the movie began.

The Headless Ghost (1959), BM's cofeature, was also supplied by Herman. The story of three exchange students who visit a haunted castle in England was cooked up after a call from Jim Nicholson. It seemed that unless Herman could supply a second feature, *Black Museum* would be sent out as a single attraction, which meant the percentage of the boxoffice would be split with another company. Herman rushed into production and supplied a 63 minute, black and white horror-comedy.

Herman's last movie for AIP was *Konga* (1961). "Not since *King Kong* has the screen seen anything like it!" screamed the ads. Herman had to pay RKO for the use of the name. Originally he wanted to call the picture *I Was a Teenage Gorilla* but the novelty of teenage titles had worn off.

The finale of the movie, highly exaggerated on the poster art, has a

Opposite, top left: Gary Conway in "I Was a Teenage Frankenstein" (1957); right: Sandra Harrison as the vampire in "Blood of Dracula" (1957). Bottom: Ad art, in time for Thanksgiving as promised.

Top: Ad art; bottom: Yvonne Lime as the 'good girl' trying to discover from Brett Halsey what she must say to 'belong' — from "High School Hellcats" (1958).

60 or 70 foot gorilla loose in London. Every night for a week, from 11 p.m. to 6 a.m. Herman and his crew photographed people running and screaming through the streets, supposedly fleeing from the giant ape. They waited until the last night to photograph Konga's death scene which necessitated the use of guns and bazookas. The citizens thought the city was under attack. The phones jumped off the walls at Scotland Yard. Herman was very apologetic but he had known all along that if he had told them what he intended to do he would never have been granted permission to shoot in the streets. A lot of flowers and candy was used to smooth ruffled feathers.

Allied Artists released Herman's next picture, *Horrors of the Black Zoo*. AIP wanted to shave the amount of his percentage. So Herman waved good-bye to Jim and Sam.

Michael Gough claims two more victims in "Horrors of the Black Museum" (1959). Above: Gough dips his analyst into a vat of acid when the poor fellow gets too close to the heart of Gough's psychological disturbance; Graham Curnow lends a hand. Below: A blackmailing old lady receives ice tongs in her neck for payment.

Eight

Bert I. Gordon

Bert was very demanding as a director. He also listed himself as the producer, the script writer, the special effects man, the optical effects man.... There was THIS by Bert I. Gordon and THAT by Bert I. Gordon, on and on ad nauseam. And he was, as I said, rather impatient on the set.

— Paul Blaisdell

He really took himself very seriously, as though he was George Pal.

— Samuel Arkoff

I always did the best I could.

— Bert I. Gordon

Next to *I Was a Teenage Werewolf* AIP's biggest moneymaker of 1957 was *The Amazing Colossal Man*, written, produced and directed by Bert I. Gordon, a young man from Kenosha, Wisconsin. In six months Bert's film grossed $848,000, playing theatres that normally wouldn't touch an AIP movie. In fact, it was the first AIP movie to play Broadway in New York.

Mister BIG they used to call him. He used his middle initial, which stood for Ira, to distinguish himself from comedian Bert Gordon, the Mad Russian. Bert moved his family to Hollywood after making a 16mm sound television commercial for Chevrolet for which he was paid $1,200. His first job in Hollywood was working on television's *Cowboy G-Men*, which only lasted a season. He cut 26 British features into half hour telecasts ("I didn't chop them. I *edited* them.") and became a production assistant on *Racket Squad*.

For a short period it seemed to Bert that Hollywood was full of nothing but doorbells. He pushed one doorbell after another but nobody was home. Then in 1954 he teamed with Tom Gries and made *Serpent Island*, a bad picture by anyone's standards I should think, with Sonny Tufts in the lead. This credit is often left off a Bert Gordon filmography and I hate to see it ignored. The next picture, *King Dinosaur* (1955), was

Bert Ira Gordon (1961): he not only produced and directed his pictures but supplied their special effects as well.

shot entirely outdoors at Big Bear Mountain and Bronson Canyon in seven days for $15,000. It grossed over a million. The equipment was borrowed. The four cast members worked for deferred payments. The story is supposed to take place on another planet. Bert had one of the actors remark how incredible it was that the place looked so much like Earth. It was one for Ripley.

Bert made three films in 1957. The first was *Beginning of the End* for AB—PT Pictures, Corp. It was a newly formed company. Bert's picture, about a swarm of giant locusts that descend on Chicago, was their first release. In *Variety's* review of the picture the writer wanted to know if AB-PT (American Broadcasting–Paramount Theatres) really believed that Bert's movie was an answer to the industry's sagging output.

"I had to get my grasshoppers from Waco, Texas. They had the only species large enough to carry focus. I could only import males because they didn't want the things to start breeding. They even had someone from the agricultural department or someplace like that come out to take a head count, or a wing count. The grasshoppers turned cannibalistic. I had about a dozen left at the end of the picture," Bert said.

The second movie Bert made that year was for RKO, *The Cyclops.* But RKO went bankrupt and it was eventually released by Allied Artists. So it's possible that he made this picture before his grasshopper picture. Maybe a year before. Who knows? Who cares?

The great thing about Bert Gordon was that he was fearless. Most low budget filmmakers never thought about tackling spectacle. It was too time consuming. Too expensive. Special effects in most B pictures of the time consisted of a puff of smoke, whatever you could hang from a wire and maybe a double exposure. Not Bert. He would try anything. When he made *King Dinosaur*, there was no way he could afford the services of an animator nor could he afford to have someone build a dinosaur suit. So he used lizards.

"I had iguanas on a miniature set," Bert remembered. "To make them appear to have size you have to overcrank the camera. You never know when an animal is going to move. I shot thousands of feet of film and the sons of bitches wouldn't move. They were like statues. Like stone. Nothing would make them move and nothing would make them angry. So I finally ended up in the library and found a book with a chapter on iguanas that said they needed extreme heat to be active. So I bought a couple of heaters and blew hot air on them with fans."

The Colossal Man, Bert's third feature in 1957, began as another project based on a short story Jim Nicholson read titled "The Nth Man." It was written during the 1920s and about a man two miles tall. Chuck Griffith wrote a treatment with Dick Miller in mind for the lead. Dick would play a malcontent, forever writing letters to editors, occasionally

Top: Dean Parkin, running amok at LAX in "War of the Colossal Beast" (1958), sequel to "The Amazing Colossal Man" (1957); Bert Gordon's travelling matte seems to have travelled a little too far. Bottom: Parkin securely bound in a hangar (split screen and a miniature), "War of the Colossal Beast."

Top: The star of "Night of the Blood Beast" (1958). The monster suit was used again in "Teenage Caveman." Bottom: "The Spider" (1958) is loose in the city.

Top: A four-eyed cat, one of the mutations in "Terror from the Year 5000" (1958).
Bottom: Peggy Webber is the only one screaming upon the sudden appearance of
"The Screaming Skull" (1958).

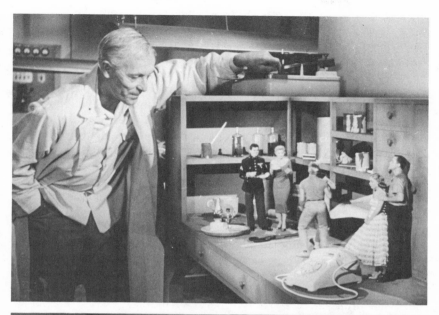

Top: John Hoyt plays rock and roll so he can watch his little friends dance. Bottom: Tired of being a little friend, John Agar tries to operate the controls that might make one of them normal size again. "Attack of the Puppet People" (1958).

offering some scatterbrained plan to set things right again. The bitcher is at the induction center, taking a physical, when he stumbles into a room full of test tubes and test animals. He's startled by two doctors entering the room and out of embarrassment hides the test tube he was looking at in his pocket. His wife, thinking he's trying to sneak booze into the house, puts it in a drink which first makes the malcontent sick, then gigantic. He travels to New York and makes demands on the United Nations, plays Navy like a kid in a bathtub, sinking real ships, and eats whales smoked over volcanoes. The Russians drop a bomb on him. He floats to shore in the Azores, madder than hell. After getting revenge on the Russians he returns to the U.S. Before he can get into politics he shrinks.

For a brief time, Chuck worked with Bert on a more conventional version of the story, but after one day of Bert dictating over his shoulder, Chuck quit. His ex-partner, Mark Hanna, took over.

The greatest challenge Bert faced was the film's climax in which his 60-foot giant supposedly attacks Las Vegas. Of course he hadn't the money to rope off the streets and pay thousands of extras to run and scream through the city but — Bert was fearless. He took slides of the city during the early morning hours, when the streets were empty. Those slides were projected on a process screen. A handful of extras were paid to stand in front of the screen and react. To all of this Bert superimposed his colossal man.

For the technique to have worked at all, two mattes were needed, one positive and one negative. Only one was used. The positive. Which meant that anything black would be transparent. So the giant's head was shaved, he wore a white sheet and he was constantly flooded with light hoping to eliminate any shadows. (For a latter film about a giant spider, he used only the negative matte.) Nothing could be done about the eyes, of course, they were doomed from the start. And even when the image wasn't transparent it was so washed out it was hardly recognizeable as being a man. Giant or otherwise.

No matter. As soon as the money started rolling in Bert was asked to start work on a sequel, *Revenge of the Colossal Man* which became *War of the Colossal Beast* (1958).

Two pictures later Bert instigated a lawsuit against AIP and Jim and Sam, claiming that the two men diverted the profits from his four films — *The Amazing Colossal Man, War of the Colossal Beast, Attack of the Puppet People, Earth vs. The Spider* — to their other companies and shaved off a $15,000 executive producer fee for themselves.

Bert's next movie was for Allied Artists.

Nine

Roger Corman

There was a stigma to B pictures. You were nothing if you were in B pictures...The only way you can be any good is to get out of B movies.

—Beverly Garland

First and foremost (I shouldn't say first and foremost) I was trying to make a film that would be profitable. At the same time I was trying to make a film that would give some satisfaction to me. I put a lot of thought into those films. It may not look like it when you see them...

—Roger Corman

Nobody had any idea about the competition because I don't think anybody went to see anybody else's pictures. None of us were interested in any of those pictures. They were just what we were doing.

—Charles Griffith

Right after *Gunslinger* Roger Corman made *It Conquered the World* (1956), about an invader from Venus, Chuck Griffith read the script Lou Rusoff had written and concluded that it was incomprehensible. Rusoff's brother was dying in Canada at the time. The man was naturally distraught.

Chuck was given 48 hours to write something they could shoot. He wrote streams of dialogue without looking at Rusoff's script again. Chuck knew Roger didn't have the money to show anything. The picture would, in essence, be one end of a radio conversation.

One scene that Chuck wrote without any dialogue was thrown out. It was supposed to be a tense moment. Four characters sat silently in a room while one of them straightened magazines. Roger didn't understand how it was possible to have a scene without dialogue. Out it went.

The first day of the shoot was in Bronson Canyon. And I'll get around to telling you about what happened there but let me tell you about Bronson Canyon first. Everybody filmed at Bronson Canyon. Roger, Bert Gordon, Eddie Cahn and every other low budget director who ever lived shot something at Bronson Canyon. It is located above Hollywood Boulevard, off Franklin Avenue near Beachwood Drive. Bronson was once a mineral quarry. Four tunnels were cut into the mountain. One out front and three in back. The exterior of one of the three rear tunnels is most often selected for filming because no matter how you angle the camera you can't find a trace of civilization. The canyon has doubled for western, African, even alien landscapes. The area has been seen in hundreds of motion pictures and television shows, the site of the battle in MGM's *Julius Caesar*, the place where the plane crashed in the new *Lost Horizon*. Someone should do a book on ol' Bronson or at least an article which would list everyting that had been filmed there.

Paul Blaisdell built the monster from Venus, which he affectionately called Beulah. Beulah had a few nicknames, Denny Dimwit being one of them. Paul's design was based on two things: Roger Corman told him that anything from Venus would be squat and low to the ground because the planet had heavy gravity; Paul heard Venus was more conducive to plant life than it was animal life. He built a preposterous mushroom with deep set eyes and a wide grin. Beverly Garland sauntered up to it the first day and said: *"That* conquered the world?" She kicked it. It fell over. She burst out laughing.

It should also be remembered that as far as Paul knew, his monster wouldn't be seen all that clearly. The script dictated that it would remain in the cave and have limited movement. There are a couple of different stories about why Roger decided to bring the monster outside of the cave and into the cruel light. He forgot the generators for the lights is one story. Another has Roger saying "I paid for it. I might as well show it."

Paul was inside Beulah, duck-walking, the afternoon Jonathan Haze stabbed Beulah between the eyes with a bayonet. Jonathan played a soldier. Lucky for Paul he had borrowed a G.I. helmet from Danny Knight, another of the soldiers. Jonathan's blade ripped right through the foam rubber and the plywood frame and scraped the top of Paul's helmet. Paul kept quiet about it until Roger yelled "Cut!"

"Hey, Jack," Paul called out.

"Yeah, Paul."

"Next time will you aim a little bit higher?"

One afternoon they hit Beulah with several rounds of explosives. Paul wasn't inside that time. Good thing too. Smoke collected inside Beulah and pored out of every orifice on its body. Roger didn't notice. He told the cameraman to stop rolling.

"Don't cut!" Dick Miller cried out.

"Cut, I said," Roger insisted.

They started a screaming match that ended when Roger happened to notice the monster's smoking effect.

"Did we get that?" Roger asked.

"No," the cameraman said dully. "You said to cut."

"Shit," Roger said.

It was up to actor Lee Van Cleef to do the job the soldiers failed to do. Armed with a blowtorch, Van Cleef killed the monster by burning one of its eyes right out of the socket. The British censor "looked askance" at this scene and only allowed it after it was determined that monsters from space weren't entitled to humane treatment.

As Van Cleef approached the monster, reprimanding it for turning the place into a charnel house, the actors off stage shouted words of encouragement.

"Give it to him, Lee!"

"You tell that big ice cream cone where to get off."

Van Cleef wheeled around. "Get off my back, will you?" he said angrily. "It's hard enough to keep a straight face without you guys horsing around."

The insert shot of the empty eye socket squirting blood was accomplished by Paul squeezing a grease gun full of Hershey's chocolate syrup. They had some trouble. By the time they were ready to shoot the syrup had hardened in the end of the gun. Paul squeezed the trigger repeatedly, while Roger screamed at him to do something, and finally Paul squeezed hard enough to clear the barrel. The gun also backfired. Paul crawled from beneath the monster, wiped the syrup from his eyes and noticed he had sprayed Roger as well.

Beulah had been trouble from the beginning. She was built in Paul's studio, located in his house. When it came time to take her outside for some panelling Paul couldn't get her out the door. Paul felt like the idiot who built a yacht in a basement. Beulah was taken apart, taken outside, and put together again. A pick-up truck was used to haul her to Bronson.

"The acting is on a minor key," said *Motion Picture Herald*, "the main ingredients of this particular attraction geared primarily to horror, both visual and anticipated." *Daily Variety* thought the movie was a cut above the usual low budget fare and compared to the other films of its kind, *Month Film Bulletin* felt it was reasonably convincing.

Roger's next three films were horror movies, though he preferred to call them science fiction. Two were made for Allied Artists. The third one, *The Undead* (1957), was for AIP. It was to be another Bridey Murphy–inspired epic. Chuck Griffith warned him that it would probably be a dead issue before they could get the film into the theatres. "Why not let me write a comedy instead?" Chuck asked.

"I've told you before," Roger said, "you have to be good to do a comedy."

The script Chuck wrote, *The Trance of Diana Love*, was in iambic
pentameter, seguing from the past to the present to the past again with
synclines performed by the Devil. It was, Chuck believed, the best thing
he ever wrote. Roger liked it until the people he showed it to said they
didn't understand it. Chuck was instructed to translate it into English. The
atmospheric tale, full of dark, brooding forests and clammy castles was
filmed almost entirely inside a renovated supermarket. The sets consisted
of a few dead branches with Spanish moss hanging from them. There was
a fog machine.

At one point in the picture, Allison Hayes was supposed to whack
off Bruno Ve Sota's head with an axe. Instead of implying the scene off
camera, Bruno suggested they cut a hole in the wall, have him stick his
head through it with the axe embedded in the wall beneath his chin. Have
somebody with his head covered fall away from the axe, pour blood on
everything and gross the audience out.

Too much time, Roger said and shot it the way he had planned in
the first place. There was never any time. A friend told Roger once that
movies weren't supposed to be track meets. But Roger couldn't think of
them any other way.

They were outside, shooting some exteriors for *Diana Love*, when
Roger noticed he was losing light. He ordered Floyd Crosby to shoot
something quick.

"I can't," Floyd replied. "There's no film in the camera."

"I don't care about that," Roger snapped. "Shoot it anyway." Floyd
laughed. Then everyone laughed. Including Roger.

As Chuck predicted the interest in Bridey Murphy had waned by
the time the film was ready for release. Roger gave the film a zombie title
(*The Undead*) and Al Kaylis designed a poster to fit, full of bats hovering
above the head of a skeleton which was menacing a pretty woman in a
nightgown. "TERROR...That Screams From the Grave!"

She Gods of Shark Reef and *Naked Paradise* were shot back to
back in Hawaii. The first picture was a project handed to Roger by a
couple of Texans. The second was initiated by Roger who figured that as
long as he was going on location anyway he might as well shoot two
pictures, which would, in effect, cut the transportation costs in half. He
talked Jim and Sam into splitting the costs with the Texans, then hired
Bobby Campbell to write a second script. Chuck Griffith did a rewrite
that became the basis for three subsequent Corman features: *Beast from
Haunted Cave*, *Creature from the Haunted Sea* and *Atlas*.

Sam Arkoff took the role of a sugar plantation owner in *Naked
Paradise* and accompanied Beverly Garland on the plane over. Bev and
Roger were dating at the time and she told Sam she was glad to be work-
ing on the picture because it was the only time she ever saw Roger.

Roger recruited a lot of local talent for *She-Gods* when he needed a bunch of people to be in outrigger canoes. "None of them could swim," Jonathan Haze recalled. "Hawaiians, you know, don't all swim. Most of them don't. The ones that work on the beach, or live on the beach or something, they do. But the ones that live back in the hills and all that, all these young girls and stuff, they're not that great at swimming. And you put them in outrigger canoes out in the ocean in the current.... What panics we had with them. It's really a wonder that Roger never killed anybody until *Von Richthofen.* * Because a lot of people took a lot of chances."

Variety thought the picture had fine color and little story. It sat on the shelf for two years before it was finally brought to AIP.

Several of the locations Roger selected for *Naked Paradise* (1957) were inaccessible by road. The equipment had to be brought in by boat with a lot of help from the local residents, and most of the picture was filmed on Kauai. Everyone stayed at a hotel there, the Cocoa Palms. Then Roger got a deal on a Boy Scout Camp on the other side of the island and many of the crew members and some of the actors were moved to the camp's barracks. Roger went with them to prove that he was no better than they were.

"I can't do this," Jonathan said after a few nights. "If you want me to act in the movie then I gotta be in a hotel where I don't have eight grips snoring in my ear all night. I don't want to go to sleep at nine o'clock at night. I don't want to have to sit in the toilet to read my script. I want to live like a human being. If you can do this Roger, you do it. You stay here. But I'm going back to the hotel."

Talking with the local residents, Jonathan and Dick Miller learned two important things: you don't run on the coral and you don't mess with suger cane. So when Roger ordered Dick to run into the water, Dick refused.

"You can't run on that coral," Dick said.

"Sure you can," Roger said and before Dick could stop him he dramatically splashed through the water to demonstrate. His sneakers were cut to ribbons.

"*That,*" said Dick, pointing to Roger's feet, "is why you can't."

And the reason you don't mess with sugar cane is because the stuff contains millions of little needles which are not only painful but a mother to extract. So when Roger told Dick and Jonathan to run through a field of sugar cane...

"Show us where you want us to run," they said.

Production shut down while Roger soaked the needles out of his body. Jonathan recalled the incident with a smile. "There was never a

---

A pilot was killed while making Corman's Von Richthofen and Brown *(1971).*

The 'fantastic orgy' sequence promised in the trailers for "Viking Women and the Sea Serpent" (1958).

heated discussion about anything. Roger was not that outgoing that he would express himself. He would pout and get angry and hold resentments and grudges more than anything. Let's face it. He came from a different socio-economic background than I did. He was a Stanford kid. His father was a successful accountant or something. Roger was very Christian. Very straight. Very square. I came from the streets of Pittsburgh where I had been around a lot of gamblers and pimps and boxers and various types like that. Then in New York where I was around the bands and Frank Sinatra and Buddy Rich and Josephine Baker... By the time I was 20 years old, man, I had been around. I don't think Roger had ever been exposed to anything in his life except school and being protected and being sort of a preppy. We came from much different worlds. I came from a world where you knock somebody down if they said something wrong to you. He didn't come from that world. He came from a world of agents and lawyers and professional types. It was amazing that we were able to communicate as much as we could and for as long as we did."

Naked Paradise didn't make any money until it was re-released as *Thunder Over Hawaii* in one of AIP's "Encore Hit" packages with three other titles.

Roger made a film for Allied Artists and a film for Howco before going to work on *Confessions of a Sorority Girl*, shortened to *Sorority Girl* (1957) for AIP. It was a rip-off of Calder Willingham's play "End As a Man," which had already been made into a movie that year called *The Strange One*. Roger did his old trick of changing the protagonist from a male to a female.

Looking over the production costs, Roger questioned AIP's proposed figure for set construction. He told Jim and Sam to forget the sets. He'd film in somebody's home. It looked better and it was cheaper.

It was Jack Rabin, a fellow who specialized in special effects for low budget films, that approached Roger with the idea to make *The Saga of the Viking Women and Their Voyage to the Waters of the Great Sea Serpent* (1958) which was shortened to *Viking Women and the Sea Serpent* for the posters and newspaper advertisements.

Rabin's story boards, dynamic illustrations of ships caught in whirlpools and people battling gigantic sea serpents, sparked Roger's interest, especially after Jack assured him that the drawings could be brought to life for a mere $20,000 plus a small piece of the picture. It was an opportunity to make a million dollar movie for $100,000 in ten days.

Roger showed the drawings to Jim and Sam and they told him to go for it. Roger would later complain that he'd been sold a bill of goods.

Rabin's partner, Irving Block, was almost killed shooting one of the effects sequences. An intelligent man, Block was never known for having a great deal of patience.* He was standing in the pool of water they'd built with tarps, anxious to get on with the scene, barking at the cameraman to hurry.

"Turn that damn camera on or we're gonna lose the thing!" he snapped. Unable to wait any longer, he flicked the switch on himself with his other hand still in the water. He succeeded in shorting the camera and nearly electrocuting himself.

"That was the biggest scare I had in my life," he said, "Maybe it's good for someone doing science fiction — it turns your brains inside-out."

Much of the picture was shot at Crystal Cove. The leading lady called in sick the first day. Roger moved all of the females in his cast up one notch and hired an extra to fill in the gap.

One afternoon Roger ordered several members of his cast to mount horses and ride them toward the edge of a cliff at full gallop. The camera was placed on the other side of the cliff. They ran through it once and a couple of people almost went over. The second time Roger called for action nobody budged.

"Come on. Come on," Roger called to them through his megaphone. "This will be an exciting scene."

Betsy-Jones Moreland grabbed her own megaphone and said, "It's pretty dangerous."

"It's in your contract, Betsy," Roger reminded her.

"It's in your hat, Roger," she called back.

At $300 a week SAG minimum, Roger couldn't expect too much. The scene was broomed.

It was Roger's idea to give the film a long title, embossed on a leather-bound book of the film's credits. Roger figured as long as they were making a corny picture they might as well go all the way.

It was on this picture that Roger made his record number of camera set-ups for one day: 73. "Never mind waiting for the slates," Roger said and that was when Dan knew they were moving fast.

As for those wonderful effects promised by Jack Rabin — you can pretty well guess how they looked.

Block's impatience got the better of him when he was working on a film about giant wasps. At the film's climax, the wasps were to be destroyed by lava flooding their nest. Two high speed cameras were trained on the miniature set and the order was given to pour the phony lava. The wasp puppets were dancing around and everything was going as planned until Block decided things didn't look hot enough. So he started flinging chunks of dry ice at the set. There was so much smoke that it completely obliterated the image on one camera. The other camera beautifully captured, in slow motion, Block's hands throwing the dry ice.

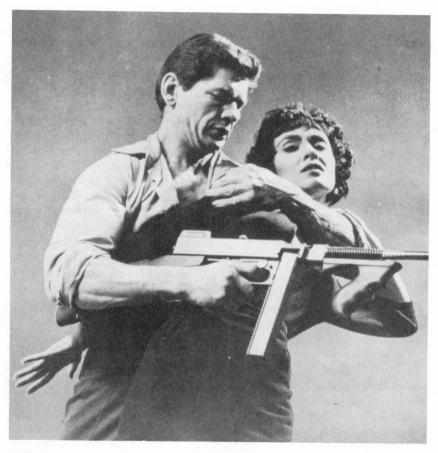

Charles Bronson as "Machine Gun Kelly" (1958) fondly embraces Susan Cabot.

A fictionalized account of *Machine Gun Kelly* (1958) was Roger's next project. It was written by Bobby Campbell for his brother, William. Roger signed Dick Miller. Bobby complained. As a result Roger decided against Dick and William Campbell. "Pay Dick off," Roger said, "and get me the names of three actors available to play Kelly by tomorrow."

Of the three, Roger chose Charles Bronson. Broson played the role of a coward ("Without his gun he was naked yellow!") who is propelled into a life of crime by his aggresive female companion, Susan Cabot. The film was just off-beat enough to be well received.

"Takes the trouble to sketch briefly, but effectively, minor characters and incidents that give weight and meaning to the otherwise sordid story," wrote *Variety*. The French critics went wild. They spoke of Roger as a real filmmaker. Roger was flattered but for him it was business as usual. He paid Martin Varno $900 to write *The Creature from Galaxy 27*, later changed by Jim Nicholson to *Night of the Blood Beast*, then took advantage of the writer by demanding constant revisions. Marty finally asked for more money. Roger refused. Marty took his grievance to the Writer's Guild. Roger was ordered to pay an additional $600, which he did, reluctantly, at the last possible moment.

Not too far from Hollywood, just across the street from the Santa Anita Racetrack in Arcadia, there is an expansive chunk of land once owned by Lucky Baldwin, called the Aboretum, the home of hundreds of plants, shrubs, peacocks and ducks. The ducks seem to stay close to a little gingerbread structure called Queen Anne's Cottage which is surrounded on all sides by a body of water that winds around a dense growth of tropical vegetation, rugged trees and vines. It has attracted movie companies for years. MGM filmed a lot of Tarzan movies there. Roger was there for one day to film scenes for another Bobby Campbell script, *Prehistoric World*.

One of the first orders of business was for Beach Dickerson to drown. Beach was hired for one week's work as an actor and as a production assistant the following week. Roger asked him to fall off a log into the coffee black water. As the actor flailed around Roger knelt beside the bank and, with his face scant inches away from Beach, said, "I don't believe you're drowning. You're not convincing me."

The water was so filthy Beach almost threw up. He decided to relax and give Roger what he wanted. He kicked and screamed and sank deep into the water, then floated to the top like a dead man, secure in the knowledge that Roger could only kill him once.

They went to Bronson Canyon to film Beach's funeral scene. Everyone in the cast sat in a half circle, many of them solemnly beating tomtoms. Beach sat in the wardrobe truck and watched.

"What are you doing here?" Roger asked.

"Well, I cannot be out *there*," Beach said. "It's *my* funeral."

"Bullshit," Roger said. "Who would recognize you anyway?"

In a matter of minutes Beach had on a fright wig and a bearskin. He sat in the front row.

A few days later it was time to shoot the sequence in which a character referred to in the script as The Man from the Burning Plains rides into camp and is stoned to death.

"Who's going to play the Man from the Burning Plains?" Beach innocently asked. Then he knew the answer. Oh, fuck, he thought, looking at the ground he was supposed to fall on. It was solid granite.

"I'm not a stunt man," Beach said.

"You're just as capable of falling off a horse as anyone," Roger said.

Jonathan Haze (left) and Leslie Bradley parade in front of Bronson Canyon in this scene from "Teenage Caveman" (formerly "Prehistoric World," 1958).

"And save you fifty bucks," Beach retorted.

He rode into camp on his sway-back horse, disguised by a beard, looking like Ulysses S Grant in bearskin. He was stoned to death and fell from his steed as written.

And he was terrific.

"I think I saw his underwear," the photographer told Roger.

Roger became hysterical. "You're wearing underwear! How dare you!"

"Of course I'm wearing underwear," Beach said angrily. "I've got a bearskin around me for crissakes."

They did the scene again.

The next day, at Iverson's Ranch, they filmed the big bear hunt.

Beach was waiting for the bear to show up until he saw a guy stepping toward him with a bear suit in his hands.

Oh my God, Beach thought. In no time at all they zipped him inside the suit and he was at the top of a hill, on all fours, his head between his legs, sweating like an iced glass.

"Okay, bear," Roger yelled. "Come down the hill."

Beach came down the hill backwards.

"What are you doing?" Roger screamed.

"I can't see anything, for crissakes!" Beach screamed back.

Roger panicked. "Well, what can we do? Think quick."

Beach suggested they make a path for him to follow with a rope. He also suggested that they do it fast because he was roasting to death inside the suit.

Down the hill he came.

"Okay, bear," Roger said. "Stand up."

The bear did.

"Okay. You're a mean bear."

The bear growled.

"You're not mean enough."

Before long Roger and Beach were screaming at each other until Roger was satisfied that Beach was mean. Then he ordered the actors to kill the bear.

The script called for the hero, in this instance played by Robert Vaughn, to kill a deer and carry it back to camp. The stuffed deer supplied for the occasion was so fake Roger decided to photograph it from a far distance, through trees. The sneak preview audience laughed anyway and Roger had to snip the scene.

The film was released as *Teenage Caveman* (1958).

"You got something for Ed Nelson?" Roger asked Bruno Ve Sota. "I want to put him on production. I'll help."

Ed had been in *Teenage Caveman*. He'd been in a number of Roger's pictures, usually in small supporting roles. Bruno asked Gordon Urquhart to write a script about a 50 year old scientific expedition to the bowels of the earth, the survivors of which return with creatures on their backs that control them. It was titled *The Keepers* but AIP changed it to *The Brain Eaters* (1958). It was shot in six days for $26,000. Ed Nelson produced and starred. He also made the monsters.

"Bru," Ed said. "I want you to look at this. See if you like it."

Bru and Ed entered Ed's darkened garage in Pomona. Ed left Bruno's side for a moment then returned. He flicked on a flashlight and pointed the beam at a furry little creature crawling on the cement floor toward them. Whatever it was it was breathing. Its antennae moved back and forth.

It looked terrific.

Ed explained that he used a motorized toy ladybug, covered with fur from an old used coat. The antennae were pipecleaners.

The picture was already completed when Bruno got a call from Roger saying that author Robert Heinlein was going to sue for plagiarism. Bruno rushed to the library to read Heinlein's *The Puppet Masters*. The stories were similar, but not enough to worry about.

Even though Ed's little furry monsters looked terrible on film (once they were flooded with lights), Roger asked him to make the suits for *Attack of the Giant Leeches* (1959). Another acting job called Ed away. Whoever did make the suits (Jay Sayer said it was the producer's wife) forgot to leave room for the airtanks. The suits ripped throughout the picture.

The last picture Roger made for AIP in the 50s was perhaps his best, a horror comedy called *A Bucket of Blood* (1959). It all started with Roger giving Chuck Griffith a tour of the sets built for another AIP production, *Diary of a High School Bride* (1959).

"You see these?" Roger said. There was a coffee house, a living room, an apartment, and a police office. "They're going to be standing for an extra week. Write a horror picture for these sets."

Chuck hammered out the first 20 pages of *The Yellow Door* and gave them to Roger to read.

"This is comedy!" Roger said furiously. Chuck was always trying to sneak comedy in on him.

"Roger. You're going to make it for $30,000. How can you lose?"

Roger thought a moment. "All right. How do you shoot comedy?"

"Just shoot it straight," Chuck instructed.

Juvenile delinquency might have been a dead issue by 1959, but no one had taken a good look at the folks too old for rock and roll and hot rods, the ones who hung out in dingy coffee houses instead of malt shops, who wore sweat-shirts, smoked dope, and listened to free-form poetry and progressive jazz, a group of people collectively known as Beatniks. Chuck's script opened with a speech delivered by one Maxwell H. Brock, aged 35, stocky, unkempt, dour and hidden behind thick, black-rimmed glasses.

"I will talk to you of art," Brock intones with cool intensity," for there is nothing else to talk about, for there is nothing else... Life is an obscure hobo, bumming a ride on the omnibus of art... Burn gas buggies and whip your sour cream of circumstance and hope, and go ahead and sleep your bloody heads off... Creation is. All else is not. What is not creation is graham crackers. Let it all crumble to feed the creator... The artist is. All others are not. A canvas is a canvas or a painting. A rock is a rock or a statue. A sound is a sound or is music. A creature is a creature or an

Dick Miller proudly displays his new work of art to Antony Carbone who knows there's a real head beneath the clay. "A Bucket of Blood" (1959).

artist. Where are John Jake Joe Jim Jerk? Dead dead dead dead dead. Before they were born. They were not born. They were not born. Where are Leonardo, Rembrandt, Ludwig? Alive alive alive. They were born. Bring on the multitude with a multitude of fishes. Feed them to the fishes for liver oil to nourish the artist... Give them hair upon their heads, so that he will have brushes... Stretch their skins upon an easel, to give him canvas... Crush their bones into a paste that he might mold them... String their tendons to a lute, that he might play them... Let them bleed, that he might have paint... Let them love him, and he will be inspired... Let them weep, that his thirst may be slaked. Let them feed him that he will be satisfied... Let them caress him, that he will be soothed... Let them fall beneath his feet, that he might walk in comfort... Let them kill that he might be avenged... Let them steal that he might be recompensed... Put them in chains, that he might be free. Let them die, and by their miserable deaths, become the clay within his hands, that he might form an ashtray or an ark... Man is the tissue of majesty. We mold him to the diadem of the eye, the finger's gold, the glory of the heart. Pray that you might be his diadem gold glory paint clay. That he might take you in his magic hands, and wring from your marrow wonders. For all that is comes through the eye of the artist. The rest are just blind fish, swimming in the cave of anonymity. Swim on, you maudlin, muddling, maddened fools. And dream that one bright and sunny night some artist will bait a hook and let you bite upon it! Bite hard and perish! In his stomach, you are very close to immortality."

Julian Bruton, the actor who played Maxwell Brock, received a round of applause from everyone on the set when he finished the speech. Roger took Chuck out to dinner that night and said: "We've got to do another one right away. I don't want a sequel or anything else. I want exactly the same picture. Just change the names and locations."

Chuck went to work on *Gluttony*, the story of a salad chef who serves up people. It was dropped because cannibalism was against the production code. He wrote *The Passionate People Eater*, about a hungry plant; it was retitled *The Little Shop of Horrors*. The legend surrounding the film is that it was made in two days. That was how long it took Roger to finish the interiors. The exteriors, which Chuck directed, took an additional four days. The film gained a cult following and recently became the subject of a Broadway musical.

"*Bucket of Blood* is still my favorite picture," Dick Miller said. "None of these are great pictures understand. But I always thought if *Bucket of Blood* had had another chunk of money in production it would have ranked with any of the top horror films. It's the best script Chuck ever wrote."

Variety was less enthusiastic. "During the first half of the picture there are many opportunities for gruesome humor, of which writer Charles B. Griffith takes full advantage. In the latter half, the humor becomes lost...." But Dick Miller, according to the reviewer, was able to "sustain a sense of poignancy while acting conceited and committing atrocities" and was largely responsible for the picture's appeal.

The night Roger finished shooting the picture he told his crew to leave all of the equipment, that he and his brother Gene might be shooting something on the weekend. Once everyone was gone Roger and Gene packed it all themselves. No sense paying the crew an extra hour's wages.

"Roger's a tight man with a buck," Dick Miller said. "I don't mind you printing that so long as you also add that once you've made a deal with him you don't have to worry about anything afterwards. I mean he'll do his best to get the most for the least while the deal is being made but once it's done you can work on a handshake."

The picture was sent out with *Attack of the Giant Leeches*. The package lost money. AIP was in trouble.

Midway in the "Attack of the Giant Leeches" (1959).

In 1957 American International Pictures released 22 motion pictures, 11 combinations, all of them successful. In 1958 they released 20 motion pictures, 10 combinations, slightly less successful. By 1959 they were starting to bottom out. Other companies were imitating their genre combinations, not just schlock outfits like Howco and Allied Artists but the majors who were picking up independently made horror films and J.D. films. And the majors had more clout getting them booked, played and paid. The competition had taken a large bite out of AIP's revenue.

Also the exhibitors weren't paying their bills or they were taking too damn long to do it. It was Sam's belief that the exhibitors would look at the money they'd made from an AIP picture and start thinking of it as their own. AIP? Why that wasn't an expensive picture. Why should they get 50%? 40%? 35%? It doesn't cost them as much. It really wasn't that good a picture. So why not use the money, interest free, to invest in hotels and fast-food restaurants?

There were times an exhibitor wouldn't agree on the settlement figures. "If you guys want your money now you can have it as long as you take 25%." Sometimes Jim and Sam would have to take it although Sam fought like hell for the full amount.

Less profit to be made because of the competition and the revenue shortage caused by the exhibitors' reluctance to pay caused the quality of AIP's product to nosedive. For example *The Naked Invader*, which became *The Astounding She-Monster* (1958) to please the censor, was made in four days by Ronnie Ashcroft, the owner of an editing service. Most of the story took place in one room with four or five people talking each other to death. Exteriors were shot in pantomime so Ronnie wouldn't have to worry about synch sound. A narrator was used to explain the visuals that didn't make any sense. The "She-Monster" was a woman in a skin-tight glittery costume which turned out to be a little too tight. During the first day the actress bent over and ripped the zipper. She was instructed to always face the camera so she would often exit a scene walking backwards, as there was no time to repair the costume.

"It was kind of a piece of junk," said the film's hero, Robert Clarke. "Certainly I couldn't be very proud of having been in it."

It taught Bob one thing. If Ronnie could do it, he could do it. Bob went out and made *The Hideous Sun Demon*, shot on six weekends to take advantage of the fact that most camera stores were closed on weekends so equipment rented on Friday didn't have to be returned until Monday but the rent was still for one day.

AIP's war movies were equally impoverished. Director Sherman Rose did *Tank Battalion* (1958) with only one tank. *Suicide Battalion* (1958), which had a great tag line—"To hell with orders...we ATTACK!"—was shot almost entirely inside the studio on small, unconvincing sets. By the time *Operation Dames* (1959) was ready for release AIP wasn't sure how to sell it so they tried two different approaches. It was sold as a straight war epic and a comedy. One advertisement depicted a woman fighting a Japanese soldier with the tag line: "No fury like four girls trapped behind enemy lines!" Another ad showed a woman bathing in a stream with cartoon drawings of G.I.s trying to get a peek while the tag line claimed the picture was the "wild, wacky adventures of four gorgeous U.S.O. girls and their lovin' G.I.'s...when the cold war turned hot!"

Below, the radio spot for *Hell Squad* (1958):

ANNOUNCER: Roaring through the hell of battle, they were as tough as

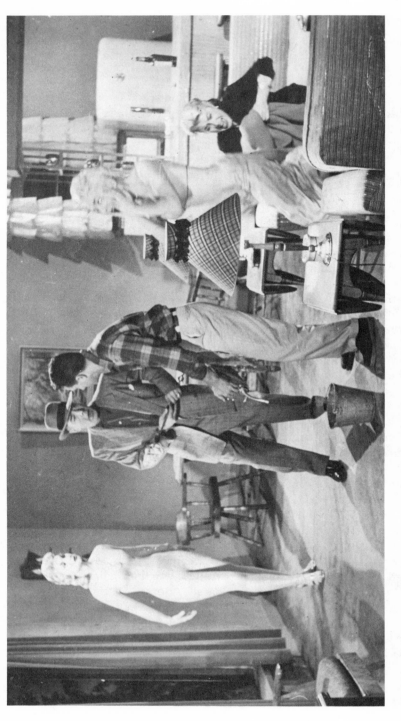

Shirley Kilpatrick (left), "The Astounding She-Monster" (1958), dare not turn around or the audience will see that the zipper is ripped on her costume. Kenne Duncan, Robert Clark and Marilyn Harvey already know.

For the last time Paul Blaisdell dons his She-Creature outfit for "The Ghost of Dragstrip Hollow" (1959).

their name, these men of the Hell Squad. And when the battle was over, only two men remained alive—the American sergeant and the German officer. And they were alone in a sea of desert sand.

OFFICER: What is the matter, American? Caught in the minefield? You can't get out maybe? You should light my match, ya?

SERGEANT: An maybe you'd like my water? Ya?

OFFICER: (under his breath) Water? (Louder) You throw me your canteen. I come get you.

SERGEANT: Listen, Kraut. You want my water? You come and get it.
(Sounds of machine gun blasts)

ANNOUNCER: *Hell Squad!* Learning the only war is the dirty war and will last as long as one man remains alive to hunt the other. *Hell Squad!* And on the same program...

(More machine gun blasts)
...a squad of men pinned to the earth by the white hot bullets of the enemy's machine gun. One by one they went for help. And one by one they were slaughtered until...
(Explosion)
Two shattering war action hits! *Tank Battalion* and *Hell Squad*.
(Fade out with machine gun blasts)

As the returns on the pictures dwindled so did the quality. It wasn't at all surprising to see Paul Blaisdell donning his She-Creature outfit again, modified of course, for *The Haunted Hot-Rod*, which was released as *The Ghost of Dragstrip Hollow* (1959). He was between takes with the head off, catching some air, when one of the actors walked by and told Paul he looked like an old condom.

Director Spencer Bennett (left) and Alex Gordon. They made "Submarine Sea-hawk" (1958) together.

Ten

Sword and Sandal

There's one thing you've got to understand if you're going to understand AIP. The exhibitors didn't want us to get bigger. They wanted us to stay in that little niche where we'd make pictures that they could buy for 25% and then say, "Look how we've helped the boys." They didn't want us to get bigger because they liked us where we were, serving a function. We made a lot of money for them. Whenever we'd branch out into something bigger very often they'd write us: "No. No. No. No. No. This is not for you!"

—Samuel Arkoff

Jerry Wald once asked Jim Nicholson and Sam Arkoff to lift their horizons, a suggestion they understandably ignored. But the time had come for them to *expand* their horizons. The ten-day black and white combinations were dying at the boxoffice. To stay alive Jim and Sam were going to have to gamble and upgrade their product. Instead of making two black and whites for $100,000 apiece they were going to have to invest $300,000 in a single feature, produced in color and CinemaScope. This new and improved production needed to be respectable looking, at least enough so that it could command a percentage of the boxoffice without being part of a combination. It would have to stand on its own. Jim and Sam gambled that Roger Corman could pull it off.

In the meantime, Jim and Sam needed pictures. They were, after all, the president and vice president of a distribution company. To stay in business they needed something to distribute. Most of their money, however, was tied up in the film Roger was making. They couldn't really afford to make another picture.

It was Joe Levine, their Boston distributor, the man who offered to pay for the privilege of burning *Beast with 1,000,000 Eyes*, that gave Jim and Sam the solution to their problem. Joe had just been to Italy where he picked up, for peanuts, the U.S. distribution rights to an Italian muscleman fantasy titled *The Loves of Hercules* starring Steve Reeves, a former Mr. Universe. Joe shortened the title to *Hercules*, dubbed it into English and spent $1,000,000 to promote it. The picture was cleaning up. Jim and

There wasn't a gladiator in the picture when Nicholson and Arkoff purchased "The Sign of Rome" for U.S. distribution—but there was after they dubbed the Italian epic; hence the new title "Sign of the Gladiator" (1959).

Sam flew to Italy to pick up their own bargain. They bought two pictures: *Sign of Rome* and *The Revenge of Hercules*.

Jim changed *Sign of Rome* to *Sign of the Gladiator* (1959), a title that promised a lot more in the way of excitement. There was only one small problem. There wasn't a gladiator in the picture. Jim and Sam fixed that by giving one of the characters a new background when the picture was dubbed into English. Sam explained it this way: "We conceived that this man, this Roman consul, had been a slave tossed in the gladitors ring. When the Roman blood got thin, which happened along about 300 A.D., they brought people who had been successful gladiators and put them in the Roman Army. Whether or not anybody ever got up to the position this Roman consul did in our picture... Anyway, the queen of Syria, played by Anita Ekberg, gives this Roman consul the old sex play to get him to betray himself. If he doesn't overcome the Queen, who he's in love with, he could wind up back in the gladiator ring. Now there was a gladiator in the story. You didn't really have him in the picture but that made the thing work. And we had a modest success with that picture." This was in spite of the fact that the film's negative was fogged, making it impossible to strike a decent print.

At a press conference in New York Jim Nicholson announced that the success of *Sign of the Gladiator* prompted AIP to switch from exploitation gimmick pictures to blockbuster gimmick pictures, to be released at a rate of one every two months. *Horrors of the House of Usher* was slated for March, *Aladdin and the Giant* for May, *Circus of Horrors* of July and Jules Verne's *In the Year 2889* for September. All the pictures were to be shot in CinemaScope and color. (*Aladdin* and *2889* never materialized.)

The switch to blockbusters was going to necessitate expansion of the company's distribution and publicity staff. Regional sales managers were to be supplemented by division managers which were to be appointed for the West Coast, the central states and the Southwest. National advertising campaigns of $500,000 to $1,000,000 were anticipated for each major production, to include radio, television and picture magazines. Sunday supplements would coincide with regional playoffs. Advertising campaigns were expected to exceed twice the cost of the pictures.

Scheduled to kick off this new wave of blockbusters was *Goliath and the Barbarians* (1959), the new title for *The Revenge of Hercules*. It would have been more advantageous to retain the original title but Jim and Sam didn't want to step on Joe Levine's toes. In fact, Joe was invited to see the picture before it was dubbed into English. He slept most of the way through it and declared at the end that it wouldn't make a dime. There was a way, however, to capitalize on Joe's picture as exemplified by the following radio spot:

ANNOUNCER: When brutal barbarian hordes savagely slashed across the face of the earth, pillaging and ravaging, through it all their leader had one cry...

LEADER: Kill them!

ANNOUNCER: Into the bloodshed stepped a fearless leader, young and powerful. Steve Reeves, Mister Hercules himself, in his greatest role.

STEVE: I will have my revenge. I swear it. This murderer shall have no peace.

ANNOUNCER: He revenged his father's death by killing 10,000 barbarians. They called him Goliath, the greatest of all warriors. *Goliath and the Barbarians*, the giant of giants of all great spectacles.

Jack Zide opened the picture at the Detroit Palms theatre on Christmas Eve. Expecting an empty house he gave his employees the night off. Jack pulled in $3,500 that night. It was the best single day gross in five years.

Duncan R. Kennedy, the vice president of the Publix Great States Theatres, fired off the following telegram to Leon Blender:

GOLIATH AND THE BARBARIANS OPENED IN FIFTEEN OF OUR TOWNS TO BLOCK-BUSTER GROSSES. THIS ENGAGEMENT IN ALL SITUATIONS EXTENDING THROUGH CHRISTMAS SHOULD SET RECORDS EVERYWHERE.

Jim and Sam received the following telegram from Raymond Willie, the vice president and general manager of Interstate Circuiting:

"GOLIATH AND THE BARBARIANS" OPENED IN DALLAS, HOUSTON, SAN ANTONIO, FORT WORTH AND GALVESTON ON FRIDAY, DECEMBER 18TH, TO THE BIGGEST GROSSES OF ANY PICTURE IN THE HISTORY OF OUR COMPANY PRE-CHRISTMAS PLAYING TIME. THANKS TO AMERICAN INTERNATIONAL FOR THE AVAILABILITY OF THIS ATTRACTION AT THIS PARTICULAR SEASON.

The picture literally saved AIP. Its soundtrack became the first released by AIP's newly formed record company.

Opposite; Two victims of Shuller's circus, also known as the Jinx Circus: top, Yvonne Romain after being mauled by lions; bottom, Vanda Hudson in a scene censored in American prints. From "Circus of Horrors" (1960).

Top: Whilst out rampaging, "Konga" (1960) startles a group of firemen. Bottom: he studies his next line with producer Herman Cohen and actress Claire Gordon.

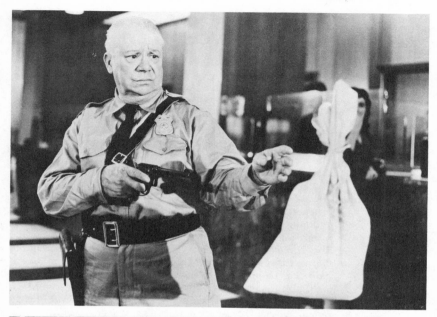

Top: Perhaps the silliest still in the book, from "The Amazing Transparent Man" (1960). Bottom: Bob Ball and Frank Ray try to be funny in this scene from "Invasion of the Star Creatures" (1962), in roles originally intended for Dick Miller and Jonathan Haze.

Eleven

The Poe Pictures

There's a story out about me that I didn't want to do the Poe picture. That's all bullshit. That's something Roger made up. The fact of the matter is, if I may say so, and I don't mean to toot my own horn, I happen to have a bigger background in all that kind of stuff than any of them do. I'm talking about reading and so on and so forth. Look, I'm not going to take credit for everything. What difference does it make? And I don't take anything away from Jim. Jim had a very good knowledge of former pictures and was terrific in his own areas. And it really doesn't make any difference. If people want to believe that old business that I didn't want to make House of Usher *because it didn't have a monster—Jesus Christ some of the classic horror pictures ... I was the only one of them that had ever seen M—it doesn't make any difference. Because it's all bullshit. It's so ridiculous. As if somehow posterity's gonna give a shit.*
— Samuel Arkoff

The $350,000 color and CinemaScope feature that Jim and Sam decided to gamble on was *House of Usher* (1960), based on Edgar Allan Poe's "The Fall of the House of Usher." There's no way to know who it was that picked Poe. Roger Corman said that idea was his, inspired by the bound volume of Poe's short stories that his father had given to him as a child. In fact, Roger said it was his idea to abandon the black and white combinations, having become restless with the format. But Sam was against adapting the Poe story because there wasn't a monster in the story. Not wanting to lose the project Roger told Sam that the house was the monster. During the shooting of the picture the film's leading man, Vincent Price, stepped over to Roger between takes and pointed to a couple of lines he was supposed to say—*The house lives! The house breathes!* It made no sense to Vince and he wondered why he had to say it. Roger explained that the lines had been included to persuade Sam to let them make the picture. Vince promised to bring life to those lines. When questioned about it Vince didn't recall the incident but added that after over 100 pictures he remembered very little about any of them. Sam Arkoff dismissed the whole business as bullshit.

110

It seems unlikely that it was Roger's idea to stop making the black and white combinations. Between *A Bucket of Blood* and *House of Usher* he produced and directed *The Wasp Woman, The Little Shop of Horrors,* and *The Creature from the Haunted Sea,* and produced *Beast from Haunted Cave,* all black and whites for his own company Filmgroup. Whether or not the choice of the Edgar Allan Poe story was Roger's or Jim's or Sam's (one source credits Sam with having selected Poe because the author was in the public domain) is anybody's guess.

There's another yarn that Jim Nicholson was agreeable to the idea only if the title of Poe's story was shortened to fit the marquee, which it was, but during production it was known as "The Mysterious House of Usher" and "Horrors of the House of Usher." So who knows if that story is true either.

Jim Nicholson contacted Richard Matheson about writing the script. The author had had a number of successes in the fantasy field as a novelist and a screenwriter. His novels included *I Am Legend* and *The Shrinking Man,* the latter made into a successful motion picture which Matheson had scripted. He'd also written several teleplays for "The Twilight Zone," often based on his previously written short stories.

AIP's breakthrough to the big time (1960).

Behind the scenes of "House of Usher" (1960). Top: Pat Dinga sprays the joint with spider webs while Vincent Price and Harry Ellerby look on. Bottom: Price and Myrna Fahey get into position for the climax while technicians dirty up the place.

Matheson was made aware of the limited budget allotted to the film but didn't feel restricted by it. There were, after all, only four characters to worry about and they were stuck in one house for most of the story so there wasn't much to spend money on. In fact the only exterior sequence took place at the very beginning of Matheson's script, when the visitor arrived at the Usher mansion. Roger filmed that sequence on the site of a recent fire in the Hollywood Hills. The scarred and barren landscape provided exactly the right setting, far more atmospheric than anything Dan Haller could have recreated inside the studio.

Milton Mortiz fired off a letter to all of AIP's subdistributors:

Dear Mr. Exhibitor:

I am happy to enclose a proof of the newspaper campaign that has been prepared for the Edgar Allan Poe classic HOUSE OF USHER in CinemaScope and color starring Vincent Price. As you will note from these proofs, we have included a little of everything to reach the largest possible audience.

At this time I would also like to advise you that the radio campaign for HOUSE OF USHER was prepared by Gordon McLendon, who has a reputation for turning out some of the most powerful radio campaigns ever heard. The radio spots on HOUSE OF USHER are among the most impressive he has ever done.

We are sure that with the quality of the advertising material that will be made available to you in addition to the national promotion of this feature, HOUSE OF USHER will be one of the top grossers of this year.

The radio spots mentioned in Milt's letter were indeed unusual for AIP, not at all conceived in their usual all-stops-out manner. The spots opened with an unusually restrained announcer describing the Usher house:

Only once did I risk the most distant glimpse of the grim and forboding house of Usher. The mere sight of that awesome structure, huge and menacing, struck me chill with fear. It lay like a malignant sore that festered in the middle of the wasteland. Overhead the clouds hung low and a ghastly vapor rose from the ground. It seemed that the roots of the house touched the very coals of Hell.

Vincent Price stepped in to quote a line or two from the film and the announcer returned to make sure everyone remembered what the title of the film was.

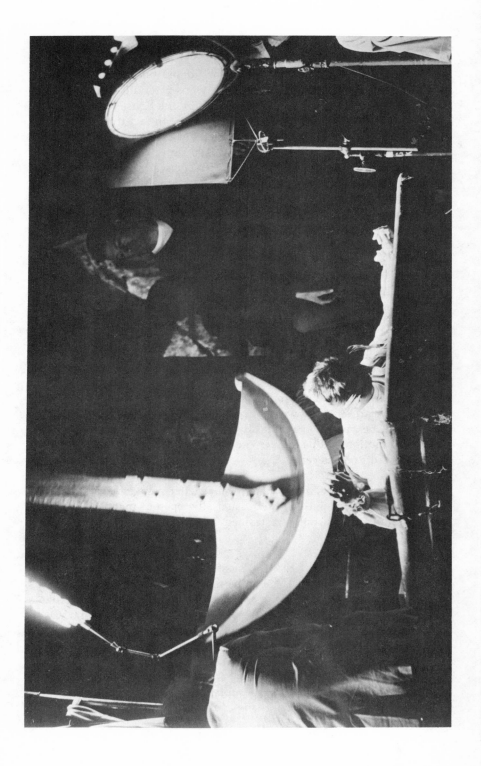

Vincent Price shares a bottle with Barbara Steele and Antony Carbone, in "The Pit and the Pendulum" (1960).

Although the feature was released with *Attack of the Giant Leeches*, most theatres chose to separate the package. *Usher* was, as Jim and Sam had hoped, able to command the percentage money regardless. It was often teamed with *Psycho*, playing theatres that normally didn't book AIP movies.

"It is a film that should attract mature tastes as well as thoses who come to the cinema for sheer thrills," wrote *Variety*. "It's also a potent, rewarding attraction for children. All things considered, pro and con, the fall of the *House of Usher* seems to herald the rise of the House of AIP."

Betty Martin of the *Los Angeles Times* found that the production managed "a fair amount of suspense throughout," the settings were "lavish" and the color photography "flamboyant." She added that it was a "Better than average" horror film "if that's saying much," which was her way of reminding everyone, as do many critics when reviewing horror films, that no matter how good a horror film might be it was still, after all, just a horror film.

Opposite: John Kerr struggles to free himself as the blade descends. "The Pit and the Pendulum" (1961).

The New York Herald Tribune complained about some of the dialog but didn't feel it seriously damaged "the mood set by the art work, the music, the direction and the acting of Price, whose intellectual grasp of this bizarrerie is fine to see." The whole business was "a heartening move in the right direction, a restoration of finesse and craftsmanship to the genre of the dread."

The moment Jim and Sam realized they had a boxoffice hit on their hands they asked Roger Corman to make *The Pit and the Pendulum* (1961). Richard Matheson used Poe's story as the climax and concocted his own first and second acts. The action was again restricted to a single setting, this time a castle in 16th-century Spain.

Dan Haller, Roger's art director since *War of the Satellites* (1958), was the one who had to bring the story's title elements of life. The first thing he did was remove the catwalks at Producer's Studio which gave his set more depth and heighth. The pendulum he installed, which was supposed to descend on actor John Kerr, had a rubberized blade which, much to everyone's dismay, stuck to the actor's belly. Dan switched to a metalized blade. It had to be positioned in such as way that it could slash Kerr's shirt without slashing Kerr. A steel band was wrapped around his waist as a precaution. It took four men to swing the pendulum. The manual operation gave them better control. The actor was a good sport about it all but Dan noticed that he perspired a lot.

"Edgar Allan Poe would have been proud of the treatment American International has given his short story," wrote Len Simpson in *Limelight*. "*The Pit and the Pendulum* is even more inventively made and edited than *House of Usher*," said Robert Roman of *Films in Review*. *Time* magazine called it "a literary hair-raiser" and the critic for *The New York Times* said it was "Hollywood's most effective Poe-style horror flavoring to date," and complimented the "rich colors, plushy decor and eerie music." The movie earned more money than its predecessor. Roger figured he was entitled to a bigger slice of the profits.

It just so happened that the folks at Pathé Labs wanted to start their own distribution outfit. They figured a Poe/Corman movie would be a fine way to start. They offered to grubstake Roger on terms sweeter than AIP's. In every respect it would be like the two previous Poe pictures — Marjorie Corso would handle the costumes, Floyd Crosby would be in charge of the art direction, Jack Bohrer would be the production manager, Floyd Crosby would handle the camera — with one major exception: Vincent Price. He was under contract to AIP (and according to an article in the *Herald Tribune* the actor received $125,000 per picture plus a percentage of the profits). Ray Milland was hired in his stead. Ray Russell and Charles Beaumont adapted Poe's story and Ronald Stein filled in for Les Baxter on the score.

Two days into production of *The Premature Burial* (1962) Roger saw Jim Nicholson and Sam Arkoff enter the sound stage. He didn't know if they had come to cause trouble or congratulate him. As they approached him Roger felt uneasy. But there was a smile on Sam's face and he was reaching out to shake Roger's hand.

"Welcome back to American International," Sam said grinning.

"What do you mean, Sam?"

Sam had called Pathé and politely reminded them that AIP supplied a lot of their lab work. It would be a simple matter for AIP to take it somewhere else. And so Pathé sold their interest in the picture to Jim and Sam. It wasn't as easy to bargain with Roger.

After two months of negotiations Roger received $500,000 plus an immediate $50,000 profit for his half-interest. The film was brought in for $450,000.

"Key exploitation stunt for *The Premature Burial*," suggested a section in the movie's pressbook marked Seat Selling Slants, "which will result in top space in all newspapers and on television, is an actual burial alive demonstration by a man or pretty girl. Should you have difficulty in contacting a stunt-man or woman in your area for this purpose, get in touch with publicity department, American International Pictures, 7165 Sunset Blvd., Hollywood, Calif."

"Taking a cue from the seat-selling success of the marquee cut-out of a pendulum for *The Pit and the Pendulum*, and use of the swinging pendulum to control seating of crowds, the same kind of device can be used for *The Premature Burial*. In this case a cut-out of a coffin, with ropes raising and lowering the box can be used as was the pendulum for *Pit*. Set a cut-out of a coffin, made of heavy cardboard or similar material with a pully device for raising and lowering. Advertise in ads and in theatre that 'No one will be admitted or seated while the coffin is being lowered' to make a striking attention-getting crowd puller."

There was also a suggestion to have a special midnight screening for gravediggers.

The New York Times thought the film was "static, slack and starchily written" while *Variety* felt it was all too familiar. "By this time, many film fans (and at least one reviewer) are as familiar with Corman's downstairs dungeon as they are with their own basement hobbyshops...." *The New York Herald Tribune* called it "handsome," and "no less attractively designed or tastefully colored" than the two previous entries.

"The Facts in the Case of M. Valdemar," "The Black Cat" (combined with "The Cask of Amontillado") and "Morello" became the basis for *Tales of Terror* (1962). By the time it reached the screen the first and last story had switched order.

For the middle segment writer Matheson completely strayed from

Vincent Price thinks Peter Lorre is only joking about walling him up. He doesn't realize that the woman next to him (Joyce Jameson) is already dead. *The Cask of Amontillado* **sequence from "Tales of Terror" (1962).**

Poe by injecting humor into the proceedings. It featured Vincent Price as a professional wine taster who falls in love with Peter Lorre's wife, Joyce Jameson. The scene where Lorre stumbles into the room where Vince is demonstrating his abilities as an authority on fine wines is absolutely delightful. Lorre challenges Vince to a contest to see which of them is the real expert, which is nothing but an excuse for Lorre's alcoholic character to get free booze. The two get stinking drunk trying to out-do each other. A professional wine taster demonstrated the proper procedure for the two actors. Roger Corman sat back and watched them run away with it.

"Roger was good at letting people do anything that they said they could do," Jonathan Haze remarked. "You would come in with whatever you wanted to do and you'd rehearse it and show him. Most of the time he would let you do whatever it was you wanted to do. A lot of times it was a mistake. But most of the time it worked out well."

"Corman was very good with pace and giving the things an interesting look," said Dick Matheson, "but he didn't work with actors, and the actors in the Poe films were not usually very good. There were exceptions in each film—Price always did a professional job—but in *The House of Usher* I think all three of the other people were not particularly good and that was the whole cast!"

A similar complaint was registered by Boris Karloff who would work on Roger's next Poe film, *The Raven* (1963). "Corman expects an actor to get on with it himself," Boris said. "He said, 'You're experienced actors, get on with it. I've got the lighting and my angles. I know how I'm going to put this together.' And if you asked him about advice on a scene he'd say, 'That's your pigeon. Go on. I'm busy with this.'"

The critics were not so pleased with *Tales of Terror* but it earned $1.5 million in domestic gross rentals, not as much as the previous pictures but enough to warrant another entry in what was turning out to be a series. It was determined that the middle portion of the picture had been the most successful so it was decided that the next Poe picture would be a comedy. That was fine as far as Richard Matheson was concerned. Another serious script would have been more than the writer could stand.

"I had to do them for laughs by then," Matheson said. "I've never had a particular interest in Poe, nor did I develop one while working on those films."

The Raven turned out to be the biggest success of all, though not with the critics, of course. "Strictly a picture for the kiddies and the birdbrained," said Bosley Crowther in the *New York Times*. *Time* magazine called it a "sappy little parody." *Variety* liked it. "The screenplay is a skillful, imaginative narrative and Corman takes the premise and develops it expertly as a horror-comedy, climaxing with Price and Karloff engaging in a duel to the death."

During the "duel to the death," Boris Karloff tosses a scarf at Vincent Price which transforms into a snake. Not being a lover of elongated reptiles, Vince asked Roger how he intended to handle the scene. Roger introduced Vince to a snake trainer.

"Okay," Vince said skeptically. "I've met you. Now I want to meet your snake."

The trainer displayed his boa constrictor and said, "Don't worry. It's a very tame snake."

"I'm tame too," Vince replied. "But strange things can happen."

It took over an hour and half to film the scene. Roger wanted the snake to face the camera but it wouldn't cooperate. The snake didn't bite but it took a little prying to unravel it from Vince's neck.

AIP announced that its next Poe film would be *The Masque of the Red Death*, to be scripted by Robert Towne. Towne, who would later script *Shampoo*, *Chinatown* and *Personal Best*, had previously written *The Last Woman on Earth* for Roger Corman's Filmgroup. The writer hadn't finished the script by the time Roger was ready to shoot so Roger hired him to act in the two movies he was shooting back-to-back in Puerto Rico. (Roger always shot two movies whenever he went on location.) Towne can be seen in *Woman* and *The Creature from the Haunted Sea* under the name Edward Wein. But he did not write *The Masque of the Red Death* (1964). That assignment went to Charles Beaumont and to Bobby Campbell for a rewrite. Nor was *Masque* the next Poe film. Well, technically it was, but in between *Masque* and *The Raven* Roger made a film based on H.P. Lovecraft's "The Case of Charles Dexter Ward," with Vincent Price, Debra Paget and Lon Chaney, who replaced an ailing Boris Karloff. It was going to be titled *The Haunted Village*, then it was changed to *The Haunted Palace* (1963) which was the title of a poem by Edgar Allan Poe. And so the movie became another in the series.

Masque received warm critical reception for a number of reasons which had nothing to do with its actually being more entertaining than its predecessors. It was filmed in England by Nicholas Roeg, had a five week shooting schedule, and made use of the elaborate sets left over from *Becket*. So what it actually was, was *better looking* than any of the previous Poe entries.

"Of all the pictures that Roger Corman has made from the supernatural tales of Edgar Allan Poe, *Masque of the Red Death* is the most ambitious in concept as well as the most lavishly produced," wrote one reviewer who called it one of the most elegant fantasy horror films ever made. "On its level," said Eugene Archer, "it is astonishingly good." *The New York Herald Tribune* critic wrote: "The film is beautifully costumed, the sets are lavish, the props exquisite." *The New York Daily News* speculated that Roger might just "out-horror all the horror filmmakers." Mandel Herbstman, in *Film Daily*, thought the film was "novel" from the beginning to its "imaginative" and "thoroughly exciting and pregnant climax." And James Powers believed it would gross more in one week from one theatre than Poe earned in his lifetime.

Sam Arkoff was amused by the reaction. "Don't you believe Roger's arty facade," he told a magazine reporter. "The important thing about him is that he's a good, competent businesslike producer."

Top: Lon Chaney replaced Boris Karloff, who became ill shortly before "The Haunted Palace" (1963) went into production. Bottom: Hazel Court discovers witchcraft isn't all it's cooked up to be, in "The Masque of the Red Death" (1964).

Many years later Roger Corman said that *Masque* would have been his choice to follow *House of Usher* if Ingmar Bergman hadn't made *The Seventh Seal* around that time. Both stories contained the hooded figure of death. This may be true but Roger has never appeared to be reluctant when it came to lifting plots and gimmicks from other people's films. Perhaps somebody at AIP had nixed the idea because, shortly after *Usher's* release, Alex Gordon announced his own plans to film *Masque of the Red Death* with Vincent Price in the lead role. (A few months later Barney Woolner said he wanted to film the property in Spectra-Scope at Producers' Studio, having relinquished the rights to Poe's "Premature Burial" to Roger.)

Alex sought an injunction to stop the release of Roger's film, charging AIP and Anglo-Amalgamated with plagiarism. Alex's script, adapted by his wife and written by Mildred and Gordon Gordon, had been submitted to and rejected by AIP. Judge Macklin Fleming denied the petition saying there was only coincidental similarities between the two properties.

While Roger was still shooting *Masque* he hired Chuck Griffith to adapt Poe's "The Gold Bug," which was to star Vincent Price, Peter Lorre and Basil Rathbone. Chuck turned it into a comedy, a variation on *A Bucket of Blood*.

Basil was to be a visiting English carpetbagger who, after the Civil War, comes to call on Vince, the owner of a burned-out mansion which has been turned into a hock shop. Vince has two servants, one of them with squeaky feet. "Sometimes I squeaks and sometimes I doesn't," the woman remarks after Vince discovers the problem is not with her shoes. Peter is Vince's other servant, a little guy who carries a gold bug around in a matchbox. At night Pete lets the little critter out to play the gold bug rag on the harpsichord in the front room. Anyone bitten by the bug turns to gold. Vince tries to melt one of the victims but in doing so breaks the spell and the gold returns to flesh. So he simply sells the victims as gold statues.

Peter Lorre died before Chuck finished the script, which was over 300 pages long. Jim Nicholson and Sam Arkoff were less than pleased. Years later Chuck ran into Sam in the streets of Rome and was surprised to learn that the cherubic movie mogul had still not forgiven him for writing such a lengthy script. When Chuck suggested that AIP buy a bunch of gladiator movies to turn into comedies, Sam gruffly replied. "Why don't you write me a picture about the Civil War?" and walked away.

The Tomb of Ligeia (1964) was Roger's final Poe picture, filmed in a 12th century monastery in East Anglia, written by Robert Towne who turned it into a gothic love story. Vincent Price had always wanted to do a picture in a ruin, using the ruin as an actual place with furniture in it. But they weren't allowed to put furniture in the monastery because the place was a national monument. So only the exteriors were shot there and the interiors were created at Shepperton Studios. Good thing too since the climax of the film called for the whole place to go up in flames. The walls of the set were coated with liquid cement. Everyone was warned not to smoke. Vince and his costar, Elizabeth Shepherd, were positioned under some debris, getting ready for the next shot when somebody lit a match. All at once the place was an inferno. Vince dragged Liz to safety as fast as he could. Naturally the shot and the set were ruined.

In his book *Classics of the Horror Film*, William K. Everson described the Poe series as "horror films first, Vincent Price vehicles second, showcases for Corman's tired and repetitive techniques third, and of only negligible interest as adaptations of Poe."

"Repetitive" is the word. Years later when *House of Usher*, *The Pit and the Pendulum*, *Tales of Terror* and *The Raven* were shown together in a single night, the audience I sat with started laughing at the repetition by the third feature and they didn't stop until the program was over. They laughed at the shock whip pans that introduced sinister figures. They laughed at the insert shots of the ocean bathing rocks, the clouds racing past the matte paintings that were supposed to be the castle exteriors, the endless scenes of people parading around to show off the sets and the fires that always marked the climax of almost every Poe picture. Often, it was the same fire. Roger set fire to a burning chicken coop for the first Poe feature and that up-angle shot of the skinny, flaming wooden planks was inserted into every fire thereafter.

When Chuck Griffith was explaining one of his "Gold Bug" sequences to Vincent Price, in which the actor was supposed to show off a series of family portraits, Vince exclaimed: "Oh! No! Not again!" That too, had become one of the clichés.

"Wait," Chuck said. "They're all *famous* paintings. You look at the Mona Lisa and tell Basil it's your mother and say, 'Don't you think she has an enigmatic smile?'"

"Oh," Vince said, heaving a sigh of relief. "I get it. Then you must include The Laughing Cavalier."

Supposedly, it was because of the repetitiveness that Roger decided not to make another Poe picture although dwindling boxoffice returns may have played a part in his decision. His next film was a contemporary one.

Four years later Poe's name was attached to a movie originally called *The Witchfinder General*, which starred Vincent Price as the real-life Matthew Hopkins, the son of a Puritan minister who, between 1645 and 1646 (with the help of his partner John Stearne), executed 200 people as witches. In the climax of the film Hopkins is bludgeoned to death. In real life he simply fell out of favor with various religious and political figures and spent the last years of his life writing *The Discovery of Witchcraft*, a defense of his murder spree.

Director Michael Reeves was able to thwart Vince's tendency to overact by covering the actor's face with a beard and a hat. All of Vince's dialogue was looped so that Reeves could restrain Vince's performance. The result was effective and in this author's opinion *The Conqueror Worm* (1968), as the film came to be called, was the best picture Vincent Price made for AIP and was probably the actor's finest portrayal.

The story that director Reeves and writer Tom Baker made out of Ronald Bassett's novel is more chilling than any of AIP's previous exercises in horror, largely because it feels more realistic. Hopkins doesn't believe that the people he tortures and murders are actually witches. It's simply a job he does for the money and power it brings him, not to mention the sexual favors bestowed upon him by the women who offer themselves as bribes to save either themselves or someone they love.

On the other end of the scale is Richard Marshall, played by Ian Ogilvy, a soldier who will stop at nothing to kill Hopkins and his partner for raping Richard's fiancée and murdering her father. By the time the story has run its course, Richard is crazy with bloodlust and his need to kill Hopkins becomes stronger than his love for Sara. I have no desire to spoil the ending by blurting it out here except to say that if it doesn't leave you exhausted and horrified then you and I weren't watching the same film.

Besides the misleading title, Vince was asked to read the phrase from Poe's poem whence the title was derived. No matter. It couldn't hurt the film.

The Conqueror Worm was blasted by critics who thought it was all in bad taste but then so were the witch-hunts themselves so what did they expect? It surprised the hell out of Jim and Sam by grossing $1.5 million in distributors' domestic rentals. They figured it was time for a new cycle of Poe pictures. Money was poured into a curiously arty project for AIP, a European production based on three Edgar Allan Poe stories, *Histoires Extraordinaires* (*Tales of Mystery and Imagination*). Roger Vadim, Louis Malle and Orson Welles were sought to direct the three stories but Welles dropped out of the project and was replaced by Federico Fellini. The critics were not impressed.

"Vadim's *Metzengerstein* was made apparently because he had some kinky costumes left over from *Barbarella* and an undaunted desire to continue his campaign of publicly degrading his wife, Jane Fonda," wrote Richard Schickel.

"While preview audiences have been uncommonly, vocally rude, they have not responded without provocation," admitted John Mahoney in his review for *The Hollywood Reporter*. "The best accomplished

Director Gordon Hessler discusses a scene with his star Vincent Price, "The Ob-long Box" (1969).

segment of the trilogy is Louis Malle's 'William Wilson,' in which Alain Delon stars as the Austrian officer who kills the conscience which pursues him as a double, and thus sentences himself to death."

Michael Ross, of the *Los Angeles Herald Examiner*, thought the film was one big joke that refused to laugh at itself. "The original idea was quite insane: Round up three famous European directors...surround them with beautiful people...mix with Gothic horror and then force-feed the whole conglomeration to a shell-shocked audience." Kevin Thomas, writing in the *Los Angeles Times*, said: "The only real accomplishment of this shoddy trilogy ... is to make Roger Corman's Poe pictures look awfully good in comparison."

In an effort to save what appeared to be a hopeless endeavor, the film was given a new title, *Spirits of the Dead* (1969), a song by Ray Charles and some narration by Vincent Price. The posters promised an "Ultimate orgy of evil and unbearable horror."

Poe's name was attached to three more AIP movies: *The Oblong Box* (1969), *Cry of the Banshee* (1970) and *Murders in the Rue Morgue* (1971). One reviewer complained about the cavalier use of the author's name: "A phrase, a verse, is cribbed from Poe, tacked on the film's main title and sprinkled into the ads," wrote John Mahoney in the *Los Angeles Times*. "The tormented poet takes the rap again."

Cry of the Banshee, originally scripted as *Cry of the Banshees*, did very well as a summer release. It pulled in $25,348 during its first six days at the McVickers Theatre in Chicago. On its opening day at the Meadow Glen Drive-In in Medford, Mass., it grossed $1,548; $878 at the South Shore Drive-In in Braintree, Mass., $644 at the Saco Drive-In in Portland, Maine, and $605 at the Center Theatre in Boston, Mass.

Murders in the Rue Morgue, minus Vincent Price, was the last in the second string of Poe pictures. Thank God!

Peter Lorre and Basil Rathbone goof around between scenes of "Comedy of Terrors" (1963).

Ray Milland doesn't look as if he is enjoying himself as "'X'-The Man with X-Ray Eyes" (1963).

Top: Janet Blair has to die first before she is able to convince hubby Peter Wyngarde (here about to conduct a ceremony to bring her back to life) that they both need witchcraft to survive—in "Burn, Witch, Burn" (1961). Bottom: Astronauts are terrified to find the remains of a gigantic creature on the "Planet of the Vampires" (1965).

Twelve

Sid Pink and Cinemagic

I try to get an off-beat touch to my films. I usually do my own original stories and try to sign directors with a special flair for a particular kind of story. Today's audiences demand the unusual — and I try to provide it.

— Sidney Pink

After *House of Usher*, AIP's next big release was *The Angry Red Planet* (1960), which, like *Horrors of the Black Museum*, boasted a new screen process, this time something called Cinemagic. Cinemagic was supposed to make real objects appear like line drawings, the advantage being that if the performers could be made to look like line drawings then almost everything else could actually *be* a line drawing. Any concept, no matter how extravagant could be brought to life on a shoestring budget.

Cinemagic was conceived by Norman Maurer who, I'm told, is somehow related to one of the Three Stooges. Originally called Artiscope, it was still in the experimental stage when producer Sidney Pink saw Norman's 16mm tests. Erroneously assuming that Norman would bring the concept to fruition in a few months, Sid went ahead and wrote a treatment called "The Planet Mars." He needed a writer to make sense out of his sketchy outline so he hired Ib Melchoir who was looking for a way to break into the director's union. Ib told Sid that he would write the screenplay but only if he could direct it. Sid agreed.

And so the comedy of errors began.

One of the monsters in the story was described as looking like a giant amoeba with "two roughly circular nuclei, almost like eyes in its center, which revolve constantly." Herman Townsley, in charge of building the monsters, took that to mean rotating eyeballs and proceeded accordingly.

Another monster called the bat-rat spider (or rat-bat spider, whichever you prefer) was so light in weight that it bounced everytime it took a step, which rather destroyed the gigantic illusion that everyone was trying to create. Howard Weeks, Herman Townsley's assistant, built the creature out of the lightest resin he could find because a heavy monster

129

meant heavy supporting wires and the heavier the wire the more difficult it was to conceal.

Howard was carving the claws for the bat-rat when Sid Pink stopped by to check on the progress. He stood behind Howard, looking over his shoulder, and then, after a few minutes, said, "That isn't what I had in mind at all."

Without a moment's hesitation Howard dropped the thing into the nearest trashcan, turned, and calmly asked, "What *did* you have in mind?"

Not long after that the critter was fished out of the trash.

The sequence which was to feature the bat-rat was placed in serious jeopardy. A key moment in the sequence, a shot of Les Tremayne being squeezed by the bat-rat's claw, still hadn't been photographed when the money ran out. The large prop claw had already been constructed. The only thing they needed was the motor to operate it. Ib Melchior cut the claw in half, mounted the pieces on some two-by-fours, laid the thing on a shopping cart, and had two guys roll the thing into the frame.

Another sequence left to be shot was the giant amoeba attacking the spaceship. Ib was told to rewrite the story in such a way that the bit could be deleted but that was impossible. Everything leading up to and away from the amoeba attack had already been photographed. Ib bought five packages of Jello, some finger paint and a plastic spaceship and set up shop in Norman Maurer's garage. They mixed the Jello, froze it and placed it on a hotplate. The plastic ship was stuck in the middle. They photographed the Jello melting away from the ship which was printed in reverse to give the illusion of the gunk engulfing the ship. Some of the Jello was then poured onto a piece of glass. The camera was placed beneath the glass, shooting up. Ib mixed some fingerpaint into the Jello then ran his fingers through it. That image was matted onto the portholes of the ship to serve as an insider's point of view of the attack.

Before the amoeba attacked the ship it chased the four astronauts — Gerald Mohr, Nora Hayden, Jack Kruschen, Les Tremayne — who were in a rubber raft, across a Martian lake. Director Melchior called for action and the four performers paddled like crazy but they didn't make any headway. The tank they were in was too shallow. They were scraping bottom.

The audience at a sneak preview laughed out loud during the scene where Nora Hayden ejected Les Tremayne's corpse into space. She whispered a sad "Goodbye, Professor" as she pushed the eject button. The sound effect was as if she had flushed a toilet. The scene was clipped.

And what of Cinemagic? It was employed only during the moments when the explorers were outside of the spaceship on Mars. Those scenes were photographed in black and white then printed through a red filter on color stock. The performers wore white make-up to enhance the stark look that Norman Maurer was trying for. (Roger Corman went for a similar effect in *House of Usher* for a dream sequence, only he used blue filters. It was just one more effect he turned into a cliché by the end of the Poe series.) Unfortunately, Cinemagic didn't work.

"The much-ballyhooed 'new' Cinemagic process ... it is sad to report, is scarcely anything to shout about — or even talk about," wrote critic S.A. Dick. "While it may take considerable ingenuity to produce this effect, the result isn't really worth it," reported *Variety*. "It doesn't seem to have any special properties in its present use that would lend itself to sales or exploitation," Jack Moffitt said.

Nor was the response to the film itself particularly favorable. "The script by Sid Pink and Ib Melchior is — simply embarrassing," wrote *Los Angeles Times* critic Charles Stinson. "Melchior's direction is not too imaginative and the potentially clever blurring process is rendered useless by producer Pink's use of cheap, clearly unreal backdrops."

S.A. Dick said the acting was "on the level of a high school play" and Jack Moffitt thought the monsters were "weird enough to please the juveniles but a long, dull seemingly endless prologue occurs before director Ib Melchior begins trotting them out."

The publicity department proceeded as if Cinemagic *did* work, as evidenced by the following radio spot:

ANNOUNCER: A great new motion picture in the world's newest motion picture process — Cinemagic, the wonder of the added fourth dimension. With Cinemagic you are actually on the first rocket ride to Mars in *The Angry Red Planet*. You'll feel the dizzying heights of their fantastic mile-high buildings. You'll shiver as you ride the river of the dead. Your depth perception will increase a thousandfold as you look into the waters that lead into foreverness. And the terrors you meet on Mars are beyond man's imagination. The rat-bat spider, so real in Cinemagic you'll feel the crazed stare of its blinded eyes, the tearing shock of its iron claws. The giant amoeba, like an earth germ, only a hundred million times larger. Thrills. Shocks. Terrors. And your first glimpse of the world and the life of Mars all are yours to experience in *The Angry Red Plant* in Eastman 52-50 color from American International.

Held over for three weeks at the Four Star and United Artists State theatres in the Los Angeles area, its longevity was one more piece of evidence that AIP was emerging as something more than a hit and run operation. Prior to *Horrors of the Black Museum*, an AIP movie would come and go within a week's time, mostly at drive-ins. Now, instead of word of

Above: The bat-rat (or rat-bat) spider — "The Angry Red Planet" (1960).

mouth killing one of their pictures, Jim and Sam were counting on it to keep them around awhile. The pictures may not have been any better but they seemed to be trying a little harder.

Sid Pink realized he could shoot the same calibre of picture for a lot less cheaper abroad. "Some locales can't be duplicated on Hollywood stages," he told a reporter from the *Los Angeles Times*. "And shooting abroad is a challenge. Many of the cameras are as old as 18 years, and quality is achieved through the use of imagination. The cost of

Opposite: Nora Hayden looks a little under the weather, or maybe it's just the phony backdrop. From "The Angry Red Planet" (1960).

production abroad, aside from salaries for the cast, is about 40 percent of costs in Hollywood. Instead of unions, guilds prevail for film workers. And they work as teams, rather than as individuals to a specialty." So Sid took another script by Ib Melchior and went to Sweden to make *Journey to the 7th Planet* (1961).

To help soften the blow of foreign faces, Sid imported John Agar and Greta Thyssen to star in his picture. They had a bit of trouble working together. Whenever they would play a two shot Greta kept upstaging John by inching to the rear so that John's back would eventually be facing the camera. Finally John backed her to the edge of the backdrop so she had no other choice than to play it 50/50.

Greta was on an afternoon game show to plug the picture. The host asked her about her recent motion picture activities. After hearing the title the host said, with a smile much broader than the situation warranted, "I'll bet it'll be great science fiction."

"Well," Greta replied, her face and voice dead pan, "it's science fiction."

Before the film was fit for release, it required some additional special effects footage, as the work originally done for the film in Sweden was too tacky even by AIP's standards. To supplement a sequence in the picture in which the astronauts are attacked by a giant spider, footage was lifted out of Bert Gordon's *Earth vs. the Spider*. Bert's black and white scenes were tinted blue. Another sequence, featuring a one-eyed monster, required the services of an effects house called Project Unlimited, a small company that had previously added some footage to Jim and Sam's *Goliath and the Dragon* (1960) import.

Project Unlimited was owned by Gene Warren, Tim Barr and Wah Chang. They received an Academy Award for their work in *The Time Machine* in 1960. Tim, who had a deformity that caused him to be hunched over, asked Gene Warren to hang back a little on the night of the Awards. Tim couldn't walk as quickly and he wanted to reach the stage around the same time that Gene did if they should win. When the announcement was made Tim was on stage before Gene had a chance to hit the aisle.

The job of animating the one-eyed monster for Sid's film was handed to Jim Danforth, who would later be nominated for an Academy Award himself—twice in fact. To defray the amount of money normally required to build a stop-motion puppet, Jim used the skeleton armature built for one of the puppets in *Jack the Giant Killer*. The first sequence Jim shot was rejected. AIP had approved the monster's design but after seeing it in action they decided it looked too much like a giant teddy bear. Jim stripped the fur off the puppet and added scales instead. He had to work around the clock, on the weekend, to finish on schedule. Jim wasn't too happy about this. As far as he was concerned he'd given them what they asked for the first time. And he'd done it right.

He was still working at six o'clock in the morning when some people from AIP stopped by. Jim didn't know they were coming. If he had he would never have hung that sign on the camera, the one that read: *AIP Can Go to Hell.*

Neither Jim nor Project Unlimited could fix Sid Pink's next picture, *Reptilicus* (1962). Before AIP filed a lawsuit against him, Sid was bragging about the picture.

"For this we used 9,000 members of the Danish army and navy," Sid said. "And the government permitted us use of a huge new bridge in Copenhagen off of which some 3,000 players tumble into the water below. We get all sorts of cooperation from foreign government, and that helps."

All very spectacular when seen, but the rest of *Reptilicus* was unwatchable. Unwatchable by AIP standards no less. The complaint against Sid was that he had agreed, by contract, to produce and deliver a picture called *Reptilicus* which would conform to "several physical requirements" by a certain date. Said AIP, the requirements weren't met and Sid was late to boot. The judge sustained Sid's objection and gave AIP thirty days to file an amended complaint. The amount of money AIP was asking for was $3,500,000. Then Sid turned around and sued AIP for using his name on what was essentially a pornographic book. The amount of money he asked for was $250,000. Sid said the novelization of his movie, written by Dean Owen, contained passages of "such lewd, lascivious and wanton nature as to inflame unsavory and lascivious desire in the reader." As a result Sid said he was held up to "public contempt and ridicule." The suit was dismissed on the grounds that the federal court had no jurisdiction in the matter.

Eventually Sid's unreleaseable film was released so one assumes AIP's complaint was dismissed as well, since apparently they'd been able to conform the picture's physical requirements. What they did was re-dub all of the voices. The Swedish cast spoke English but with such a heavy accent they were often hard to understand. It was also feared that their accents would sound funny to U.S. audiences. Ib Melchior took six parts himself when it came time to dub. It was also necessary to remove many of the special effects scenes, including any scenes of the monster flying. (In Melchior's script Reptilicus flaps around an amusement park, causing trouble, which apparently was filmed.)

"I suppose it would be supercilious to say that 'Reptilicus' is ridiculous," wrote the *Citizen News*. "But in critical essence, it ranks far below most films of this nature, failing even in the technical department to register any appreciable degree of surprise or horrifying suspense."

One good thing that can be said for *Reptilicus* is that is *did* provoke Monarch Books to issue that pornographic version of it, deceptively packaged and priced like a regular monster item, made available to children. Monarch being a subsidiary of Charlton Publications, Charlton would run ads in their two monthly monster magazines, thereby hitting their target audience. This little kid bought every one of those books — *Reptilicus, Gorgo, Konga, Brides of Dracula* — and read them right under my parents' noses. Those books were the best. "He took her with the savage lance of his manhood" is still my favorite line.

No matter how hard they tried, they couldn't make an A feature out of Sid's monster movie. And they had another not-so-hot Italian beefcake picture they weren't sure what to do with. So AIP returned to the days of the double bills and promoted both films equally. Two A pictures for the price of one.

Sid's next feature played the bottom half of a bill headlining *Goliath and the Vampires* (1964). And Sid had learned his lesson. He hired two American performers this time to play the lead roles. But the picture didn't provide much for AIP to over-sell. The story didn't provide enough horror elements. It was about Martha Hyer and Barry Sullivan who fall in love. But he's married. So she burns his house down to kill his wife and kids. She succeeds but he's burned trying to save them. So he spends the rest of the film trying to do the same to her. But AIP can't peddle it like a revenge film. They had to advertise it like a horror film. *So a Cold Wind from Hell* became *Wheel of Fire* and finally *Pyro* (1964), sometimes called *Pyro, the Thing Without a Face*. Barry Sullivan became a monster whose soul was a cauldron of hate. And Martha Hyer: "..the strange desire that feeds on her cannot be quenched by love alone!"

Variety thought the film was "so weighted with stilted dialogue and plot absurdities" that its status as second feature material was in jeopardy. *The Citizen News* suspected it would appeal to "people who enjoy gawking at roast meat."

Thirteen

Foreign Affairs

Jim and I had lunch together virtually every day. We spent a lot of time together. We would talk about what we wanted to do and we'd have these specific things but we'd go our way separately when it came to the legal and the business, which I would handle, and the advertising and merchandising, which he would handle. Occasionally, he would have some thought in regards to what I was doing. And, occasionally, I would look at the advertising or the title and I would have something to say.

—Samuel Arkoff

Jim sat behind the immaculate desk in a big office, in a suit and tie and a smile. He was the one that invited you in. He was the one who asked you to do the picture. He'd tell you how good it was going to be. Then you'd go see Sam in his shirttails, with his coat off, and he'd start talking hard facts. "Tits and ass. Sex and violence. That's all we need. Anything else is arty farty." Sam was the dynamo.

—Charles Griffith

The Italian imports became steady income for AIP. Not only could Jim and Sam buy the muscle-man epics they also picked up a few dandy horror items. *La Maschera del Demonio* (*The Mask of the Demon*) retitled *Black Sunday* (1960) was able to pass as a main feature in spite of being a black and white film. Its director, Mario Bava, carved a niche for himself among horror movie fans.

"Please note," cautioned the ads, "the producers of *Black Sunday* recommend that it be seen only by those over 12 years of age!" The film's opening credits cautioned that the picture would shock like no other and therefore might be harmful to "the young and the impressionable."

Announcer: The sound you hear is dripping blood. This is the start of Black Sunday. Black Sunday comes but once every 100 years. On that day the undead demons of hell rise to unleash an orgy of evil on the world. American International presents *Black Sunday*, the most frightening motion picture you've ever seen.

Barbara Steele is about to have a devil's mask nailed to her face, in "Black Sunday" (1960).

It was far more outrageous in its depiction of death and murder than American audiences were used to seeing. Spiked masks pounded into faces. Maggots crawling from empty eye-sockets. Rotting corpses. It premiered at the Allen Theatre in Cleveland on February 15, 1961.

"A classic quality permeates this gruesome, shocking, horrifying story of a vengeful, blood-thirsty vampires," wrote Sam Berns in *Motion Picture Herald*. "Effectively photographed in low key black and white against rich settings of macabre design ... achieves frightful elements of surprise through clever makeup and performances...."

"The technicians and artisans ... are to be highly commended for creating moods and illusions with skilled sets, props, costumes, cinematography, musical score and particularly editing," wrote *Citizen News*.

Kay Proctor of the *Los Angeles Examiner* called it a "honey of a horror" for adult eyes only, and only those "who can take their macabre straight and strong."

"There is sufficient cinematographic ingenuity and production flair ... to keep an audience pleasantly unnerved," wrote *Variety*. *Time* called it "a piece of fine Italian handiwork that atones for its ludicrous lapses with brilliant intuitions of the spectral." *The Hollywood Reporter* said it was made with "the same care and purpose as any other kind of film story." Bill Everson thought it was "a marvelous exercise in baroque horror," although he felt it exploited sadism and pain unduly. It was an incredible picture.

To promote the film, Jim and Sam held a contest to find the 10 best ghouls in the United States. All women between 18 and 35 were eligible and all they needed to enter was originality in their ability to make themselves as ghoulish looking as possible. And if one of them should also be attractive, why Jim and Sam might be "scared" into giving her a contract.

Before stopping in Italy on that first trip, Jim and Sam paid a visit to Nat Cohen in England. The first picture they'd cofinanced with Nat was *The Cat Girl* (1957), for which they paid something like $25,000 plus Lou Rusoff's services as a writer and producer, for the Western Hemisphere rights. The second film had been *Black Museum* but that had been in connection with Herman Cohen. Jim and Sam wanted to cofinance another picture. It became *Circus of Horrors* (1960), a fanciful color production that *Hollywood Citizen News* thought was "better-than-average chiller-diller." The *Times* critic found it "adequately paced" though the writing was "tissue thin in characterizations." The song "Look for a Star," heard throughout the picture, was simultaneouly recorded by Gary Mills, Gary Miles, Deane Hawley and Billy Vaughn. It wasn't a big hit by any of them but it received radio play. The film was trimmed for U.S. distribution, the first cut rather jolting. New credits were shot for the film which abruptly cut, music and all, to a shot of a woman wearing a black bra and panties and a flimsy white nightgown, smashing mirrors. The cut was made to eliminate as much footage of the scantily clad woman as possible. Most of the other cuts were of a sexual nature, footage of buxom starlets parading around in low-cut brassieres. There was only one violence cut, a close shot of a woman with a knife in her neck, curiously remaining in the film's trailer, covered with a title plate.

Anglo-Amalgamated and AIP's next collaboration was *Burn Witch, Burn* (1962), a title borrowed from an old A. Merritt novel. For a while Jim Nicholson thought of calling the picture *Devil Doll* which was an old MGM title. The film's original title was *Night of the Eagle*. It died as a cofeature to *Tales of Terror*. But the critics loved it.

"Quite the most effective supernatural thriller since *Village of the Damned*," said the *New York Times*. The *Los Angeles Herald Tribune* thought the acting and direction were excellent. William Everson thought, atmospherically, that the film "had several really chilling sequences." He explained that the somewhat erratic editing was due in part to the hero's insistence on wearing tight pants. The director was forced to shoot him in either extreme long or close shots. "Direction is fresh and exciting," said the British Film Institute, "skillful in its reliance on suggestion, naggingly effective as a study of psychic attack."

Based on Fritz Lieber's "Conjure Wife," already made into one of Universal's Inner Sanctum series in 1944, the remake was scripted by Richard Matheson and Charles Beaumont.

A special screening of the film was shown October 28, 1962, at the Lytton Center Theatre to the members of the Writers Guild. Bill Everson assembled some horror film clips for the occasion. Ray Bradbury made a speech.

Jim and Sam were able to buy U.S. distribution rights to *Two Faces of Dr. Jekyll* from Hammer Films of England, a small company that had had quite a success in America with their color remakes of classic horror films. Their Jekyll and Hyde, however, was short on horrific elements. That's why nobody else wanted it. But to Jim anything was salvageable. His advertising campaign exploited the film's hedonistic aspects.

ANNOUNCER: Buried alive in each man is a strange, depraved creature that turns the soul into a battleground of sin and violence, turning life into an inferno. In Dr. Henry Jekyll it was his knowledge. Or perhaps it was his quiet ways, his unloving wife, his simple homely face that drove him to unleash this inner presence. This is *Jekyll's Inferno*. Dr. Henry Jekyll gave life to the unspeakable evil of Mr. Hyde. Rich, handsome, decadent Mr. Hyde erupted to spew adultery, viciousness, murder in the greatest macabre spectacle of all time. American International Pictures presents a fascinating new Dr. Jekyll, a terrifying new Mr. Hyde. Robert Louis Stevenson's study in terrifying evil, *Jekyll's Inferno*, in color and Megascope.

Later Jim decided to shift the focus from sex to violence and changed the title to *House of Fright* (1961), "the nerve shattering story of a man who committed every outrage in the book...living a holocaust of horror beyond imagination! A shock ending that you dare not reveal!" If, that is, you could remember it.

Although it would be some time before AIP and Hammer joined forces again, Jim and Sam continued to cofinance films in England, Italy, and Japan.

Above: Director Norman Taurog discusses a scene with Susan Hart, "Dr. Gold-foot and the Bikini Machine" (1965). Opposite, top: Burt Lancaster atop the ladder and director Dan Taylor (right), filming "The Island of Dr. Moreau" (1977) in St. Croix, Virgin Islands; bottom: another Italian import, Mario Bava's "Baron Blood" (1972).

Fourteen

The Beach Party Series

When we did the beach pictures, AIP was more cognizant of an image. We depicted the California surfing crowd as a bunch of fun-loving kids. Always Cokes. No beers. Nobody smoked. They even asked us not to smoke between takes.
—John Ashley

Our position as regards complaints from the self-appointed guardians of public morals is that there are no overtly sexy sequences and no sex talk among the kids. In fact, the stars of AIP's beach pictures are always talking about getting married. And that, to us, is the epitome of morality.
—James Nicholson

There are some unkind people who say we made pictures that pandered toward youth. That's a matter of semantics. We did make pictures that appealed to youth, and in doing so we took a different position from other producers and didn't moralize.
—Samuel Arkoff

The Girls Are BARE-ING...The Guys Are DAR-ING and the Surf's RARE-ING to GO-GO-GO.

A Beach Party movie was a teenager's fantasy. It was summer without parents. It was a summer without a job. The sun was out and the surf was up — every day. It was a summer on the beach where people dressed in as little as possible, and the only trouble came from a gang of over-the-hill cycle bums who were a danger only to themselves.

The Beach Party series was uniquely an American International item. It combined the Rock Hudson–Doris Day comedies with Mack Sennett slapstick and pop music. The prime purpose of these movies, according to one of the pressbooks, was to entertain young moviegoers; send them out of the theatre whistling one of the movie's songs. And, of course, to make money. Which the pictures did. There were seven in all.

William Asher, the director of the series, remembered how they came about. "I was called to come in and talk to Jim and Sam about something. They had a screenplay written by Lou Rusoff that was like the kind

143

of films they'd been making at the time, an exploitation thing, kids in trouble, parent-kid relationships, the generation gap, those kinds of things. And I didn't want to do that. I asked them if they'd do a film based on kids having a good time and not getting in trouble. Where they don't have to make up their minds right away about what they're going to do with their lives. The kids in the beach pictures were right out of high school, a time to be free before they made a commitment. Commitment, as we all know, is difficult because there might be something better down the road. I wanted to use that time and just let them enjoy themselves. Jim had a little more enthusiasm for the idea than Sam. But Sam was certainly not opposed to it because we did the pictures."

10,000 kids meet on 5,000 beach blankets! The inside story of what goes on when the sun's gone down...the moon's come up...and the water's too cold for surfin'.

"They had a great system. Those guys knew how to make movies. And they knew how to sell them. They were just great. AIP should be in existence today. They'd make up their minds that they wanted to do a certain kind of picture then they'd go out to the theatres, through their chain of distributors, and get commitments from the theatres. They'd say we'll be there on such and such a date with such and such a film and the exhibitors could count on it cause Jim and Sam would always be there."

Every summer when the sun is hot and the surf is up, the younger generation, like a horde of lemmings, wends its way seaward. Once on the beach they pair off on blankets to participate in a pagan rite common to all societies both civilized and savage. This is known to sociologists as the "post-adolscent beach party" and to parents as "'oh Horrors!" If you don't know just what happens on a beach party (or why it's so much fun) here's your chance. We dare you to take it. You may be shocked to death...but you'll die laughing!

"Sam has a wonderful sense of going forward. I love that. He didn't vacilate. We were committed to *Beach Party* [1963] and we didn't even have a cast. Well, we did have a cast. We had, hopefully, Frankie and Annette. But Annette was the property of Disney. And we had thirty pages of script. I took it to Bob Cummings and he read the thing and said 'This is amusing. But what happens?' And I said, 'I'm going to say the worst thing in the world: trust me.' I didn't know what else to say. Then Disney had to approve it. Not having all the material he was concerned about Annette's image. I told him that there wouldn't be anything that would offend, that it wasn't that type of picture. They were a little wary because it was AIP. Their background had been a different kind of films."

A confidential message to parents (or a definitive defense of a popular, healthful outdoor sport). Beach Blanket Bingo, as you might guess, is a game. Sociolgists would call it a "mating game" or a post-

Ex-Mousketeer Annette Funicello and pop singer Frankie Avalon — the Doris Day–Rock Hudson of the sand 'n' surf set — in "Beach Party" (1963).

adolescent puberty rite — with rules, yet. You may have played a version of it when it was called Spin the Bottle or Post Office. Now the contest is a bit more modern and the rules and prizes are more up-to-date. But it still puts the girls against the boys — just as close as they can get. So don't worry if your kids go out for the B.B.B. Team. Come see for yourself what it's like. You might even try a round — yourself.

"Lou Rusoff's script had to do with marijuana and kids getting into the fruition of sex, all of the things that a lot of the kids were doing. I was a surfer. I wondered why we couldn't do a picture about kids *not* in trouble. I guess in its own funny way the pictures made a statement that I wanted to make, that there was such as thing as kids *not* in trouble."

"Bob Dillon nor I took credit for the first picture. Lou Rusoff was very ill at the time and Sam asked us about credit. He knew that Lou would see the picture and it meant a lot to him. (Sam is a warm, wonderful family man. He really is. We haven't worked together for years but I always get a Christmas card from him showing the growth of his family in pictures.) So Bob and I let Lou get the screen credit. I mean the man was ill. How could we argue with that."

Leon blender, genl sales mgr
          American international pictures 7165 sunset blvd hollywood calif.

Dear leon:
          Four of our houston drive-in theatres opened your beach party first run multiple to such outstanding business that first five day grosses well ahead of such outstanding grossing pictures as hud, tammy and the doctor, nutty professor and the birds to name a few. hud, tammy, professor and the birds were terrific grossers for our texas drive-ins, so it looks like you have a definite winner in beach party. eagerly looking forward to playing your beach party throughout our texas zone of some thirty seven drive-ins.

With best wishes,
Brandon doak
Stanley warner management corp.

"There was no real fruition of sex. There was no booze. No cigarettes. The nucleus of the beach gang just weren't in trouble. The pictures were very thin as far as the stories went. They were full of activities; the gang's experiences. The theme was almost like a Doris Day picture I guess. Frankie wanted to bed down Annette and she wouldn't until they got married. But she wouldn't consider marriage until he made a commitment to something like work or his life."

          Predictable enough, Avalon seeks to make Annette jealous and takes up with Eva Six, a local waitress, and Miss Funicello in turn pursues Cummings. Also involved in this fast-moving story is Morey Amsterdam as the owner of a beat dance hall, Harvey Lembeck as head of an invading gang of motorcycle toughs, and Jody McCrea as a friend of Avalon's. — Edward Lipton, The Film Daily.

"Harvey would come in with little vignettes for his group. Some of which were terrible and some of which could be used, at least in part. He was very helpful. Bob Cummings would bring in his own material too, a lot of which was very good. But at one point he wanted to pursue an idea and I said, 'Bob, there's not time for this. Let's operate on a yes/no basis. If it strikes me as good we'll do it but if I don't like it we can't keep talking about it.' You see he had made pictures at another level for a long time and was the star of his own television show. Anyway, I was in a set-up that was an over-the-shoulder past Annette. And he said, 'If we don't discuss it, I won't make the shot.' I said, 'Well Bob, then I'll go on to the next one." So I went on to shoot other scenes. I had quite a bit to do without him, and he went storming off to his dressing room. This all happened in the morning. Then he came out and went to the stage phone and talked to his agent about how he was quitting the picture and how awful I was so I could hear it. I just kept on shooting. Around four I'd run out of stuff to do. So I went into his dressing room and I said 'Bob, we have this picture to finish. It's a fifteen day schedule so it'll be over soon. So let's just get through it. The problem here, I think, is that you want Billy Wilder for a director and I want Cary Grant for an actor. But you've got me and I've got you and that's life. That's the way it is. I can't deliver what you want and, baby, you can't deliver what I want. But I'll take you for what you are and I think you're terrific. Why don't we just bite that bullet and make the picture.' He kept looking at me with a semi-pout and wouldn't say anything. I finally said: 'So I'll see you out there.' A few minutes later he came out and walked over to me and said, 'Okay, Uncle Bill. Let's go.' From that time on he called me Uncle Bill."

William Asher has carefully directed the picture with an eye on his potential market. It moves quickly and easily and has been dressed with handsome production values, including spankingly clean camera work by Kay Norton. — Anby, Variety.

"I went over schedule. And at the end of one day's shooting I suddenly noticed a lot of people around. I'd been so involved in what I was doing that I didn't realize that there was something out of the ordinary for a long time. Then I found out that all the people were part of the wrap party. Sam said, 'If nothing else comes in on schedule, the wrap part will. So we had a wrap party. We had about three more days left to shoot. I didn't have the time to go through the editing process that I wanted to afterward because I'd done a television pilot with Patty Duke that had sold and we were shooting it in New York. I had to go back there and get started. Sam said, 'If you go to New York that's it. We haven't got time to fool around.' I told him I needed one weekend to tighten the editing which meant double time pay. He said, 'You can have the weekend but as far as I'm concerned the picture is finished. So you'll pay for it.' So I paid for it. Not begrudgingly because he was right."

With the Princess Theatre, Jesse James, Starlite and Parkside Drive-Ins literally staging their own "Beach Parties" at the theatres, the Toledo multiple is off to a tremendous gross. In addition to the regular use of paid media, newspaper, radio and TV, the promoted gimmick of a beach party at the theatres paid off handsomely on opening night. In effect, the theatres imported a truck load of white sand and created their own beach setting. The addition of tree stumps, derelict boats, fish nets, a band for dancing, and the offer of free admission to the first fifty couples who showed up in bathing suits spelled B-E-A-C-H P-A-R-T-Y and any way you cut it also spelled D-O-L-L-A-R-S at the box *office. The Seven-Up Bottling Company was contacted and went along on the beach party by supplying the drinks FREE, the theatre gave FREE "promoted" hot dogs to go with the drinks for the fifty couples only and a jolly time was had by all. At the drive-ins the parties were held at the concession stand for a forty-five minute period prior to the start of the regular showing. The PAYING crowd turned out en masse to view the doings which was, in effect, an additional attraction...AND...the local television station televised the whole deal...also FREE...You just can't beat a deal like that and the box office figures prove it... The four-theatre unit turned in a record $4,557 for a Wednesday opening and has broken every existing record for these theatres, according to theatre owner Jack Armstrong, who is also President of Allied States Association Exhibitors Group. Seven-Up was so happy with the deal, that they tagged all their regular radio spots and television spots before opening and continuing through the run with the copy "FRESH UP WITH SEVEN-UP WHEN YOU GO TO A BEACH PARTY." The entire success of this run can be based on the facts above...It's the get-up and go with the extra effort that paid off. This same deal as outlined above can be worked at any level, in any theatre, with the same success. IT IS A MUST DO AND MUST BE INCLUDED INTO EVERY CAMPAIGN FOR EVERY PLAYDATE.*

"Jim was on the creative side. Not being behind-the-scenes you don't really know what face they brought to those meetings they had but I felt that. Jim would come to the set. Sam never would. Sam was not worried about how good a film was as much as he was concerned with how entertaining it was."

Not only has 'Bikini Beach' set new records for an AIP picture in every area, but in most cases its grosses have equalled and even exceeded previous house records set by the top pictures of recent years. — Leon Blender.

"Everyone's talking about E.T. today. The truth of it is that it's a very simplistic work. The morality concept is there. It's a film that Sam Arkoff could have easily made. Easily. Whether or not it would have been executed the same way, who knows, but if you look at it very objectively, it's very basic. Nothing complicated about it at all. But very entertaining. It was very busy. A lot was going on. But it was all simple. I think that's what Sam went for. He'd have done *Poltergeist*. Not just because it was horror but because it was about family."

The trend setting, record breaking hit "Beach Party" and its equally successful sequel "Muscle Beach Party" will be re-issued to bolster exhibitor's pre-Christmas box-office receipts, according to AIP vice president in charge of sales and distribution Leon P. Blender.

"I had two pictures that opened on Broadway the same week:

A makeup contest was held by *Famous Monsters*; the winner got a role in "Bikini Beach" (1964). Jim Nicholson (left), contest winner Val Warren, and editor Forrest J Ackerman.

Beach Party was at the Astor and *Johnny Cool* was at the Ambassador. My wife and I went down the second day, the eight o'clock showing, to see how they were doing. There was line around the block for *Johnny Cool*. They had to turn the air conditioning down in the other theatre. There were four people in there. I thought one out of two wasn't bad."

   Actor John Ashley drew mammoth crowds to airports and autograph parties in San Francisco, Omaha, Denver, Kansas City and Washington, D.C. Giant sign emblazoned airport observation tier in Kansas—all activities contributing largely to record grosses for "Bikini Beach."

   Sam Riddle, emcee of KHJ-TV's "9th Street West," hosted a Zody's Department Store "Bikini Beach" Dance Party which drew more than 5,000 to a Conoga Park shopping center. Laura Nicholson, Luree Holmes, Connie Ducharm and Carrie Foster were some of the film's bikini-clad starlets on hand along with the film's star, Annette Funicello.

   Johnny Cool went on to make its money back and maybe a little more. *Beach Party* took off. But I was not aware it was doing well until I got a letter from AIP that had a check in it in the amount of money that I had spent for the editing that weekend. I told Elizabeth [Montgomery, his wife] that I had a feeling the phone was going to start ringing. Sam finally called and asked if I would meet with Jim on his boat in Miami to talk about another picture. I said sure."

A teenage romp on the beach somewhere in Southern California, complete with song and dance, Technicolor and Panavision, names that look well on the theatre marquee and a lively yarn of no consequence but reasonable amusement make up the ingredients of American International Pictures' first big musical. It speaks well for the James H. Nicholson–Samuel Z. Arkoff combination that the resulting picture looks ready-made for the teenage crowd, whose numbers are legion, and also looks like lots of box office for the exploitation-minded showman. —Motion Picture Daily.

"We met Jim in Miami, Bob Dillon and I, and we concocted another story that weekend. The first inclination was to grow with the characters. And I said, 'What are we going to grow with? This is comic strip. They don't have to be a year older. They don't have to be in jobs now. It can be the longest summer on record.' There was some discomfort with that but they agreed. So I would concoct activity for them to do."

The real trouble is that almost the entire cast emerges as the dullest bunch of meatballs ever, with the old folks even sillier than the kids... We suspect that the youngsters in the audience may find it all pretty laughable. In any case, the coproducers ... have kept the proceedings flat, contrived and neatly and serenely suggestive... —The New York Times.

"When each picture opened it was summer. Bam! You're on your way. They were still trying to figure out what they were all about. I guess you could say they were six years out of high school but we never said that. Annette had that speech in every picture, that boring speech that we had to give her. Or that I felt we had to give her."

We are fully aware that our beach bunnies in bikinis are a prime attraction for the teenaged boy who brings his teenaged girl friend to the theatre to see the barechested surfers. —James Nicholson.

"The motion picture industry did not look upon the beach pictures, no matter how much money they made, as anything but sub-motion pictures. Sub-distributors. Sub. Sub. Everytime I told Columbia that I had to bring in some help on 'Bewitched' because I had another Beach picture to make they would always ask: 'Why do you want to do those?' They looked upon it as low grade."

AIP contract star John Ashley bolsters his claim as "Hollywood's most traveled personal appearance personality" this month as he begins another extensive tour to attend conventions and plug his latest film "Beach Blanket Bingo." —American International Pictures News Clips.

Top: Vincent Price is flanked by his bikini clad robots (from left, Salli Sachse, Leslie Summers, Issa Arnal, Luree Holmes) and his idiot assistant Jack Mullaney, in "Dr. Goldfoot and the Bikini Machine" (1965). Bottom: The rat-pack headed by 'Eric Von Zipper' (Harvey Lembeck in dark glasses), in "The Ghost in the Invisible Bikini" (1966).

"In *How to Stuff a Wild Bikini* [1965] there was a character in the South Seas someplace that was using witchcraft and jungle magic. Since you didn't actually see the character until the end of the picture, I knew I could use a double for most of it, so I asked Elizabeth if she'd like to play the part if I fashioned it in such a way that she liked it. She read it and liked it and said, 'Sure.' Then Columbia stepped in and said they didn't want her to do it. They didn't want her in that kind of picture."

The bearer is hereby assigned all rights and privileges as an accredited member of the "How to Stuff a Wild Bikini" Association of America and agrees to follow the laws of the organization.

1. How to...with dignity search for material that is proper BIKINI stuffin'.

2. How to...properly react when sighting aforesaid material and blow official BIKINI stuffin' alert whistle.

3. How to...with foresight review American International Picture's "How to Stuff a Wild Bikini" and report reaction to club president.

"There was a thing I used on 'Bewitched' that Elizabeth did to activate the witchcraft that was something Elizabeth had done that I remembered that we called the Witch Twitch. Columbia found out we were going to use it in the picture and said it was copyrighted. She can't do that, they told us. Of course, the harder they tried to keep her from doing it and the picture the more determined we were. Finally we said that she'd be in the picture. Period. And she was. And she did the Witch Twitch. And they didn't sue. But they started saying it was going to ruin her career. That she was respected, had a big series and all...I hated them for that."

Theatres Nationwide are having a picnic with Beach Party.

Framington, Mass.	1st 5 days	$3,156
Waterbury, Conn.	1st 5 days	$8,894
Providence, R.I.	1st 7 days	$16,322
Brockton, Mass.	1st 5 days	$4,023
Hartford, Conn.	1st 5 days	$12,079
Dartmouth, Mass.	1st 5 days	$4,784
Flint, Michigan	1st 5 days	$14,204
Lansing, Michigan	1st 5 days	$7,187
Toledo, Ohio	1st week	$32,340
Fremont, Ohio	1st 5 days	$3,497
Appleton, Wisc.	1st 5 days	$4,441
Fond Du Lac, Wisc.	1st 5 days	$2,253
Madison, Wisc.	1st 5 days	$7,381
Houston, Texas	1st week	$38,000
Dallas, Texas	1st 4 days	$43,000

San Antonio, Texas	1st 4 days	$7,745
York, Pa.	1st 5 days	$3,223
Wilmington, Del.	1st 5 days	$5,597
Dayton, Ohio	1st 5 days	$21,618
Baltimore, Md.	1st 5 days	$40,000
Oklahoma City, Okla.	1st 5 days	$13,066
Chicago, Ill.	1st week	$25,341
	2nd wk, 1st 3 days	$13,148
Salt Lake City, Utah	1st 6 days	$14,638

"People have always looked at Jim and Sam as being second grade. And that's not true. They didn't spend as much money but they dealt with things that were pertinent to the audience. And they made a lot of money. But they weren't respected in the industry."

Jody McCrea, Harvey Lembeck and Morey Amsterdam, as sideline comics, are downright embarrassing. Mr. Cummings has to be seen to be believed and Miss Malone had better hold tight to that Academy Award. — The New York Times.

As a study of primitve behavior patterns, Beach Party is more unoriginal than aboriginal. In comparison, it makes Gidget's Roman Misadventures look like a scene from Tosca. — Time Magazine.

"Every major studio made a beach picture, trying to capitalize on AIP's success and none of them were successful. Columbia eventually wanted me to do one, I forget what it was, but I didn't want to for a couple of reasons, one being that I was already doing them in a way that I wanted to do them, good or bad. Paramount made one, MGM, they all made a beach picture and none of them succeeded because they were making them *better*, better meaning that they were doing all the things that were formula concepts that nobody wanted to see. They didn't go for the feeling of it, they went for the mechanics of it. They put in parents. The reality of parents. What would *really* happen if kids spent the summer at the beach. Parents would be concerned about the whereabouts of their kids, their behavior, what they were involved in and so on. Our pictures were fantasies," concluded director William Asher.

Opposite: Two examples of why Hammer Films was able to stay in business long after they'd dried up as horror experts. Left: Valarie Leon in "Blood from the Mummy's Tomb" (1971). Right: Ingrid Pitt in "The Vampire Lovers" (1970). Above: Behind the scenes of Hammer's "The Vampire Lovers" (1970), which AIP imported; in multiple poses is Dawn Addams.

Fifteen

Television

Our first ten years in feature production and distribution have been so eminently successful and we were so thoroughly entrenched in this branch of the film industry that we felt now is the time to enter this new field of distribution.

—James Nicholson

There was more talk about AIP's television excursions than there was action. At least that's the way it seems to me after researching the matter. There was some talk of making *Beach Party* into a TV series but nothing came of it. AIP talked about making a series out of Dr. Goldfoot (the subject of two AIP films), but nothing came of that either. And I think Vincent Price was supposed to host an evening of Edgar Allan Poe.

What did happen, television-wise, was a series of 16mm color remakes of old AIP movies, made in Texas for $40,000 apiece by Larry Buchanan.

The Day the World Ended became *Year 2889* with Paul Peterson in the Richard Denning role. *The She Creature* became *Creature of Destruction* with Les Tremayne in the Chester Morris role. *Zontar, the Thing from Venus* was *It Conquered the World* with John Agar filling in for Peter Graves. *The Eye Creatures* was John Ashley doing Steve Terrell's role in *Invasion of the Saucer-Men*.

"I was the only actor from Hollywood," John Ashley recalled. "All the rest were local people from Dallas who had had little theatre background and that sort of thing. We shot it on Gordon McLendon's ranch. I think it took three or four weeks. I was going to do another one right after that, *Mars Needs Women* (a remake of the 1964 *Pajama Party*) but I got tied up with something else and Tommy Kirk did it.

"To be very honest I was very well paid. More than half of the budget went to me. What the hell, it was the money. I had no illusions about it. But, once again, these are feelings I would say to you now, but you don't verbalize them while you're in the middle of working on

156

somebody's picture because ... well, you know, Larry was very conscientious and it was very important to him. So, you go in and try to do the best job you can. Which is what an actor should do. He accepts a role and takes the people's money. There's no point in being condescending about it. You try to make it as believable as you can. In the final analysis, *you're* the one that people are going to be seeing so you try to make it come off as well as you can. I saw the picture not too long ago, on television, at four in the morning. You would be amazed at the number of people that sit up and watch those damn things. Of course, the funny thing is the kids, cause they're so honest. My older boy, Tony, he's eighteen now and kind of laid-back, so he doesn't rag me too much. But my younger son, Cole, will say: 'Dad, you're so corny'."

In addition to the remakes, Larry produced and directed a couple of originals. He made all of the pictures between 1966 and 1968. To say that all of Larry's pictures were not very good is being extremely kind. Not generous, but kind.

AIP purchased a number of Mexican and Italian movies to release directly to television. *Epicolor '64* was a package of sword and sandal features liberally sprinkled with "Hercules," "Samson" and "Ulysses" titles.

An undated brochure I came across, which looked to be vintage '64 or earlier, advertised AIP-Television's line-up: Hal March's "Gold Record" with headliners Henry Mancini, Connie Stevens, Frankie Avalon, Paul Revere and the Raiders, Harpers Bizzare, etc.; "Young Adult Theatre," 26 swinging action-packed films in color; 200 old "Adventures of Ozzie and Harriet;" "Holiday Story Book of Fables"; "Domiant," ten fast paced, thrill-packed exciting stories with top-drawing names; "Cinema 20," a package of distinguished motion pictures combing the most exciting award-winning talents in the entertainment industry (which may have been the films Jim and Sam bought from Ely A. Landau and Oliver A. Unger—*La Dolce Vita*, *The Pawnbroker*, *The Umbrellas of Cherbourg*, etc.—for which Jim and Sam formed another company, Trans-American Films); "Sinbad Jr." 130 five-minute swashbuckling action-packed cartoons; "Real Life Adventure Specials," all color documentaries of high adventure and fierce action. "Make the now television scene with those switched on, tuned in *In*" people," the brochure said. "It's the grooviest— get with it...." Interested parties were to contact Stanley Dudelson, who was persuaded to leave his job with Screen Gems to become AIP's television representative.

Sixteen

Keeping Busy

I keep thinking I'll leave them. But I sort of have a stake in the company. I have this recurring nightmare where I think I've made some picture for AIP long ago and they still owe me money. The trouble is I can't think of the name of the picture.
—Roger Corman

Roger Corman produced and directed eight Edgar Allan Poe movies between 1960 and 1964, which accounted for less than half of his output during that period. He produced and directed six movies for Filmgroup, two for United Artists, one for Pathé American, and three more for AIP. He had a hand in several more in one capacity or another. (The Pathé American film, *The Intruder*, tackled the problem of racial prejudice. It received good reviews but died at the boxoffice. Roger still uses this film to excuse the fact that he hasn't upgraded his product since.)

Jonathan Haze approached Roger with an idea around this time. Since *The Little Shop of Horrors* had done fairly well, Jonathan wanted to write a comedy for himself and Dick Miller to star in. Roger asked Dick about it.

"Fine," Dick said. "But I want to be involved with the writing of it."

Dick and Jonathan went to work on *The Monsters of Nicholson Mesa*, a script which used the names of people who worked for AIP as characters or places in the story. Discussions about the script went along fine but when the two actors got down to business they discovered they couldn't write together. Jonathan wanted to write one quick draft then go back and make the corrections. Dick wanted to make the corrections as they went along.

"I'm going to have to write it myself," Jonathan finally told him. "You can rewrite it if you want to."

Dick got miffed and refused to appear in the picture. Roger lost interest so Jonathan took his script to Jim Nicholson. He loved it. But Roger intervened.

"He's asking for more money than I was going to pay him," Roger told Jim. "Just hold on. I can get it for less."

Top: Richard Basehart (left) as Sayer of the Law and Fumio Demura as Hyenaman, in "The Island of Dr. Moreau" (1977). Bottom: Composer Robert O. Ragland (right) with Ray Milland behind the heads (Rosie Greer and Milland) made for "The Thing with Two Heads" (1982, photo Jack McCarthy).

While Roger was waiting for the price to come down, Jonathan sold the property to Mel Welles who had just formed a production company. But the company went bust and AIP ended up with Jonathan's script after all. The finished product was called *Invasion of the Star Creatures* (1962). Burt Schoenberg, the artist who supplied the weird paintings for the Poe movies, made the monsters out of burlap bags dyed green. "Crappy" was the word Jonathan used to describe the picture.

In the meantime Roger purchased a Russian science fiction picture which he called *Battle Beyond the Sun* (1962). For $250 Roger hired a young UCLA student named Francis Ford Coppola to write the English language version. The original story concerned the race for space between the U.S. and the U.S.S.R. Francis stripped the script of politics by creating a future world divided into two countries—North Hemis and South Hemis. At the point in the film where one of the characters sees the astronauts holding "the golden torch of truth" Roger wanted monsters fighting instead.

"What kind of monsters?" Francis asked.

"Something phallic in concept," Roger said casually. "Might make it interesting."

"Fine," Francis said and had some of his UCLA film student friends build two monsters—one of them looked like a vagina with teeth, the other a penis with eyes. Roger was taken aback when he first saw the footage of the monsters in action.

"We can't put this in the picture," he said.

"Nobody will know," Francis replied. "The only reason it seems raw to you is because you know what it's all about."

After working for Roger as a dialogue director and an assistant director, Francis volunteered to be the soundman on *The Young Racers* (1963). Francis knew nothing about the job. Right after volunteering he went home and read a pamphlet on the Perfectone sound recorder. Roger, Francis and Floyd Crosby were looking at some of the rushes in Paris when Floyd commented on the fact that you could hear the camera over the cars. Francis immediately became defensive and said it was Floyd's fault. Roger knew whose fault it was but admired Francis for thinking on his feet.

The film had quite a crew besides those already mentioned. Menachem Golan, by the early 1980's president of Cannon Films and owner of Israel's largest studio, was the second grip. Robert Towne was the assistant director. Bobby Campbell wrote the script which started out as a story about bullfighting. His brother, William, was the film's lead.

Roger made a deal with Sunbeam to use one of their sports cars, a Sunbeam Alpine. But he needed someone to drive it to Paris. He got Chuck Griffith to do it.

Top: Shelley Winters as "Bloody Mama" (1970). Bottom: David Carradine and Barbara Hershey in "Boxcar Bertha" (1972).

Chuck was stranded in Israel at the time. He and Mel Welles had started a war movie that the unions shut down. Some of Chuck's Israeli friends told him to finish the picture in Israel. Chuck arrived in Israel flat broke. He lived on rooftops. Roger promised him a job as assistant director on the race picture plus work as director on a horror script that Francis was writing if he drove the Sunbeam Alpine.

Chuck totalled the car somewhere near Provence.

It was Roger's policy to make two features whenever he went on location but with Chuck in the hospital, and himself returning to the U.S. to make *The Raven*, there was nobody left to make Francis's horror movie, *Dementia 13* (1962). Nobody, that is, except Francis. He was given $20,000 to make it. If he needed more money he'd have to raise it himself. Francis shot the picture in Ireland. Roger left him alone. Until the editing stage. That was where Roger got his way. He added voice-overs to simplify some of the scenes. And he wanted some more violence. Another ax murder, which was eventually shot by Jack Hill.

After finishing with *The Raven*, Roger was compelled to make another movie on the same sets before they could be dismantled. He had Boris Karloff under contract for three more days. Leo Gordon was asked to write unrelated scenes for Boris, Jack Nicholson and Dick Miller to enact.

"But you haven't got a story," Boris told Roger, trying to talk him out of the project.

"That's all right," Roger told him. "I know exactly what I'm going to do."

For three days the three actors paraded back and forth across props and down long, dark corridors with no where to go and nothing to do when they got there. Dialogue was exchanged without meaning. They all dashed around Producers Studio one or two steps ahead of the wreckers.

"He nearly killed me in it," Boris remarked. "The last day he had me in a tank of cold water for about two hours...."

Since most of the Poe films ended with a fire, Roger thought it was time for a change of pace. Instead of burning his castle he flooded it. Although his realization about the need for change was correct, his response was impotent.

After three silly days Boris returned to England. He'd finished his contractual obligation. That was okay with Roger. He figured on fleshing out the rest of the story without Boris. Roger told Jack Nicholson and Dick Miller he'd be calling as soon as he got the rest of the script together. Three or four months later Monte Hellman, Francis Ford Coppola and Jack Hill all took turns directing new pieces of a puzzle without a picture. A scene was finally written in which Jack grabbed Dick by the collar and

Jack Nicholson is looking for a copy of the script to see if he can figure out what the hell is going on in "The Terror" (1963).

demanded to know what the hell was going on, as if serving as a spokesperson for the audience. The film's title was *The Terror* (1963).

* * * * *

The following production fact sheet was sent to the exhibitors:

The story of *"X" — The Man with the X-Ray Eyes* is one which might actually have happened only yesterday, which may be happening today, or which quite possibly might happen tomorrow. It is the personal, human story of a brilliant doctor who, in his endless striving for healing powers in the true tradition of the medical profession, seeks to improve upon the limited and imperfect mechanical devices which assist the doctor in his work.

"He stripped souls as bare as bodies!" the ads claimed. The critics were happy. *The New York Times* found it "level-headed and persuasive." It won the Trieste Science Fiction Film Festival Award for best picture of 1963. But it was filmed on a $300,000 budget and it needed more like a million. It was generally deficient in most departments, but none more obvious than in the special effects.

"I feel it was an opportunity that was slightly missed," Roger said. "The original idea to do a picture about a man who could see through objects was Jim Nicholson's and then the development of the basic idea was mine and Ray Russell's. I almost didn't do the picture for two reasons: one, I felt the script had not turned out as well as I had expected; and two, the more I got into it, the more I felt we were going to be heavily dependent on the special effects. The picture was shot in three weeks on a medium low budget and I felt we were not going to be able to photograph what Xavier could see, and that the audience would be cheated. The picture turned out reasonably well but I think, when finished, it did suffer from that. The effects just weren't there. We did the best we could. To show a man seeing through a building I photographed buildings that were in various stages of construction, on the basis he could see through the outer skin — which was a reasonable cheat — but it still was a cheat."

By the time Roger Corman stopped making Edgar Allan Poe movies, AIP had grown almost as gigantic as the Colossal Man. From a one-room office in Los Angeles, AIP spread to New York, Lisbon, Berlin, Buenos Aires, Paris and Palm Beach, with employees numbering at least 300, not counting the 30 domestic exchanges and franchise holders. The company had 15 foreign distribution outlets.

From *Chicago's American*, Vol. 65, No. 74, section 1, page 1:

American International Pictures, which has been celebrating "a decade of progress" this year, has the biggest grossing picture in its history, the musical comedy, "Bikini Beach."

However, this is but one of numerous significant events making 1964 a memorable year for A.I.P.

A 10th anniversary sales drive in July and August saw an A.I.P. picture showing 83 percent of the theatres in the world during the concentration period.

In addition to company offices in every major domestic exchange center, this year's A.I.P. expansion activities added representation in 30 foreign nations.

Star personalities and A.I.P executives chalked up

more than a million air miles meeting with exhibitors and ballyhooing releases in all parts of the world.

The company also launched a program of signing young contract players to long term pacts and, according to A.I.P. Executives James H. Nicholson and Samuel Z. Arkoff, plans are for the strongest line-up of productions and largest financial outlay for their filming in company history.

"We at American International have never bought negative prognostications, but we have aggressively sold positive and imaginative values to the hilt," wrote Jim Nicholson. "The history of our company indicates that we launched our world-wide distribution and production organization during the blackest period in Hollywood history. The perennial pessimists were sounding the death knell to the most fabulous industry the world had ever known. Having grown up in this entertainment business and matured through exhibition, distribution, promotion and production, we listened to the crepe-hangers, made our own evaluations, but wouldn't believe a word of it. Our judgement has been substantiated as we review the past twelve years of our growth and expansion.

"You see, I've always believed that motion pictures are a great business. Sometimes there was little or no effective planning and markets were not analyzed properly. Many times there was too wide a gap between creative enterprise and sound economic values, but these matters of proper and carefully thought out business structure and procedures. Why damn the film business as a whole?

"It's an ancient filmland cliché that no one starts out to make a bad picture. I am convinced that this is essentially true. [Your author is likewise convinced, although equally so that there are many in the business who never set out to make a good picture either.] What happens so often though is that a motion picture story is selected, cast and made with too little attention to its audience market areas or the ultimate selling campaign. Just before it reaches the exhibitor, there is a wild scramble to quickly adapt a selling campaign which has no particular rhyme or reason and is not aimed at any particular segment of its world-wide audience. Many artistic triumphs have failed to score at the box office due to inefficient planning and market analysis.

"At American International we firmly believe that the promotional campaign, which includes publicity, advertising, exploitation and merchandizing, begins at the point of story purchase. When you are selecting the subject matter is when you must be acutely aware of where you are going in the matter of audience direction, marketable assets, merchandising possibilities and the areas of publicity, advertising and promotion suggested by the subject.... In other words we want to know at the outset exactly why we are making a certain motion picture, what we have to sell, what the exhibitor can do with the property in his territory and what inherent exploitable values are available for immediate development.

"In other words a sales blueprint emerges from the first story, cast and production discussions and we are moving in a single purposeful direction from the inception of a film idea. Just as a rudimentary example, how in the world can sound merchandising tie-ins be effectively executed so that all participants may reap full benefits unless they are conceived before the picture reaches the sound stages? Just as in all phases of promotion, it's a case of setting the stage before the curtain goes up. With such merchandising virtually built-in to the story structure, we are ready with complete promotional material even for a quick release date after filming.

"Also at American International we are highly in favor of 'beating the bushes'. Sam Arkoff and I do it all the time. We take our stars with us and get out and meet exhibitors and press all over the nation. By doing this through the years of AI's company development, I am now able to count many theatre men throughout the country among my personal friends. The association becomes much more than a business arrangement. Personal appearance tours are certainly not a new thing in motion picture promotional history. We used to have some great national junkets in the old days, but when the economy wave hit Hollywood, the various companies pulled in their horns and curtailed such expenditures. We've kept going with the 'rubbing elbows in the field' business. In fact we've doubled up and its been highly rewarding at the box office.

"Showmanship through the years hasn't changed much in essence. We maintain it's extremely important, however, not only to keep up with the times, but to keep ahead of them. It has been said that each era in world history has its own literature and its own language. We believe it is American International's business to interpret this age in which we live and to communicate in these understandable terms. We adhere closely to this both in topical subject matter for the screen and in all of our advertising, publicity and promotional activities.

"But coming back to the original theme, I do believe that the only completely successful results in a promotional campaign will be achieved when the preproduction planning board or blueprint technique is applied. You know what you have to sell and how you're going to sell it before you make it." — Jim Nicholson.

Seventeen

Protest Pictures

The Italians read all kinds of symbolism that wasn't there into every scene — things we never dreamed of. Angels will be by far the biggest profit maker we've ever produced — probably half again better than the best of the beach pictures.

— Samuel Arkoff

From the standpoint of my own standards of morality, I've never made a picture I'd be ashamed to show my children. But we would be idiots to think that Mary Poppins *is the limit of their interest and knowledge. My daughters have been offered LSD on the grounds of their high school. This is a fact of life, and we'd damn well better start discussing it out in the open so we can do something about it.*

— James Nicholson

It was Milt Moritz who first saw the magazine spread on the Hell's Angels in *The Saturday Evening Post.* He showed it to Al Kallis. They both agreed it was a natural for AIP. They took the magazine into Sam Arkoff's office. Roger Corman was called the next day and it wasn't long after that the trade papers announced that *All the Fallen Angels* was in the works.

George Chakiris was signed for the lead, primarily because he'd been the leader of a gang of toughs in *West Side Story.* Nancy Sinatra was to be his costar. Peter Fonda was in New York trying to raise money to make a movie when he was offered the part of Loser. Peter read the first forty pages of the script and discovered Loser was dead for more than half the picture. For $10,000 Peter figured he could play a stiff.

Peter entered Roger's office wearing hexagonal glasses, the top quarter of the lenses silver mirrors, an old leather jacket and a huge sheriff's badge that read: I BELONG TO NAVY INTELLIGENCE. CHICAGO BRANCH, BADGE #7.

"He wanted to do something I also wanted to do very much," Peter said. "He wanted to make a film straight, without any message. Merely film. When I heard this, then I wanted to do it with him."

Roger called Peter Bogdanovich, who was working on a script for Roger, a combination of *The Bridge on the River Kwai* and *Lawrence of Arabia* on a slightly smaller scale. He told Peter to put the script aside and go searching for locations. Never having done any location scouting before, Peter wanted to know what to look for.

Shortly before shooting began, George Chakiris was told he'd have to ride a motorcycle. He took a quick ride and decided once was enough. He was willing to do the picture but only if they'd hire a double. Roger asked Fonda if he'd like the lead. Fonda said yes but wanted to change the name of his character from Jack Black to Heavenly Blues. Roger was agreeable but wanted to know why Fonda wanted to be called Heavenly Blues. Fonda explained it was a drug made from morning glory seeds. Three hundred fifty Heavenly Blue morning glory seeds, nicely crushed, equalled a buzz. Fonda was so worried about the name change he forgot to ask for more money for the larger role.

Chuck Griffith wrote the script. It contained less than 120 lines of dialogue and paralleled motorcycle cops and the scungey bikers. It was Chuck's intention to show they were both motivated by the same impulses. Roger was enraged. He didn't want a movie about cops. Chuck wrote a second version which was ultimately rewritten by Peter Bogdanovich. Much of the dialogue and story situations came from a meeting with actual Hell's Angels at a place in Venice Beach called the Gunk Shop. Chuck brought along a tape recorder and Roger brought a grin which he pasted on his face for the bulk of the evening in an effort to hide the fact that the bikers made him uncomfortable. He ended up hiring some of them to be in his picture, which attracted the attention of the police.

They were on location in Mecca, a town near the Salton Sea when the state police started tracking them. There were warrants out for most of the Angels. Jack Bohrer pointed out that the bikers were earning an honest day's pay but the police were not impressed. They told Jack to finish what had to be done in a hurry and then get out.

Roger completed the film in fifteen days. It was previewed at the Theatre Owners' Association convention in New York under the title *The Wild Angels* (1966). It was after dinner and very few members of the audience were in the age group for which the film was intended.

"The picture you are about to see will shock, perhaps anger you!" cautioned the film's pre-credits opening. "Although the characters and events are fictitious, the story is a reflection of our times."

It certainly shocked the TOA audience. The picture hadn't been on for long before Jim and Sam saw people exchanging disapproving glances. The frequency increased until they couldn't take it anymore. Jim and Sam waited outside in the lobby and watched the folks trickle out.

"It's too strong for my theatre," one chap said as he strolled into the

First of the motorcycle films, "The Wild Angels" (1966), starring Peter Fonda, also kicked off a wave of protest pictures.

lobby. His wife was less kind. She stared at Jim and Sam a moment then asked: "What kind of people are you to make a picture like this?"

By the time the sequence in the church came on the screen, where the bikers stage an orgy, there was a mass exodus. "We wish you luck," one fellow said on his way out. "That was a dirty picture," someone else remarked.

Peter Fonda was on his way to his car when he was accosted by a woman whom he recognized as being the same woman who stood outside the theatre every night when he was on Broadway. Now she struck at him with an umbrella, screaming at him, calling him a Nazi. Peter drove to the Lincoln Center where his arrival was "booed" and "hissed" by the exhibitors. Except for a table of about fifteen people from Canada who knew they were going to make a pile of money from the picture.

The film was shown, by invitation, at the 27th Venice International Film Festival. It caused a stink among the American representatives. Roger defended the festival invitation, contending that the film supplied proof that, in a democracy, artists have the freedom to show whatever they wanted. (*The Wild Angels* won an award at the Cannes festival.)

The critics were not pleased. Bosley Crowther called it a "brutal little picture" and "an embarrassment." *Newsweek* said it was an "ugly piece of trash" that revelled "in the shock value of murder, mob violence, gratuitous brutality and a squalid rape in a chapel during a funeral." *The Saturday Review* thought that the film's lack of psychological or social background made the film irresponsible. Even *Variety* warned that it carried "shock impact of the sort that occasionally stuns," although a "lush take" was predicted. *The Hollywood Reporter* concurred. But the requests for bookings were scarce. The exhibitors were afraid of the film.

"You have all received one Promotion Kit on *The Wild Angels* which is to be used to service newspaper writers etc.," AIP's *Weekly Hi Liter* reminded the branch offices. "So far we have only received a very, very limited number of requests for additional kits. What happens to these when you get them? Do they just hit the shelves to collect dust? Or is it you only have one newspaper in your one-horse town? Let's get on the ball and get this material out and then watch the columns for items and send us some tear sheets. Do you realized how important free publicity is? It makes you extra money!"

San Francisco	Esquire Theatre (1st 7 days)	$15,292
	Spruce D/I (1st 7 days)	$10,588
	Crown Theatre (1st 7 days)	$7,657
San Jose, Calif.	United Artists Theatre (1st 7 days)	$8,960
	Bayshore D/I (1st 7 days)	$13,854
Oakland, Calif.	Stadium Auto D/I (1st 7 days)	$16,222
	Auto Movies (1st 7 days)	$10,938
	Grand Lake Theatre (1st 7 days)	$6,570
	Rancho D/I (1st 7 days)	$11,043
Palo Alto, Calif.	Sunnyvale Theatre (1 7 days)	$7,981
San Rafael, Calif.	#101 D/I	$5,502
Reno, Calif.	Crest Theatre (1st 7 days)	$5,067
Sacramento, Calif.	Fox Theatre (1st 7 days)	$7,702
	Thunderbird D/I (1st 7 days)	$12,222
Salinas, Calif.	Auto Movies D/I (1st 7 days)	$6,190
Belmont, Calif.	Auto Movies D/I (1st 7 days)	$4,769

San Mateo, Calif.	Peninsula D/I (1st 7 days)	$5,531
Berkeley, Calif.	California Theatre (1st 7 days)	$4,555
Fresno, Calif.	Sunnyside D/i (1st 2 days)	$3,072
Carbondale, Ill.	Waring Auto D/I (1st 7 days)	$6,026
Nashville, Tenn.	Paramount Theatre (1st 7 days)	$13,697
	(1st 3 days 2nd wk)	$6,784
Jacksonville, N.C.	Center Theatre (1st 7 days)	$6,245

In Europe, where some of the critics had started to think of Roger as an artist, the response to the film was more favorable. They were far less outraged than their American counterparts.

The money continued to roll in. And so did the requests for bookings.

"What am I going to do?" Leon Blender asked.

"What's the trouble?" Sam wanted to know.

"I just got a call from an old customer," Leon explained. "He wants to book *The Wild Angels.*"

"So? Let him have it."

"But it's the guy who told you he'd never book it," said Leon. "You remember. The one in the lobby that night at the TOA convention. I booked it to his competition. I don't know what to tell him now."

Sam reached for the phone. He took a great deal of relish in explaining the situation. "You said you couldn't play it in your theatres. Remember?"

There was a moment of silence before the voice at the other end of the line said, "You didn't have to take me seriously."

The Hell's Angels sued Roger Corman for defamation of character. They said they were portrayed in the picture as an outlaw gang. They were, they claimed, a social organization dedicated to spreading technical information about motorcycles. Because of the "false and derogatory" image the film projected of them it was virtually impossible for them to appear unharmed in public. They wanted $2,000,000 in damages. They settled for $2,000. According to Roger they threatened his life.

Big Otto Friendly, the Angels' leader, called Roger to say they were going to snuff him out. "But, Otto," Roger reminded him, "you're sueing me. How are you going to collect if I'm dead?"

The Wild Angels spawned a rash of biker dramas. The first from AIP was *Devil's Angels* (1967), written by Chuck Griffith, produced by Burt Topper and directed by Daniel Haller. Roger was asked to make it but he was already busy with another. Roger was a little miffed at Chuck for giving Danny what he thought was a better script. Chuck didn't think it was better, just more conventional. His idea this time was to present the bikers as a bunch of technologically inclined Oakies. Shooting began on Tuesday, January 10th, 1967, on location in Arizona. The following day a full page one-color ad appeared in the *Weekly Variety* and a two-color announcement appeared in *Exhibitor*.

From 1967 to 1972 there must have been at least two dozen motorcycle dramas, a goodly portion of them from AIP. As the writers searched for new activities to involve the bikers in, the stories became more and more like westerns. James Gordon White borrowed the plot from *Winchester '73*, a Jimmy Stewart western, for his *Hell's Belles* (1969). Jeremy Slate took Jimmy's role and the rifle Jimmy pursued became a motorcycle. Jock Mahoney, television's "Range Rider" and star of a number of U-I oaters, seemed right at home in White's *The Glory Stompers* (1968). He simply traded his horse for a chopper.

One of the most popular biker dramas was *Hell's Angels on Wheels* (1967) starring Jack Nicholson, who stepped into the lead role after John Ashley turned it down because he thought he was too old for it. Richard Rush, who went on to bigger pictures—*Getting Straight, Freebie and the Bean, The Stunt Man*—directed it. He told the producer, Joe Solomon, that he would include all the "razzle-dazzle fights and action" that Joe wanted, so long as the producer would let him "play a little bit." One critic took delight in pointing out it was far more damaging to the image of Hell's Angels than *The Wild Angels* yet it was made with the approval of Angel leader Sonny Barger, who reportedly saw it ten times. Barger, in fact, volunteered to make personal appearances.

Tom Laughlin made his first appearance as Billy Jack in an AIP biker movie, *Born Losers* (1967). Laughlin directed the film under his pseudonym T.C. Frank. The story was based on two incidents: the ex-Marine from Philadelphia who was fined $1,400 and sentenced to 180 days in jail for wounding two of the hoodlums who were molesting three ladies (the assailants were fined $50 apiece and set free); and Kitty Genovese who was repeatedly stabbed in front of dozens of apathetic onlookers. AIP was naturally delighted when Laughlin's *Billy Jack* hit big in 1972. *Born Losers* went out again as "the original Billy Jack." Laughlin demanded, but didn't get, $5,000,000 in damages.

The fact that *The Wild Angels* became AIP's most commercially successful film had everything to do with the company's decision to produce what it called protest pictures. "We make films until they quit paying," Jim told *The Atlanta Journal*. "Like the Poe horror shows. We made a number of them and they went great.* Then one day one didn't

*They were still going great at the time the article was written in 1969. The first five Poe pictures were re-released as a Dusk to Dawn package in 1967 and grossed $5,863 at the Acres drive-in in Phoenix, $3,931 in three days at the Edgemere in Shrewsbury, $5,436 for the same number of days at the Sherman drive-in in Indianapolis, $4,145 in four days at the Geneva drive-in in San Francisco, $3,566 in four days at the Vallair drive-in in Denver, and $65,000 after a week in nine Los Angeles theatres.

Roger Corman and Susan Strasberg (right) on the set of "The Trip" (1967).

sell. We quit. The same with the beach party films. For three years they were great. Then one didn't sell. We quit."

The *National Observer* was informed that AIP would make more documentary style pictures like *The Wild Angels*. On the boards was something called *The End*, a look at futuristic automated society. *Sunset Strip* was to be "a look at the frenetic fringe of today's youth." *The Trip* (1967) was to be an impartial look at LSD.

Before making *The Trip*, Roger Corman (at Chuck Griffith's insistence) decided to drop acid. He'd read Timothy Leary's book, which suggested a beautiful setting with friends for a good experience. Roger chose Big Sur.

"I was the most conservative of a very wild crowd," he said. "What started out as a couple of us going up to Big Sur ended up as a caravan when they found out I was going to take LSD. There must have been twenty people or more. We had to draw up the equivalent of a production schedule — who was going to be taking acid and at what time."

Everyone but Roger stayed in a tent trailer. Roger rented a motel room.

Nothing happened to Roger at first. He thought he'd been swindled. "Nothing's happening," he told Chuck Griffith. "It's a rip-off."

His rage subsided and suddenly he sat in silence. "Excuse me a moment," he said. He lay face down in the dirt and had a wonderful trip. He remembered later thinking that the way to create art was to spread out on the ground and touch as much of it as possible. That way you could create a piece of art in your mind and others could experience it by simply touching the ground. "I'm humping the earth," he said at one point. "The earth is a woman." A group of nuns walked by and were unimpressed. When Roger was informed that the park was closing and they would have to leave, he said he had enough money to buy the park. "It's a good thing I made all my money before this happened because now I don't care about it."

The next day the plan was for Chuck to drop the acid and for Roger to observe. Chuck thought the whole thing was too ridiculous and took off through the woods as fast as he could travel under the circumstances.

The first script was about three inches thick, largely because Roger wanted all of the social issues of the 60s crammed into it. The second version concentrated on drugs and music.

"I can't sell dope to fifty million people," Roger concluded. "What would you do if you were doing it yourself?"

Chuck thought a moment. "I would just have the lead character drop acid at the beginning and follow him through the trip."

That's precisely what Roger did. Only he hired Jack Nicholson to write the final draft. The movie was completed in three weeks for $100,000. Peter Fonda is reported to have assisted in the editing of the final three reels. The result was the most objective treatment of LSD in a commercial film, even after AIP got cold feet and added a disclaimer that warned the audience against drug experimentation. Roger's open-ended finale was also altered. An optical was added which shattered Peter Fonda's image like a cracked glass, to suggest that his drug experience had irreparably damaged his life. Roger was a little surprised. His movies had never been tampered with before.

Even with the concessions many critics were pissed. NBC's pinch-butt critic called it a 90 minute commerical for LSD. *The New York Times* called it a big put-on. Hollis Alpert thought it was the best picture Roger ever made.

AIP continued to explore topics that would appeal to the youth market just as they always had. When it became obvious that marijuana was gaining popularity among high school and college students AIP released *Mary Jane* (1968). In terms of its accuracy and authenticity it was sort of an updated version of *Reefer Madness*.

"Are you saying that marijuana leads to the hard stuff?" a concerned teacher asks at one point.

Max Julien (left), Susan Strasberg and Jack Nicholson in "Psych-Out" (1968).

"Big time scientists say no," a self-righteous policeman replies. "But statistics show that every hardcore addict started with marijuana [which the actor playing the part pronounced *mary-wana*]." Unlike Roger's teen-age dramas, *Mary Jane* was preachy and pompous, much like the scenarios Lou Rusoff once wrote for the company.

Two locales inhabited by hippies were used as backgrounds for *Riot on Sunset Strip* (1967) and *Psych-Out* (1968). The first exploited the actual riot that took place when the merchants along L.A.'s Sunset Strip complained that the flower children were chasing their customers away. The police tried to disperse them which resulted in a riot. The movie was made by "Jungle" Sam Katzman for MGM but the studio couldn't move fast enough to get the picture into theatres in time to take advantage of the topicality of the event so Katzman took it to AIP.

The latter film took place in San Francisco's Haight-Ashbury section, another stomping ground for the hippies.

Racial tension in the public schools, brought about by integration was the subject tackled by *Born Wild* (1968). But the most successful of the "protest" pictures was *Wild in the Streets* (1968).

Sam Arkoff (left), Hilda Arkoff, Susan Hart Nicholson, and Jim Nicholson, in 1966.

It began as a novella in *Esquire* magazine by Robert Thom titled "The Day It All Happened, Baby." MGM and Paramount expressed an interest in the property but it eventually found its way to AIP. The title was changed to make use of an advertising campaign previously designed for another project that had fallen through. The movie was completed in 20 days for $700,000. It had a solid cast: Christopher Jones, Diane Varsi, Hal Holbrook, Millie Perkins, Richard Pryor, Shelley Winters, Bert Freed, Larry Bishop, Kevin Coughlin, Michael Margotta, Don Wyndham, Sally Sachse, Ed Begley, Melvin Belli, Louie Lomax, Dick Clark, Walter Winchell, Pamela Mason, Army Archerd and Paul Frees.

Diane Varsi played Sally Leroy, an ex-child star elected to Congress with the help of Christopher Jones, who played Max Frost, the rock idol of Thom's scenario who eventually becomes President.

Miss Varsi was the actress nominated for an Oscar for her performance in *Peyton Place* in 1959. Educated in convents, raised by strangers, married at 15 and again at 17, Diane added to her troubled life by walking out on her contract at 20th Century–Fox, which made it nearly impossible for her to return to acting when she decided to. The Associated Press had a little fun at her expense:

> Diane Varsi, reporting for a wardrobe fitting for her new movie, *Wild in the Streets*, found it rather wild on the set too. Her costume for an important scene was one very skimpy apron to be worn over skin and talcum...to which was added a rather large sweet-heart bow. More cover was needed, so her naval was decorated with a peace symbol and her breasts painted in the manner of flower children.

The picture, about a 24-year-old rock star president who orders everyone over 35 into concentration camps, went into national release May 29th. It premiered at the Oriental Theatre in Chicago on May 17. It could not have been better timed, coming as it did a few months prior to the Democratic Convention. Thousands of young people came to Chicago to protest the choice of Hubert Humphrey for President. Mayor Richard Daley decided to deny their right to protest and sent his drones out to silence them. Police began bashing skulls, a piece of Americana telecast by all three networks. Daley would later tell the press that cops weren't hired to create disorder but to preserve it. Daley expressed concern over the possible repercussions that *Wild in the Streets* might cause. Aware that the movie contained a sequence in which Washington's water supply was spiked with LSD, Daley ordered guards and barbed wire around Chicago's reservoirs. Apparently he didn't notice the "Max Frost for President" signs in the Democratic Convention Hall.

"*Wild in the Streets* is one of American International's most ambitious and expensive productions, but it assumes a look several times its budget through extensive and diverse set-ups, admirably researched and utilized newsreel footage and the presence of a sizable recruitment of authenticating media personalities," wrote *The Hollywood Reporter*. "Barry Shear, handling the directorial reigns ... has gotten some fascinating performances from his cast," said *Film Daily*. *Variety* called it "a neat package."

Once again AIP insisted on messing with the picture. It was to have ended on a shot of Shelley Winters, clinging to a barbed-wire fence, singing "The Battle Hymn of the Republic." An epilogue was added which showed Max Frost bullying a small child. The child turned to the camera and said: "Everyone over ten ought to be put out of business."

Robert Thom wrote and directed *Angel, Angel, Down We Go* (1969). "Here again I want to say something about society," Thom told *Variety*. "It deals with a court reporter who concentrates on tax evasion to get the Mafia."

The picture was produced by "Jungle" Sam Katzman (so nick-

Christopher Jones (center) as the 24-year-old rock star president in "Wild in the Streets" (1968).

named for the low budget "Jungle Jim" series he produced) and his son, Jerry. *Angel* was to mark a change of pace for "Jungle" Sam. After three decades worth of carelessly made pot boilers ("Lord knows I'll never make an Academy Award movie," Katzman once told the press, "but then I'm just as happy to get my achievement plaques from the bank every year!"), he was going to make movies with "depth and a point of view."

"The day of the exploitation picture is gone," Jerry Katzman said. "We learned that with *Riot on Sunset Strip*. We learned that people are no longer interested in headlines. [Heaven forbid he should conclude that people simply weren't interested in his movie.] There is so much sensationalism on television it doesn't work anymore.

"AIP is trying to go much more highbrow. They have made a fortune, but this is a business of money as well as art. This will be one of the first pictures in an effort to change their image."

But it's not easy for a man who earned a reputation as being "the master of stock footage," "the king of anachronism and blithe, internalized actions of murky motivation" to change his own image, much less anyone else's."Jungle" Sam saw his picture open exclusively at one of the more prestigious Hollywood theatres. One week later it was withdrawn and shelved for a year. It emerged again, recut, as *Cult of the Damned* and played as a second feature to a semipornographic vampire movie.

Not so Christopher Jones' follow-up to *Wild in the Streets*: *3 in the Attic* (1968), costarring Yvette Mimieux, Judy Pace and Maggie Thrett, became AIP's top grossing film. It earned $354,401 in Philadelphia alone and $60,177 in Kansas City, Kansas in the first seven days at 11 theatres. The story, by Stephen Yafa, began as a screenplay that nobody was interested in. He turned it into a novel and it won an award from the Writers Guild of America. Two years later Richard Wilson directed the film version in North Carolina.

> Inherent in the story of "Three in the Attic" are angles which strongly suggest some of the same "with it" manner and satirical mood of "The Graduate," one of the biggest hits of recent years.
>
> The story is provocative — and not just because of its interracial sex angles. Teenagers and young adults are certain to be buzzing about the reasons for the young man's imprisonment, its justification (if any) and his refusal to submit to the demands of his beautiful captors, while the oldsters will be set to pondering the ethics and moral values of today's younger citizens.
>
> Audience predisposition figures to be high at all levels, from teenyboppers to curious oldsters, from the ballyhoo trade to, most especially, the college crowd. The ultimate response in the more discriminating class sectors will depend on the film's quality and its ability to provoke controversy, but the initial lure should be quite strong. — Film Bulletin

It inspired the less successful *Up in the Cellar* (1970), later retitled *3 in the Cellar* and shipped out with *3 in the Attic*.

One of the last of AIP's youth-in-revolt protest pictures was *Gas-s-s-s! or, We Had to Destroy the World in Order to Save It* (1969). It was *the* last film that Roger Corman made for the company.

It began as a serious science fiction idea about an experimental gas that kills everyone over 25. Writer George Armitage turned it into a satire and the picture was filmed in four weeks on location in New Mexico and Texas for $260,000. The cast was largely assembled from local college drama departments. The film's editor was recruited from UCLA's film department. Roger and George von Voy were looking at one of the sequences on a moviola, in a cutting room in an alley behind the Sunset

Strip, when Roger noticed George had cut the beginning of a scene in which a bunch of Texas warriors throw rocks through a showcase window to loot a store. Roger asked him why he had done that.

"Well," von Voy replied, "I just thought that the sight of those rocks bouncing off the window sort of destroyed the illusion of the scene, Roger."

"The rocks bounced off the glass?" Roger asked with surprise. Von Voy nodded. "Well, I guess that wouldn't be too good."

With the picture finished, Roger flew to Europe to make *Von Richthofen and Brown* for United Artists. While he was there, AIP recut *Gas-s-s-s!*, eliminating one of the main characters as well as anything that might be considered offensive. The film flopped. Roger bid farewell to Jim and Sam and AIP and started his own company, New World Pictures. Nobody would mess with his pictures now. Instead, Roger became the one who messed with everyone else's pictures.

Eighteen

A Samuel Z. Arkoff–James H. Nicholson Production

Around about '68 or '69, Jim didn't have the energy he used to have. He seemed to be more tired. He wasn't as enthused. I don't know if he didn't like the fact that the company was getting bigger—I don't think he minded that—or if he didn't feel like he could cope with it. Ultimately, he decided he wanted to be an independent producer. He came to me with it and I must admit that the idea kind of floored me. So he got a deal at Fox. I would have given him a deal if he wanted it, but I think he felt like he wanted to get away.

—Samuel Arkoff

In September of 1969, American International moved from 7165 Sunset Boulevard to 9033 Wilshire Boulevard in Beverly Hills. The new building, a four-story affair with an underground garage and a penthouse, was a far cry from AIP's office on Selma. Two years after the move Jim Nicholson resigned as the company's president. One year later he was dead.

The newspaper accounts of Jim's decision to leave were suspiciously free of politics. He simply wanted to get into independent production. AIP had grown so big that there wasn't time for him to do anything but grease the wheels. He signed a six picture deal with 20th Century-Fox. First on the agenda was *When the Sleeper Wakes*, which AIP had threatened to make every year since 1965. Instead Jim made *The Legend of Hell House*, based on a novel by his old friend Richard Matheson. The movie was released after Jim's death.

To better understand why Jim Nicholson left the company he built, it is necessary to digress a bit, back to 1964 when he and Sylvia filed for divorce. Sylvia was depicted by the press as the wounded party. Jim was running around with some young starlet and Sylvia just couldn't stand it any longer. Yet Jim claimed they had agreed on a discreet Mexican divorce months earlier and that her announcement to the press

181

was a bit of a shock. And some of the people I spoke with flat out said Sylvia had been seeing other men for years. Since I was unable to get in touch with the woman there's no way for me to know the truth of the matter. The divorce is only mentioned because the settlement stripped Jim of his power of AIP. The company stock was divided—172,500 shares for Jim and an equal amount for Sylvia, which left Sam Arkoff the principal shareholder. Sam was elected chairman of the board. His name appeared before Jim's on the pictures they made. Prior to the settlement it had been the other way around. People were hired and decisions were made without Jim's approval. So he stayed home more often. If Sam wanted to run things, then let him. And so he left.

"Jim occupies a special niche in our industry and justifiably so," said Gordon T. Stulberg, the president and chief operating officer at Fox. "He is an astute showman, possessed of an uncanny ability to anticipate trends. He has time and again demonstrated a remarkable insight into the entertainment wants of today's audiences. We welcome him not only for his talents as a picture maker, but for his great experience in marketing and in current merchandising know-how." Stulberg wanted Jim to produce six pictures for his company.

"Once Jim left," Sam said, "it changed AIP. And I didn't really realize it for years. Jim and I used to have lunch at least four days a week. And we'd spend a couple of hours a day, generally, together, planning this and that, so on and so forth. See, Jim and I were equal.... So when I talked to Jim he could be in error about something or I could be wrong about something but, fundamentally, neither one of us had any particular axe to grind. It wasn't like when you were talking with any of the other people in the organization. (We had some very good people, you know, who were with us for a long time and so on and so forth and all fine people but still there was never the same relationship that there was with Jim.) It got a little bit lonely. Because instead of being able to make mutual decisions—even though on some things, like advertising, Jim would be the first among equals. On business matters I would be the first among equals. None the less we were equals. With the others, no matter how much you liked them (and it was a family company really) once Jim was gone there were no equals. We used to be close, even after he left. He'd tell me his problems and so on and so forth. He could have come back and made pictures for us at any time he wanted to. Actually, he was offered a deal at Fox which was probably a little better than I could have afforded, but he could have come back. And he might have. Who knows? I always suspected he might have come back if they didn't give him an honest count."

Jim had a seizure at the Cock 'n' Bull Restaurant. He ordered a drink with a peculiar name then became disoriented. The waitress urged

Susan Hart, Jim's wife, to get him to a hospital. On the way to the car he kept bumping into the parking meters. At the hospital a priest thought he was drunk. Shortly after, he died of a malignant brain tumor. Susan and Elizabeth, Jim's sister, were at his side.

On November 25, 1973, the Variety Children's Heart Center at the UCLA School of Medicine unveiled a bronze nameplate that officially changed the name to the James H. Nicholson Variety Children's Heart Center. Jim had been a chief barker of the club, often screening AIP movies to raise money for the club's various charities, as he had done as a teenager for the Red Cross. AIP produced a 50 minute documentary in 1969 called *The Heart of Variety*, narrated by Greer Garson, Charlton Heston, Vincent Price, Ed Begley and Burt Topper (who also wrote the script). It showed, modestly and hauntingly according to *The Hollywood Reporter*, how the $165,000,000 raised by Variety since its founding was spent to ease the suffering of afflicted and/or deprived children.

Jim Nicholson was buried at Inglewood Park Cemetery. David Melamed, Joe and Milton Mortiz, Leon Blender, Micky Zide, Norman Herman, Al Simms and Salvatore Villitteri were his pall bearers. Sam Arkoff delivered the eulogy.

Billed as "The Adventure You Will Never Forget!", this deadly dull import came from Amicus, in England (1975). Also see page 185.

Above and opposite, bottom: Bert I. Gordon came back to AIP to mess with H.G.
Wells; this page shows Robert Lansing attacked by mutant ants in "Empire of the
Ants" (1977); the other has Ida Lupino looking as if she were about to become
"The Food of the Gods" (1976). Opposite, top: Doug McClure makes a desperate
attempt to rescue Bobby Parr from a pterodactyl in "The Land That Time Forgot"
(1975).

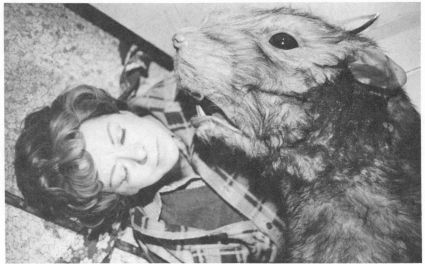

Nineteen

Samuel Z. Arkoff Presents

*When you come down to it, I don't think there are any of us in
the film industry making anything today that will be of more
than passing historical interest fifty years from now. There are
times when, probably, if we at AIP were a little more pompous or a little more serious about the sheer earth-shattering
importance of what we're doing we'd be better off—because
most people in this business are so fornicatingly serious about
the importance of these little ships that pass in the night.*

—Samuel Arkoff

Sam Arkoff never wanted to go public. AIP had always been a
family-type operation. He didn't want a bunch of strangers all of a sudden
telling him what to do. But AIP needed the capital that could be garnered
from selling stock. "Others in the company felt it would make their own
stock interests more *meaningful*," Sam remarked, "to use one of those
words that isn't meaningful." Sam believed the company could remain
independent by a public sale of 20 percent of its stock.

One prospective financier glanced at all of the posters around
Sam's office and asked: "Are all these posters we see around us supposed
to support the claim of 'three years in the making,' like so many Hollywood film companies do?"

"No," Sam replied. "We're trying to be more honest."

Sherrill C. Corwin, the Variety Club convention chairman,
announced AIP's plans to go public at a luncheon sponsored by Jim and
Sam at the Beverly Hilton. By June of 1969 it had become a reality.
American International authorized 2,500,000 shares of common stock
(20¢ par value) and an aggregate of 75,000 shares reserved for purposes of
the company's qualified stock option plan (which was adopted on May 1,
1969: selected employees could purchase common stock at the fair market
value upon the date of the grant, if they desired).

From *Daily Variety*, June 12, 1969:

Principal Stockholders

New York, June 11 — Following is breakdown of common stock now held and to be held after the public offering of AIP stock, as itemized in prospectus issue by underwriters. It lists each person who owns of record or is known by company to own beneficially more than 10% of stock and all officers and directors as a group. Shares held include those owned by minor children.

	Owned Prior to Offering			To Be Owned After Offering		
	Owner of Record and Beneficially (plus shares held in voting trust)	Percent of Class	Held in Voting Trust	Owner of Record and Beneficially (plus shares held in voting trust)	Percent of Class	Held in Voting Trust
Samuel Z. Arkoff	...345,000	33.8%	251,300	345,000	29.2%	251,300
James H. Nicholson	...172,500	16.9%	86,250	172,500	14.6%	86,250
Sylvia Nicholson	...172,500	16.9%	......	72,500	6.1%	......
Joseph Moritz	...110,000	10.8%	55,000	72,500	6.1%	55,000
TOTAL	...800,000	78.4%	392,550	662,500	56.0%	392,550

The following month AIP announced plans to move to Beverly Hills.

The company continued to run smoothly after Jim departed. In the early 70s much of its revenue was garnered by tapping the black exploitation market, not to the liking of The Coalition Against Blaxploitation. They asked AIP's vice president, Richard Zimbert, if any of the profits from the black films were going into black banks. They also wanted to know if there were any blacks hired to work behind the camera. Writers. Directors. "We've got black publicists," Zimbert told them. "We've got black people all throughout the country. We advertise in black media. *Blacula* [1972] had an all black cast, black director...."

Zimbert's car was torched. It was in the AIP parking lot at the time. The head of the coalition, Junius Griffin, assured Zimbert it wasn't they who had done it. "I disavow it and I will not condone it," Griffin told the reporters. He also said that whoever was responsible was trying to discredit the coalition. "You cannot preach against violence and actually partake in it yourself." And so on. And so forth.

The success of *Blacula* led to a sequel, *Scream, Blacula, Scream* (1973) and a rash of other films: *Black Mama, White Mama; Slaughter, Black Caesar* (all 1972), *Coffy, Slaughter's Big Rip-Off, Hell Up in Harlem* (all 1973), *Sugar Hill, Foxy Brown, Truck Turner* (all 1974), and *Sheba Baby, Cooley High, Cornbread, Earl and Me, and Bucktown* (all 1975). The queen of many of these epics was an actress named Pam Grier.

"I took the parts no other Hollywood actress would because they didn't want to be demeaned or mess up their nails," Pam Grier said. "If I held out for those sweet, pretty, demure parts I'd still be waiting."

Roger Corman was the one who gave her her first break, in one of his New World Films, *Women in Cages*. AIP took over from there.

"Sam gave me my biggest break," said Pam. "People always ask me if I had to go the casting couch route with him and I say with Sam Arkoff there is no such thing as a casting couch."

Top: AIP drifted away from the sort of exploitation quickies that had been their mainstay. Example: "Hennessy" (1975) with Lee Remick and Rod Steiger. Bottom: Warren Oates in John Milius' "Dillinger" (1973).

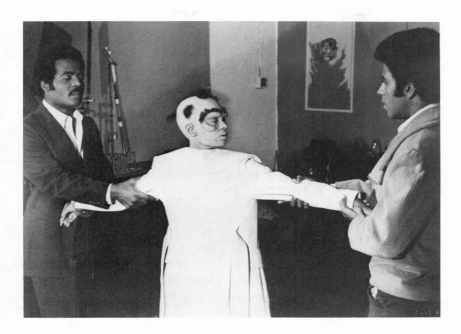

Carol Speed possessed by the Devil in "Abby" (1974), which was withdrawn after Warner Bros. threatened a lawsuit: too much like their "The Exorcist."

"American International is upon the threshold of the highest level of motion picture production and distribution in its history," Sam Arkoff wrote in an article that appeared in the *Hollywood Reporter* on November 29, 1974. "We will make available to exhibitors an average of one film a week, year 'round.

"Timing of a release is also a critical matter. If producers and exhibitors will remain as flexible as possible we are able to properly polish our product before offering it to the public. And we can slant our publicity, advertising and promotion to peak at the most advantageous moment."

AIP acquired a package of films from Commonwealth, Hallmark and Cinerama. The company drifted away from being a major-minor to being a minor-major.

"We have come of age and we are in the position to take on all comers!" Sam said in 1975. "We have the money, facilities, know-how and organization to welcome any film project — regardless of cost — if we like the project and its potential. This is an era of the promotion picture more than ever, but today's blockbusters are simply on larger-than-ever scales and are bigger than life. Promotion is the name of the game and it is a game we have been playing with every year success since we were born."

That same year ABC ran "Monster Beach Party—21 Years of A.I.P." on its 90 minute *Wide World of Entertainment* television program. Two years later AIP's profits dipped 12 percent. By July of the following year Arkoff signed the papers merging AIP with Filmways.

"Today is the producer's era," Sam told the press. "We must woo the producer. When AIP was formed independent producers were rare. Today, with web license fees, ancillary rights, merchandising, tax shelters, foreign government subsidies, their numbers have increased."

By that December, Sam had resigned. Jerry Perenchio, Norman Lear and Bud Yorkin bought him out. Sam walked away with $4,300,000. Reportedly he was paid less than his stock was worth but according to Sam he received $2.00 above the market price for each share. "It's not my style to sell at a loss," he remarked.

Sam's final movie for AIP, released under the Filmways banner, was *Dressed to Kill* (1980), directed by Brian DePalma (who more or less got his start when AIP released his film *Sisters* in 1973). A box office hit, it didn't win Sam any points with the panel of ladies who invited him to their Women in Film–sponsored panel discussion at the MGM commissary. Those ladies weren't happy with Sam at all. They were fired up about the shitload of movies graphically depicting the rape and mutilation of women. "Can you imagine," Susan Griffin asked, "a woman being murdered who died without doing some damage (to her assailant), without a peep? That helpless woman is a projection of the male, of that masculine mind. It's a very dangerous situation. There is a kind of art that leads to self-knowledge and catharsis. But the art of denial doesn't let you move beyond. The man who hates women doesn't move beyond his hate by making movies of it."

Puffing away on his cigar, Sam tried to make light of the whole issue by saying things like "I'm just a farm boy from Iowa." Then he reminded the fifty or so women in the audience that the bottom line of any moviemaker's conscience was money. Later he warned them against using the strategy of confrontation. "If you're going to be seen by males as strident—" Sam cut himself off. Wisely so, I think. The boy from Iowa was outnumbered.

"Fellini makes *Amarcord* because it has a chunk of his childhood," Sam once remarked. "I am not fundamentally the kind of picture-maker Fellini is. I can't make that kind of a picture. I'd have to get someone else to make it. I am not, fundamentally, a creative director of the Fellini kind. And ninety percent of all the people that make these kind of pictures aren't either.

"I think we have too much of that shit. It all came from that auteur shit, a conception made by some French journalists who intended to become directors and prophets from what they set up. It's all bullshit.

From Steve Krantz's "The Nine Lives of Fritz the Cat" (1974).

"Not entirely. Truffaut tells personal stories. And that's fine. You have to realize there is a distinction between Samuel Z. Arkoff and Darryl Zanuck or Sam Goldwyn and people like that who are legitimate producers. Jim and I made genre pictures.

"Now genre pictures don't have to be cheap pictures. *Jaws* was a genre picture. The kind of personal thing is the sort of thing I would never do. I would never even think about doing it. Sure, I have memories of my past, and if some writer ever wanted to sit down with me ... it's possible. But it isn't anything that would interest me. I don't need it as a personal monument. It's simply a difference in outlook.

"And the average picture is not a personal picture. Less and less today. When you see that they're making *Stars Wars* one, two and three, *Grease* one and two and *Rocky* one, two and three (and four if they can conceive of something or other) you will see that these are, in a sense, genre pictures, even if some of them might have started as a personal statement, like the Stallone picture.

"There are not many personal pictures made and, for the most part, they do not come in the regular commercial market. And say what you want, that's the market I'm trying to be in."

And Sam is still kicking. You can find his name on Larry Cohen's Q, released while this book was being written. I suspect Sam's name will continue to pop up now and again because Sam wants to stir it up. He likes the business too much, and by that I do mean the business, the deals with the stars, the talks with the writers, the stuff he has some control over. The other stuff, the actual making of the picture ... that's something Sam doesn't even want to worry about. Unless he has to. Unless some director goes over budget. Sam might even let a director get arty-farty if he just didn't go over budget and included all the essential ingredients — namely sex and violence. Which is not to say that Sam wouldn't like to be thought of as a producer of quality movies. I think it tickled him in more ways than one when the New York Museum of Modern Art ran a retrospective of AIP's films. Sam talks a lot about the movies they made being nothing but merchandise but a tailor can be proud of a coat, a carpenter can be proud of a chair, and I think Sam Arkoff is sort of proud of some of those pictures he helped produce.

"Altogether there were about 500 pictures," Sam said. "Of which we either made or were associated with the production of, let's say 350. I've never counted. In the early days I can name you every picture because it was new and we were experimenting. And we had the parties afterwards. Which we ultimately discontinued because they got to be a pain in the ass. Word got around how great they were along about the second year of them. We'd wind up with an enormous number of people. Everybody had 17 friends. And if you were running a little late, you were sitting with 200 people on the set. But in the beginning, each picture we sweated through and slaved through. We kept really right on top of it. We took previews. Of course, these weren't big previews. In fact, it used to get me when it would say on the marquee 'Major Studio Preview.' I would squirm because I would know when the American International title flashed on the screen there would always be some people who would give vent. I didn't mind 'Studio Preview.' But that 'Major' ... 'I'd kind of balk."

Sam wanted to know who I'd talked to about AIP when I interviewed him. I gave him a list of the names and added that I had done extensive research at the Academy Library. There were hundreds of articles written about AIP and most of them included extensive quotes from him and Jim. "All of that stuff is bullshit," Sam said with a wave of his hand.

And now I'll wave my hand to you.

Top, left: James Harvey Nicholson, AIP president; right: Samuel Zachary Arkoff, AIP vice-president. Bottom: Producer Herman Cohen admires his creations—from "How to Make a Monster" (1958).

Jim Nicholson, Vincent Price, and Barbara Steele on the lot at Producer's Studio during the filming of "The Pit and the Pendulum" (1961).

Biographies

These biographical notes focus on the various people not adequately covered in the text. Since many of these people have been overlooked for many years, it is my hope that by making the information on them easily accessible the names might one day find their way into volumes like The Film Encyclopedia *and* The Filmgoer's Companion.

Agar, John (Jan. 31, 1921). Son of a Chicago meatpacker and eldest of four children, John made front page headlines following his four years in the U.S. Navy and Army Air Corps during World War II by marrying former child star Shirley Temple. Shirley introduced her new husband to producer David O. Selznick at a party. He thought John and Shirley might make a good screen couple and asked John to come to the studio for a screen test which John remembers as being awful. He was signed to an RKO contract and made his screen debut in John Ford's *Fort Apache* (1948) playing opposite Shirley, whose career had been sagging since 1940. They were paired again in *Adventures in Baltimore* (1949) but the two didn't click. The marriage ended and after a couple of more pictures so did John's affiliation with RKO. He managed to secure a few leading parts in some low budget movies before being signed to a two year contract with Universal-International. There he was relegated to roles in the studio's lowest priority item, horror and science fiiction films. He pleaded with the studio head to give him the kind of parts being handed to the other contract players like George Nader and Jeff Chandler but Edward Muhl turned a deaf ear to him. By 1957 John was on his own again. The only parts offered him were from low budget producers who wanted to take advantage of whatever name value John still had from appearing in major studio films. He finished his career in routine horror movies, which he never particularly enjoyed, and westerns. Of his career John once said: "You can take all of those pictures that I made, and with the exception of *Fort Apache, She Wore a Yellow Ribbon, Sands of Iwo Jima*, and maybe *Breakthrough*, and throw them all away." He married Loretta Barnett, a professional dancer, in the mid-50s and they've been together ever since. Much has been made of John's alcoholism and the fact that he was never much of an actor (he once feigned sickness to avoid appearing in a high school play), but no one has ever mentioned that the man always gave it his best shot. And that ought to count for something. AIP credits: *Flesh and the Spur, Attack of the Puppet People, Jet Attack, Journey to the Seventh Planet, Zontar the Thing from Venus, Curse of the Swamp Creature.*

Adams, Nick (July 10, 1931–1968). Born in Nanticoke, Pa., educated at St. Peter's College, Nick had a spotty career playing supporting roles in movies like *Rebel Without a Cause* and *Mister Roberts* before achieving a minor success in his own television series, "The Rebel," after which he was nominated for an Oscar as the best supporting actor in the 1963 film, *Twilight of Honor*. He died of a drug overdose. AIP credits: *Frankenstein Conquers the World, Die Monster, Die!*

Asher, William (Aug. 8, 1926). Grew up in New York's lower east side; father died when he was 11. Lied about his age to join the Army during World War II, wrote some short stories during that period, then came to Hollywood. He collaborated with Richard Quine on a low budget boxing drama, *Leather Gloves* (1948). He lied about his age for that too. Figured he ought to look as if he had a little more life experience under his belt. Low on money, Harry Cohn's secretary arranged for Bill to go to Las Vegas to be a shill. "I did that for a while but there are too many temptations that I generally take advantage of," Bill said so he left Vegas to pick dates. Got a call from a man in the garment business who wanted to produce five minute short stories for television. "That sounded better to me than picking dates. A step in the right direction, off that ladder anyway." He has since directed over 100 television shows, including "I Love Lucy," "Make Room for Daddy," "The Dukes of Hazzard," and "Bewitched," which starred Elizabeth Montgomery, his wife at the time. He continues to be active in television and features and is a helluva nice guy. AIP credits: *Beach Party, Muscle Beach Party, Bikini Beach, Beach Blanket Bingo, How to Stuff a Wild Bikini, Fireball 500*.

Ashley, John (Dec. 25, 1934). Born in Kansas City, Mo., the son of Roger and Lucille Atchley. John discovered that he was adopted quite by accident when a friend intercepted a note from John's girlfriend in high school. "The fact that he's adopted," the note read, "makes no difference to me." (A local newspaper had mentioned something about Dr. and Mrs. Atchley's adopted son, John.) John graduated from Will Rogers High School in Tulsa and then went to Oklahoma State University. He changed the spelling of his name when he came to Hollywood and his first role was in *Dragstrip Girl*, which more or less typed him for a time as a villain. "My mother, who was a Baptist midwestern lady, always felt she had to defend me to all of her friends. She didn't understand why I had to play all those evil roles and told her friends that I really wasn't like that." He continued to appear in juvenile delinquency melodramas and television shows like "Men of Annapolis" and "The Sheriff of Cochise." His three marriages were summed up in the following manner: "The first time I got married it was because I thought I should. The second time I got married because I frankly had nothing else to do. The third time I got married because I wanted to." John describes himself as "kind of a homebody," is proud of his Italian heritage and wants to be a good father. For a while he left the acting profession to run a theatre chain. Then he was asked to fly to the Philippines to star in *Brides of Blood*. The picture proved so successful that Ashley and the film's director produced a series of horror pictures. Lately, John has turned to producing made-for-television movies with his partner, actor Robert Conrad. John expressed a desire not to compromise himself as a producer the way he did as an actor. AIP credits: (actor) *Dragstrip Girl, Motorcycle Gang, Hot Rod Gang, How to Make a Monster, Suicide Battalion, The Eye Creatures, Beach Party, Muscle Beach Party, Bikini Beach, Beach Blanket Bingo, How to Stuff a Wild Bikini*; (actor, producer) *Savage Sisters*; (producer) *Black Mama, White Mama*.

Avalon, Frankie (Sept. 18, 1939). Born Francis Thomas Avallone; raised in South Philadelphia where he played trumpet for a number of years, locally and on television, until he read about James Darren, another Philly boy, who was making it as a singer. Frankie hired himself a manager and before long he was signing a contract at Chancellor Records, one of the many record companies hoping to take advantage of Elvis Presley's induction into the Army by promoting a new singing idol to replace Elvis during his absence. Just for a joke Frankie held his nose during the fourth or fifth take of a song called "De De Dinah" and that version became a hit. In 1959 he earned his first gold record, "Venus," and his first gold album. Although he had appeared in a 1957 feature, *Jamboree*, he didn't start pursuing an acting career until the 60s. He didn't really click in bigger films like *The Alamo* and *Voyage to the Bottom of the Sea* but he did find a niche at AIP singing and clowning his way through the company's silly "Beach Party" series. He still pops up now and then on television and continues to perform in night clubs. AIP credits: *Panic in the Year Zero, Beach Party, Operation Bikini, Muscle Beach Party, Bikini Beach, Beach Blanket Bingo, Sergeant Deadhead, How to Stuff a Wild Bikini, Pajama Party* (cameo), *Dr. Goldfoot and the Bikini Machine, Fireball 500, The Million Eyes of Su-Muru, Horror House.*

Bakalyan, Dick (Jan. 29, 1931). Born in Watertown, Mass., Dick hung around with a pretty tough crowd in his younger days. He did a year's probation when he was 15. Not too surprising that his first part in a film was a tough in Robert Altman's *The Delinquents* in 1957, shot in Kansas City. Dick knew from the beginning that he was going to be typecast as an actor just as he had been in real life. "I always knew that I'd have a gun or a knife in my hand, so I always tried to find a different way of presenting that kind of character. When I did *The Delicate Delinquent* nobody had long hair yet. Trying to think like the character I was portraying, I thought to myself 'Why should I cut my hair? They'll cut it when I'm drafted to be killed in some crazy war. The hell with them.' It was that kind of attitude that justified the long hair and the negative behavior of the character I was portraying. Of course, by today's standards my hair *wasn't* long." Dick has continued to be active in motion pictures and television, most often still the bad guy. AIP credits: *The Cool and the Crazy, Paratroop Command, The Bonnie Parker Story, Operation Bikini, Panic in the Year Zero.*

Bava, Mario (July 31, 1914–1980). Born in San Remo, Italy, the son of a sculptor turned cinematographer. While working on *I Vampiri*, the director (Ricardo Freda) walked off the picture and Mario directed the picture himself. The moment he was offered the chance to direct his own picture he chose a horror story and remained identified with the genre until his death. "My dreams are always horrible," he told a writer from *Terror Fantastic*, a Spanish magazine. "There's a character that continuously haunts me in my nightmares; he's a musician that serenades his lover with a violin, strung with the nerves of his own arm." He wrote many of his films using the name John M. Old or John Foam. His output was visually exciting but the content of his features were generally dull. AIP credits: *Black Sunday, Erik the Conqueror, Black Sabbath, Planet of the Vampires, Dr. Goldfoot and the Girl Bombs, Baron Blood.*

Baxter, Les (1922) Probably best known for his hit pop record of the 50s, "The Poor People of Paris." He has, on several occasions, conducted the Hollywood Bowl Orchestra in something called "An Evening with Les Baxter," and composed film scores for producer Aubrey Schenck. He claimed that the secret to writing music for pictures like *The Pit and the Pendulum* was to put notes where they didn't belong. Although he was hired in the hope that his name would add a certain prestige to AIP's sleazy image, Baxter's scores were usually unexciting and inappropriate and it was up to AIP veteran Ronald Stein to compose the best score for the Poe series, *The Haunted Palace*. AIP credits: *Alakazam, the Great, Goliath and the Barbarians, Baron Blood, Beach Blanket Bingo, Bikini Beach, Beach Party, House of Usher, Black Sunday, Black Sabbath, Born Wild, The Raven, Tales of Terror, Comedy of Terrors, Cry of the Banshee, Dr. Goldfoot and the Bikini Machine, Dr. Goldfoot and the Girl Bombs, The Dunwich Horror, Fireball 500, Frogs, Ghost in the Invisible Bikini, Hell's Belles, How to Stuff a Wild Bikini, Marco Polo, Master of the World, Mini-Skirt Mob, Pajama Party, Panic in the Year Zero, Sergeant Deadhead, The Young Racers, Wild in the Streets, "X" — The Man with X-Ray Eyes.*

Beaumont, Charles (1930- — 1967) A writer of fantasy oriented stories since his early teens, he moved from Chicago to Hollywood in 1948 hoping to become a screenwriter. While waiting for a break he did a number of odd jobs like inking cartoons until he was hired by producer Ben Scwalb to write *Queen of Outer Space*, adapted from a treatment written by Ben Hecht which had been sold to producer Walter Wanger. Chuck wrote it as a satire but unfortunately the end result was unintentionally funny as if no one but Beaumont knew it was a gag. Charles Beaumont died from spinal meningitis. AIP credits: *The Premature Burial* (with Ray Russell), *Burn Witch, Burn* (with Richard Matheson), *The Haunted Palace, The Masque of the Red Death.*

Bender, Russell (1909-1969). He wasn't much of an actor but according to Sam Arkoff, who was with Russ in the Air Force during World War II, he could sing up a storm after he'd had a few drinks. Unfortunately that sort of vitality was absent from his performances. AIP credits: *It Conquered the World, Born Wild, Maryjane, Dragstrip Girl, Ghost of Dragstrip Hollow, The Amazing Colossal Man, War of the Colossal Beast, Suicide Battalion, Invasion of the Saucer-Men, Motorcycle Gang, Voodoo Woman* (screenplay only).

Birch, Paul (died in 1964). Born and educated in Alabama, he came to Hollywood in the late 40s. He went to work for Roger Corman and eventually graduated to bigger films. One of his best roles for Roger was the alien invader in *Not of This Earth.* He was a semi-regular on television's "The Fugitive." According to different sources he was either in his late thirties or forties when he passed away. AIP credits: *Five Guns West, Apache Woman, The Day the World Ended, Beast with 1,000,000 Eyes.*

Blaine, Jerry (1936). Born in Dallas, Texas, he moved to California when he was two. His two loves were athletics and music. He pursued the first by joining the King Brothers Circus as an acrobat. A year of that was enough so he went to Michigan State College for a while, then studied acting in New York. Producer Herman Cohen hired him to write songs for two movies and let Jerry sing in one of them. AIP credits: Songs "Eeny, Meeny, Miney Mo" written for *I Was a Teenage Werewolf,* and "Puppy Love" written for *Blood of Dracula* (which he sang).

From left: Russ Bender, Jonathan Haze, and Dick Miller.

Bronson, Charles (Nov. 3, 1921). Born Charles Bunchinsky, he changed his last name to Buchinski and then Buchinsky before settling on Bronson. He was the only one of 15 children to finish high school but, like his father, he went to work in the coal mines. He was a tail-gunner on a B-29 bomber during the second world war after which he joined an acting company. But the only role he could get was playing goons until after his short-lived television series, "Man with a Camera," when he appeared in films like *The Magnificent Seven* and *The Great Escape* in likeable tough guy roles. He continued, however, to be a supporting player until he went to Europe where he became a star. Eventually his success swept to the U.S. Most of his movies deal in violence but he did manage to make one decent picture, *From Noon Till Three*, which unfortunately was a flop. AIP credits: *Machine Gun Kelly, Master of the World.*

Jerry Blaine and Sandra Harrison.

Cabot, Susan (July 9, 1927). Born Harriet Shapiro, she attended college in New York where she won an award for the best young painter in the N.Y. educational system. She went to work in off-Broadway theatre and landed the lead in the Broadway musical "Shangri-La." She won the N.Y. Critics Award for her role in "A Stone for Danny Fisher." She was placed under contract to Universal-International where she played opposite Jeff Chandler, Rock Hudson, Tony Curtis, and Joel McCrea usually in the role of an Indian sqauw. She appeared on television's "Playhouse 90," "Goodyear Theatre," and "Studio One." Once married to director Monte Hellman, she went to work for Roger Corman and appeared in his *Carnival Rock*. She was a good actress but never really got a chance to shine. AIP credits: *Sorority Girl, Machine Gun Kelly, Viking Women and the Sea Serpent*.

Campo, Wally (dates not known). Born in Alameda, Calif., he graduated from College of the Pacific, where he majored in drama. There he had the opportunity of working with actress Jo Van Fleet. He was performing the lead in a little theatre production of "Night Must Fall" when he was spotted by Roger Corman. AIP credits: *Machine Gun Kelly, Hell Squad, Tank Commandos*.

Biographies

Clark, Dick (Nov. 30, 1929). Started his career in show business as a radio announcer; he saw there was money to be made in rock and roll music and thrust himself into the limelight as a spokesman for rock music. Despite the fact that he was a square he became the host of a successful television dance show, "American Bandstand." Columbia tried to make an actor out of him but after two pictures they called it quits. Clark produced a number of films for AIP and took a part in the productions now and then. He continues to be active, producing unexceptional television histories of rock music. AIP credits: *Wild in the Streets* (cameo), *Psych-Out, Savage Seven* (producer), *Killers Three* (screenplay, producer, actor).

Clarke, Gary (dates not known). Born in Los Angeles, Ca., he attended Woodrow Wilson High School. He took part in athletics and drama, had a leading role in "Quiet Summer" and was seen by Doc Bishop of 20th Century–Fox who encouraged him to follow an acting career. He was a regular on "Michael Shayne, Private Eye" on television. AIP credits: *Dragstrip Riot, How to Make a Monster*.

Clarke, Robert (dates not known). Began acting in Oklahoma, where he was born. Attended the University of Oklahoma where he appeared opposite Van Heflin's daughter, Frances, in a school play. He went to Wisconsin to get rid of his accent and after a tour of duty in the Army went to California where he was spotted by a talent scout from RKO. He appeared in a number of extremely low budget films, none of which were very good. Of those pictures *The Man from Planet X* is probably the most fondly remembered. "We felt fortunate to get into a picture that would be treated as carefully as it could be on that kind of a budget," Clarke said. "Maggie Field, Bill Schallert and I worked our tails off to make it as believable as we could. And our director, Edgar Ulmer, did everything he could to help us." He married Alice King of The King Family and lives in Hollywood. AIP credits: *Beyond the Time Barrier*.

Conklin, Chester (Jan. 11, 1888–1971). One of the original Keystone Cops, he'd worked as a circus clown and in vaudeville before being hired by Mack Sennett. His career all but ended during the beginning of the 50s (he was said to have taken work as a department store Santa) when Roger Corman hired him to appear in a western. He became sort of a good luck charm at AIP. His last picture was *Big Hand for a Little Lady* in 1967, made after he entered a nursing home where he met the woman that later became his fourth wife. His real name was Jules Cowles. AIP credits: *Apache Woman, Beast with 1,000,000 Eyes, Girls in Prison, The She-Creature*.

Connors, Touch (Aug. 15, 1925). Attended UCLA where he earned the nickname "Touch" while playing on the football team. Although he went to school to study law, after the Air Force he set his sights on becoming an actor. His first film was *Sudden Fear* (1952). He became AIP's all-purpose leading man, alternating from villains to heroes. Things were looking up for Touch when he changed his name to Michael Connors and landed a television series, "Tightrope." But after a few roles in major films (*Where Love Has Gone, Stagecoach*) he drifted back to television and had a hit series, "Mannix." He continues to be active in made-for-television movies and, at the time of this writing, has another series, "Today's F.B.I." Born Kreker Ohanian in Fresno, Ca., he was always a smooth but

Robert Clarke

unconvincing performer. AIP credits: *Five Guns West, Oklahoma Woman, The Day the World Ended, Shake, Rattle, and Rock, Flesh and the Spur, Voodoo Woman, Suicide Batallion.*

Conway, Gary (Feb. 4, 1937). Born Gareth Carmody in Boston, Mass., his family moved to Los Angeles when he was ten. He earned himself athletic letters in basketball and football during his high school years but it was playing the lead part in the school's version of "Our Town" that caused Gary to enroll in the Theatre Arts and Cinema Departments at UCLA. That's where Herman Cohen saw him and signed him for the title role in *I Was a Teenage Frankenstein*. He appeared in a couple of other low budget programmers before he found work on

Michael (Touch) Connors

television in "Burke's Law" and "Land of the Giants." He married a former Miss America, Marian McKnight and they had a daughter, Kathleen. AIP credits: *I Was a Teenage Frankenstein, How to Make a Monster.*

Conway, Tom (Sept. 15, 1904–1967). Born Thomas Charles Sanders, brother of actor George Sanders, in St. Petersburg, Russia. He was the son of British parents, educated at Brighton College in England, and after some stage experience moved to Hollywood. He was signed to an RKO contract and appeared in a number of routine B movies, Val Lewton's atmospheric horror thrillers included. Eventually he took over the lead in "The Falcon" series that had originally starred his brother. His last screen appearance was on television's "Perry Mason." During the last few years he lived a spartan life in a beatnik haven near Venice, California. AIP credits: *The She-Creature, Voodoo Woman.*

Cortez, Stanley (Nov. 4, 1908). Born in New York City, he began his career as an assistant to a number of portrait photographers until 1926 when he went to work as an assistant cameraman. *Four Day Wonder* (1937) was his first film as a cinematographer. He worked on a number of impressive films — *The Magnificent Ambersons, Since You Went Away, Night of the Hunter* — before working for AIP. His real name is Stanislaus Krantz. AIP credits: *The Angry Red Planet, The Ghost in the Invisible Bikini.*

Coughlin, Kevin (1947–1977) Made his debut on the legitimate stage on his 7th birthday in "I Remember Mama" on television, chosen over 500 other contestants. He played opposite Sidney Poiter, Bette Davis, and Tony Curtis then quit to finish college. When he returned to acting he found work in exploitation films. He died in the 70s in an auto accident. AIP credits: *Wild in the Streets, Maryjane.*

Court, Hazel (1926). Born in Birmingham, England, she excelled in school, learning three languages. Attended the Birmingham School of Drama and Art. When she was 18 she signed a five year contract with J. Arthur Rank. She appeared in 34 British productions and did stage work at the same time, appearing in "Random Harvest," "Laura," and "Othello." The star of the CBS-television series "Dick and the Duchess," she came to the attention of horror fans in America with her appearance in *The Curse of Frankenstein.* With her more than ample bosom spilling over her low-cut dresses, she was a welcome sight to a genre that often attracted masculine or cold looking actresses. She never made it as a star but she'll always be a star to me. AIP credits: *The Premature Burial, The Raven, The Masque of the Red Death.*

Crosby, Floyd (1899). Born in New York City, he worked in the stock exchange for a while before trying his hand at still photography. It was a short step to cinematography and in 1931 he won an Academy Award for his work on the documentary *Tabu.* He photographed *Of Mice and Men* and *High Noon,* to name a few. When Warner's and Universal were racing to be the first to be second with a 3-D feature — Arch Obler's independent *Bwana Devil,* in 3-D, was cleaning up — Columbia beat them both with the Crosby photographed *The Man in the Dark.* Never associated with any one studio, Floyd became one of Roger Corman's most often used directors of photography. AIP credits: *The Fast and the Furious, Five Guns West, Apache Woman, Rock All Night, She Gods of Shark Reef, Naked Paradise, Machine Gun Kelly, Teenage Caveman, House of Usher, The Pit and the Pendulum, The Premature Burial, The Raven, "X" — The Man with X-Ray Eyes, The Haunted Palace, Tales of Terror, Comedy of Terrors, Bikini Beach, Pajama Party, How to Stuff a Wild Bikini, Fireball 500.*

Damon, Mark (1935). Chicago born, he became his grammar school's best-read student but lost out on becoming one of the famed Quiz Kids by missing one of forty questions in the competition. His family moved to L.A. where he attended

Hazel Court and Boris Karloff.

Fairfax High School and UCLA. He tried out for the chorus of a musical in college, was given a part with only one line. It was enough to fire him up so he enrolled with drama coach Sanford Meisner who taught him method acting. His career was rather uneventful. AIP credits: *House of Usher, The Young Racers, Black Sabbath*.

Denning, Richard (1914). Born Louis A. Denninger in Poughkeepsie, N.Y., educated at Woodbury College, he served in the armed forces during World War II. Mostly his appearances were in routine action pictures (*The Glass Key, Beyond the Blue Horizon*) during the 30s and 40s but throughout the 50s he countinued to pass back and forth from playing leads in extremely low budget films to playing second leads in major studio features. He was active on television in "Michael Shayne, Private Eye," "Mr. and Mrs. North," "The Flying Doctor," "Karen," and

Richard Denning (right), with Alex Gordon.

"Hawaii Five-O," in which he had the longest run. "Now that the series has finally terminated," Dick has remarked, "Evelyn and I are looking forward to the eighties as a new era—'retirement and pensions.' We hope it beats working." The woman he referred to was his wife, Evelyn Ankers, an actress who was extremely active in Universal pictures during the 40s. According to the people who worked with him, Dick was considerate, dependable, and professional. AIP credits: *The Day the World Ended, Oklahoma Woman, Naked Paradise.*

Dern, Bruce (June 4, 1937). Chicago born nephew of the famous playwright Archibald MacLeish, Bruce dropped out of college to become an actor. Played his first bit part in *Wild River* (1960), then took a number of psychopathic parts on television that type-cast him in the movies he made later. (He was at his best in *The Cowboys*.) His off balance and brilliant performance in *Coming Home* earned him an Academy Award nomination. Roger Corman considered him the greatest actor he had ever worked with. AIP credits: *The Wild Angels, The Trip, Psych-Out, Bloody Mama, The Incredible Two-Headed Transplant*.

Dickerson, Charles Beach (1924). Born in Glenville, Ga., he used to stay after the movies were over and sweep out the theatre so he could come again the following day for free. He came to Hollywood in 1942, went to drama school for four years, and in 1957 lucked into a part in Calder Willingham's play, "End as a Man" in which he appeared with Robert Vaughn. Beach invited Beverly Garland who was a friend from his days with the Player's Ring. She, in turn, brought Roger Corman. He almost immediately signed Beach for a role in *Attack of the Crab Monsters* and later *Teenage Caveman* for which Robert Vaughn was also signed. Roger phased Beach into dialog directing and whatever else he needed. Made his own picture, *Shell Shock*, then went into retirement and became an architect, ended up building Roger Corman's home. He wants to get back into movies as an actor with the hope of winning an Oscar. He figures if Jack Nicholson can do it, he can do it. AIP credits: *Rock All Night, Teenage Caveman, Savage Seven, Killers Three, Dunwich Horror, The Wild Racers, Unholy Rollers, The Trip*.

Downs, Cathy (1924). A leading lady with limited exposure during the 40s, her biggest film was John Ford's *My Darling Clementine* although her part was little more than a token effort on the screenwriter's part to include a female in the story. She played Ann Howe on television's "The Joe Palooka Story," a syndicated series that ran thirty episodes. AIP credits: *The Phantom from 10,000 Leagues, Oklahoma Woman, The She-Creature, Amazing Colossal Man*.

Dunlap, Paul (dates not known). A composer of scores for many low budget features who often recycled his own themes. AIP credits: *I Was a Teenage Werewolf*, (much of the score reworked for) *Blood of Dracula, I Was a Teenage Frankenstein*, (which was used again for *The Four Skulls of Jonathan Drake* and) *How to Make a Monster, The Angry Red Planet* (used also in *Invisible Invaders*).

English, Marla (Jan. 4, 1935). Born Marleine Gaile English in San Diego, Ca., she was a professional model before making her motion picture debut in *Red Garters* (1954). She was never all that interested in being an actress and retired around 1958 to get married. AIP credits: *The She-Creature, Runaway Daughters, Voodoo Woman, Flesh and the Spur*.

Fair, Jody (dates not known). Born in New York where she attended the Childrens Professional School, then appeared in some off-Broadway shows but couldn't break into the big-time. So she came to Hollywood and ended up at AIP. AIP credits: *Hot Rod Gang, The Brain Eaters, Ghost of Dragstrip Hollow*.

Fonda, Peter (Feb. 23, 1939). Son of actor Henry Fonda; made his Broadway debut in 1961 and appeared in a couple of unimpressive films before carving a niche for himself in the youth market with his appearance in *The Wild Angels*. His

Beach Dickerson

success in that picture partially enabled him to secure financing for his own movie, *Easy Rider*, an extremely successful effort that, for a short while, made hot properties out of Peter and his costar, Dennis Hopper, who was also the film's director. However, a disappointing directorial debut (*The Hired Hand*) plus a string of forgettable action dramas (*Dirty Mary and Crazy Larry*, *Race with the Devil*, etc.) returned the actor to the same status he had had when he made *Tammy and the Doctor* back in 1963. AIP credits: *The Wild Angels*, *The Trip*, *Killer Force*, *Spirits of the Dead*, *Futureworld*, *High-Ballin'*.

Forte, Fabian (Feb. 6, 1940). Like Frankie Avalon, was another Philadelphia-born singer signed by Chancellor Records. In fact, there was a rivalry between the two, at least amongst their fans as to which was the better singer and better looking. Since Fabian had about a three-note range, he was little threat to Frankie in the singing department. Despite that he managed a few hit records, "Turn Me Loose" and "Tiger" before quickly moving to films. He was under contract to Fox where he appeared in a couple of better-than-average films (*Hound Dog Man, Mr. Hobbs Takes a Vacation*) but by the time he developed a little as an actor he could only find work at AIP. He still shows up now and then on television in shows like "Fantasy Island." AIP credits: *Fireball 500, Dr. Goldfoot and the Girl Bombs, Thunder Alley, Maryjane, The Wild Racers, Devil's 8, A Bullet for Pretty Boy.*

Fraser, Sally (dates not known). California born, she was raised in the San Fernando Valley, a graduate of Canoga Park High School. She took voice lessons to train for a career in opera when she was urged by Jeanne Halliburton, an agent, to try her hand at acting. She appeared in a number of television drams including "Schlitz Playhouse," "Four Star Playhouse," and "Hall of Fame," but wasn't often seen in major studio films. If you look real close you'll catch a close-up of her during the United Nations sequence in *North by Northwest*. AIP credits: *It Conquered the World, Road Racers, War of the Colossal Beast, Earth vs. the Spider.*

Frost, Alan (dates not known). Attended the Northwestern University School of speech and the Goodman Theatre of Chicago. Patricia Neal, Jean Hagen, and Martha Hyer were his classmates. Alan did a little summer stock before hitting the Broadway stage. He served a tour of duty in the Army during the Korean war, stationed in the Far East where he was made program director of the Armed Forces Radio Service. He appeared on television in "The Christmas Carol" and "The Passion Play." I haven't the faintest idea what happened to him. AIP credits: *Female Jungle, The Brain Eaters.*

Fuest, Robert (1927). Born in London; was a painter and graphic designer before becoming an art director for British television. After directing television programs and commercials (he did some episodes of "The Avengers") he graduated to features. AIP credits: *Wuthering Heights, The Abominable Dr. Phibes, Dr. Phibes Rises Again.*

Funicello, Annette (Oct. 22, 1942). Born in Utica, N.Y., her family moved to California when she was four. She wanted to be a ballerina and took dancing when she was five. She won the "Miss Willow Lake" beauty contest when she was nine and started modeling. She was seen by Walt Disney while appearing in an outdoor show, "Ballet versus Jive," and was made one of the original Mouseketeers on the "Mickey Mouse Club" television show. Her popularity on the show propelled her into motion pictures. She married her agent, Jack Gilardi, and has pretty much retired from the business although she does a television show once in a while. Her singing was pretty lame but she had a few hits records ("Pineapple Princess," "Tall Paul") nevertheless. AIP credits: *Beach Party, Muscle Beach Party, Bikini Beach, Beach Blanket Bingo, How to Stuff a Wild Bikini, Pajama Party, Fireball 500, Thunder Alley, Dr. Goldfoot and the Bikini Machine* (cameo).

Garland, Beverly (Oct 17, 1926). Born Beverly Fessenden in Santa Cruz, Calif., educated at Glendale College. She thought about becoming a nurse, decided to be an actress instead. Her first film part was in *D.O.A.* in 1949. Because of a casual remark she made about the picture, that she didn't think it deserved the Academy Award, the producers of the film spread the word that she was an impossible actress to work with and as a result her career suffered a setback. But in 1953 she was given a part in *The Glass Web*, a B movie. She spent the bulk of her career in B movies and was never really given a chance to prove how really good she could be. She was always sincere, rose above her material, and deserved much better than she got. She had her own television show, "Decoy," in the late 50s and became a regular on "Stump the Stars" and "My Three Sons." AIP credits: *Gunslinger, It Conquered the World, Naked Paradise*.

Glasser, Albert (Jan. 25, 1916). Chicago born, he got his start in the music business by copying music for Erich Wolfgang Korngold. He was 19 then and he thought Korngold was like a god the way he was able to manipulate emotions with a few bars of music. So Al decided to try his own hand at writing music. For $250 he scored *The Monster Maker* (1944). He was often given no more than a week to write an entire score, orchestrate it and get it copied. Since Al was generally working for practically no money, the twenty or thirty musicians used for the recording sessions were only hired for about three hours. "That meant one rehearsal and a fast take immediately," said Al. "If the take was too dirty — wih mistakes you just couldn't tolerate — we'd go for another. But near the end of the session, when we were running out of time, we couldn't even rehearse *once*." Unfortunately Al's scores generally sounded as if each member of the orchestra was still searching for the right note when the take ended. He was conducting the music for a movie called *Huk* when he was approached by Bert Gordon. "Did you write all that stuff?" the producer-director inquired and Al told him that he had. "I'm doing this movie called *The Cyclops*, and I need someone just like you." Al scored Bert's next seven pictures, as well 100 or so other motion pictures, including *Paris Model* and *Murder Is My Beat*. An album of his music was released by Starlog Records. He's retired now. "Composing film scores doesn't excite me anymore," he told the people from Starlog. "I've done everything I wanted, and I'm satisfied that I always did my best and was honest." Perhaps his greatest contribution was his theme for *The Cisco Kid*. AIP credits: *The Amazing Colossal Man, Attack of the Puppet People, War of the Colossal Beast, Earth vs. the Spider, Motorcycle Gang, Teenage Caveman, Viking Women and the Sea Serpent*.

Gordon, Leo (Dec. 2, 1922). Born in New York City, he can most often be seen in westerns or gangster movies playing a nasty sort of fellow, which he does very well. He's also a writer, however, and has penned a number of scripts including *Tobruk* and *The Intruder*. AIP credits: *Attack of the Giant Leeches* (writer), *The Haunted Palace* (actor), *The Terror* (writer).

Gorshin, Frank (1935). Impressionist and character actor, he has appeared in dozens of television shows, including a regular role as "The Riddler" on "Batman." He established himself as a comedian and a dramatic actor (*Ring of Fire, The George Raft Story*) and is still working today. AIP credits: *Runaway Daughters, Dragstrip Girl, Hot Rod Girl, Invasion of the Saucer-Men*.

Gough, Michael (Nov. 23, 1917). Born in Malaya, educated at Wye Agricultural College, he was with the Old Vic School for a while before making his

Pam Grier

stage debut in 1936. He became a favorite of producer Herman Cohen who starred the actor in a number of silly, Grand Guignol-type movies in which Mike turned in outrageously hammy performances. AIP credits: *Horrors of the Black Museum, Konga.*

Graves, Peter (March 18, 1925). Born in Minneapolis, Minn., he was a band musician and a radio announcer while at the University of Minnesota. He was in the Air Force for two years, did some summer stock. He was originally suggested for the lead in television's "Gunsmoke" but the part was eventually given to his brother, Jim Arness. (Pete's real name is Peter Arness.) The producer of the show didn't think Pete looked "American enough" after seeing him as the German spy in *Stalag 17.* "I think what burned me most," Pete said, "after hearing my brother Jim got the job, was that he'd just done a move called *The Thing* and played a vegetable in it." Pete did get his own television show, two in fact: "Fury," and "Mission: Impossible." He made his motion picture debut in *Rogue River* (1950). AIP credits: *It Conquered the World*.

Grier, Pam (1925). Born in Winston Salem, N.C., the daughter of an Air Force sergeant. Entered a beauty contest in Colorado and was urged by an agent to come to Hollywood. Was a receptionist for a talent agency before being signed by Russ Meyer for his *Beyond the Valley of the Dolls* (1970). Her first starring role came one year later, *The Big Bird Cage*. She was most active between 1973 and 1975 when Roger Corman's New World Pictures and AIP were active in black exploitation features. "I was happy when those films stopped," she remarked. "I played those parts because they had women in positions of power. It was a good positive image for black women. But the films became redundant and I don't like being redundant." She's worked little since. Most recently she could be seen in *Fort Apache: The Bronx*. AIP credits: *Black Mama, White Mama, Scream Blacula Scream, Foxy Brown, Sheba Baby, Bucktown, Friday Foster*.

Griffith, Charles B. (1930). Born in Chicago, began writing at the age of ten, amusing himself with song lyrics. During his high school years in a military academy he earned extra money from his fellow cadets by writing poetry structured in such a way as to allow any young lady's name to be shoe-horned into the rhyme scheme. Most of his film work was a writer, usually for Roger Corman. His attempt to become a producer in 1958 with *Ghost of the China Sea* was not a positive experience for him and his few brushes with direction—*Eat My Dust, Up from the Depths, Dr. Heckle and Mr. Hype*—proved disastrous. Some of his early scripts were unique and unusual, even brilliant, most notably his comedies like *A Bucket of Blood* and *The Little Shop of Horrors*. AIP credits: (as a writer) *Gunslinger, It Conquered the World* (also actor), *Rock All Night, A Bucket of Blood, The Wild Angels, The Devil's Angels*, (with Mark Hanna) *Flesh and the Spur, The Undead, Naked Paradise*; (assistant director) *The Young Racers*.

Haller, Daniel (1926) Born in Los Angeles, a graduate of Choinard Art Institute, he created backgrounds for television and commercials before becoming an art director for Roger Corman. Dan graduated to directing and works in television mostly, although he's directed a number of features. He always wanted to be an artist but painting eventually became a hobby. AIP credits: (as art director) *Machine Gun Kelly, A Bucket of Blood, House of Usher, The Pit and the Pendulum, The Premature Burial, Tales of Terror, The Raven, The Terror, "X"—The Man with X-Ray Eyes, The Haunted Palace, The Masque of the Red Death*; (as director) *Die, Monster, Die, The Devil's Angels, The Dunwich Horror*.

Halsey, Brett (dates not known). Born in California, he's the nephew of Admiral "Bull" Halsey. During his high school years Brett was active in sports but felt he'd excell better in dramatics. A two-year hitch in the Navy interrupted his pursuit of an acting career but he kept his hand in things by becoming a disc-jockey for the Armed Forces Radio. After his discharge he enrolled in the Don Martin School for Radio and television. Jack Benny took a liking to him and introduced Brett to some of his friends at U-I where he was signed to a two-year contract. He had a number of bit parts in films like *Revenge of the Creature, To*

Hell and Back, and the "Ma and Pa Kettle" series, after which he continued his career in low budget films at other studios. The last I'd heard he'd gone to Italy to make movies there. AIP credits: *High School Hellcats, Submarine Seahawk.*

Hampton, Orville H. (May 21, 1917). Born in Rock Island, Ill., he attended the University of Illinois, worked for the Moline *Daily Dispatch,* became a radio announcer and a news editor at WOC-Davenport, Iowa. Joined the Army for four years after which he began writing films for Robert Lippert. A very prolific writer, his work was generally uninspired. Many of his screenplays were written for Edward Small. AIP credits: *Riot on Sunset Strip, Friday Foster.*

Harrington, Curtis (Sept. 17, 1928). Dabbled in home movies during his teens. For a while he worked as an executive assistant to producer Jerry Wald, became an associate producer at Fox, and finally directed his own film, *Night Tide* (1963). Had a brief run at Universal when the studio hired him to replace William Castle to make suspense pictures. AIP credits: *Queen of Blood, Who Slew Auntie Roo?*

Hart, Susan (Jan. 2, 1941). From Wenatchee, Wash., she moved to Palm Springs when she was 4 years old. "I went to school there, but returned to Washington to Wenatchee Junior College. After taking dancing, singing and acting lessons for a few years and doing bit roles on television and a few movies I was discovered." She was on vacation in Hawaii when

Allison Hayes

someone spotted her on the beach and gave her a small role in a film being made there. After that Susan performed at the Palm Springs Playhouse and later the Los Angeles Actors' Theatre. She landed a few television parts on "77 Sunset Strip" and "The Alfred Hitchcock Show." Jim Nicholson saw her in *Ride the Wild Surf*, fell in love and married her. She starred in several AIP films, and recorded "We've Got to Get Something Straight," written by Guy Hemric and Jerry Styner. Retired from acting, Susan dabbles in country-western music. AIP credits: *War Gods of the Deep*, *Ghost in the Invisible Bikini*, *Dr. Goldfoot and the Bikini Machine*, *Pajama Party*.

Hayes, Allison (Feb. 22, 1930–1977). Washington's entry for the 1949 "Miss America" beauty pageant, had a rather uneventful career in films, stuck in low budget genre films. She had a short-lived television series, "Acapulco," and four years prior to her retirement from the business, she appeared as a regular on "General Hospital." She wasn't much of an actress but she was very nice to look at and was often the sole asset of the pictures in which she appeared. AIP credits: *Gunslinger, The Undead*.

Haze, Jonathan (April 1, 1929). Born in Pittsburgh, Pa., he traveled to New York after he finished high school to become an actor. "I was living in a hotel room for something like fifteen bucks a week," he recalled. "There were a lot of young people. Things were cheap. It was exciting. It was a life. There was music all night and people were out there having a good time." He met another hopeful in New York, actor Dick Miller. They ran into each other at the Bird in the Hand Restaurant and became good friends. Then Jonathan moved to California where he met Roger Corman. He appeared in a number of Roger's films, often serving as a stunt coordinator. "When I staged a fight, the other guy never got the best of me, even if he was bigger." He's in the production end of the business now. AIP credits: *Five Guns West, The Fast and the Furious, The Day the World Ended, Gunslinger, It Conquered the World, Rock All Night, Naked Paradise, The Viking Women and the Sea Serpent, The Terror, Invasion of the Star Creatures* (SP only).

Hopper, Dennis (May 17, 1936). Born in Dodge City, Kan., he idolized actor James Dean, whom he worked with in *Rebel Without a Cause* and *Giant*. Eventually Dennis became known as an actor who was difficult to work with. As a result he found little work except in low budget films. He decided to make his own movie, *Easy Rider*, which ended up costing something like $400,000. It made more than $16 million. It was less trouble for him to raise backing for his next project, *The Last Movie* which turned out to be a most prophetic title, at least as far as his career as a director went. AIP credits: *Night Tide, Queen of Blood, The Trip, The Glory Stompers*.

Hughes, Carolyn (1938). Born in New York City, attended Dwight Morrow Grammar School in New Jersey. The desire to become an actress struck her when she was 14. She quit school and became a model. Nothing clicked for her on Broadway so she came to California. Not much happened there either. AIP credits: *The Bonnie Parker Story, Paratroop Command*.

Hughes, Mary (Feb. 25, 1944). Born in Hollywood, daughter of a camera-man, Mary attended Paul Revere Junior High and University High in L.A. After graduation she sought a career as a model, which was mostly what she did at AIP. AIP credits: *Muscle Beach Party, Bikini Beach, Beach Blanket Bingo, How to Stuff a Wild Bikini, Pajama Party*.

Hunter, Tab (July 11, 1931). Born Arthur Gelien in New York City, he lied about his age so he could join the Coast Guard when he was only 15. He was eventually found out so he returned to high school to get his diploma. An ex-actor friend who had become an agent introduced Arthur to some of his freinds, which resulted in Arthur's first appearance in films, *The Lawless*. He was under contract to Warners for a while, where he made *The Burning Hills* and *The Girl He Left Behind*. He was never popular with the critics but I thought he was pretty good in *Damn Yankees*. He had his own television show for a short time but eventually all but retired from the business, raising horses at his home in the San Fernando Valley. He received an "Emmy" nomination for a "Playhouse 90" episode, "Portrait of a Murderer." AIP credits: *Operation Bikini, War Gods of the Deep*.

Hyer, Martha (Aug. 10, 1924). Born at Fort Worth, Tex., she attended the Pasadena Playhouse, eventually signed a contract with Universal where she was cast in the studio's routine programmers, westerns and Francis the Mule pictures. Finally she was given a role in one of the studio's bigger films, *Battle Hymn*. She was nominated for an "Oscar" for her role in *Some Came Running* but after fell into supporting roles in some rather silly pictures. She married producer Hal Wallis. AIP credits: *Pyro, House of a 1,000 Dolls, Bikini Beach, War Italian Style*.

Jergens, Adele (Nov. 28, 1917). From Brooklyn, she worked as a model, won "Miss World's Fairest" at the 1939 Chicago World's Fair, which was the break she needed to become a Broadway actress. She appeared in nightclubs in the U.S. and abroad. She usually played tough broads and did it quite well. AIP credits: *Girls in Prison, Runaway Daughters, The Day the World Ended, Outlaw Treasure*.

Johnson, Candy (1941). Born in San Gabriel, Calif., she took tap dancing when she was five, continued to dance until after her graduation from high school when agent Red Gilson got her bookings in Vegas, Palm Springs and other resorts. She danced her way through all of the "Beach Party" movies and certainly won this kid's appreciation. She was terrific. AIP credits: *Beach Party, Muscle Beach Party, Bikini Beach, Beach Blanket Bingo, How to Stuff a Wild Bikini, Pajama Party*.

Kandel, Aben (dates not known). Began his career in 1934 with a story for *Sing and Like It*. He collaborated on a number of screenplays—*Werewolf of London, She Gets Her Man* etc.—did a novel then adapted it which was *City for Conquest*, and began collaborating with producer Herman Cohen, both men using pseudonyms, on a series of horror melodramas that were much more vicious and brutal than the genre was used to seeing. The general message that seemed to prevail over their collaborations was, especially in the films with Michael Gough, that men are driven to murder by deceitful women. This may not have been their intention but who cares? The message is there and their films always made me uncomfortable besides boring me so wrap'em both up. AIP credits: (in colloaboration with Herman Cohen) *I Was a Teenage Werewolf, I Was a Teenage Frankenstein, Blood of Dracula, The Headless Ghost, Horrors of the Black Museum, Konga*.

Karloff, Boris (Nov. 23, 1887–1969). Born William Henry Pratt, the son of a civil servant, one of seven children, living in London. Moved to Canada in his teens and worked there as a farm hand, became an actor and traveled with a troupe. The acting wasn't paying the bills so he drove a truck. He started getting work in silent pictures but after forty films there were still damn few people who knew who he was. It wasn't until his appearance as Frankenstein's monster in 1931 that he made an identity for himself. He often expressed gratitude to the horror films for supplying him with so much work. Boris acted until the very end, long after he was all but crippled. Peter Bogdanovich did his best to give him a little boost by writing and directing the actor in a more contemporary and realistic film called *Targets*. Boris may have deserved a lot better but I must confess that I enjoyed the hell out of him and Bela in those old films like *The Invisible Ray* and *The Raven* and *The Body Snatcher*. His performance in *Comedy of Terrors* is even more wonderful. Boris was terrific. AIP credits: *The Raven*, *Black Sabbath*, *The Terror*, *The Comedy of Terrors*, *Bikini Beach*, *Die Monster, Die!*, *The Ghost in the Invisible Bikini*, *The Crimson Cult*.

Katzman, Sam (July 7, 1901–1973). Born in New York City, at 13 he was a prop boy for Fox Studios. Became a production manager and later worked for First National, Cosmopolitan, and just about every small outfit there was: Showmen's Pictures, Supreme Pictures, Victory Pictures. He roosted at Columbia Pictures for a while, churning out silly genre pictures, usually hiring directors and writers who shared his disinterest in entertaining. He learned well just how little effort needed to be exerted and how much profit he could expect. Sam always bragged that his pictures never lost money. A quick glance at his credits — *The Jungle Jim* series (for which he earned the nickname "Jungle" Sam), the serials, the Lugosi films of the 40s, his horror films like *The Giant Claw*, his costume dramas like *The Magic Carpet* — it seems pretty obvious that the man simply didn't give a shit about making good pictures. AIP credits: *Riot on Sunset Strip*, *Angel, Angel, Down We Go*.

Kenney, June (dates not known). Born in Boston, she was involved in radio at a very early age. Her mother showed her off when she was only three to producers searching for a Shirley Temple successor. Warners eventually signed her and she made several musical shorts for them in their New York studio. They wanted to bring her to Hollywood but her father thought she was too young to go there on her own and he wasn't about to give up his successful construction business to give her a chance at her career. She was 11 before the family moved to California. She sought parts in school plays and four years later went on tour with a ballet company. It was during this period she was able to secure the services of an agent. She did some television — "Loretta Young," "Hallmark Hall of Fame," and "Trackdown," — but her movie career was restricted to potboilers. I sort of liked her and wished like hell that I could have interviewed her for this book. AIP credits: *Sorority Girl*, *Attack of the Puppet People*, *Earth vs. the Spider*, *Viking Women and the Sea Serpent*.

Kraushaar, Raoul (Aug. 20, 1908). Born in Paris, the son of Rachel and Arnold Kraushaar. He was educated at Columbia University. He was an assistant to Hugo Risenfeld on many films, *Ten Commandments* and *Beau Geste* and

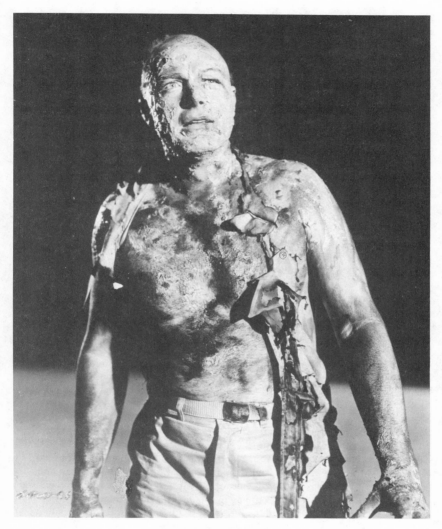

Glenn Langan

others, and in 1928 became an assistant at United Artists. Later he could be found at RKO, MGM, WB, and radio station KFWB. He was an arranger for Ted Fiorito, after which he started composing music himself. I always liked his little theme for the "Abbott and Costello" television show. AIP credits: *The Cool and the Crazy*, *Dirty O'Neil*.

Langan, Glenn (July 8, 1917). Born in Denver, he was educated at Wheatridge High. His career began as an assistant manager at the Elitch Gardens in

Denver. He traveled to New York and worked at a number of odd jobs until a small part in the play *Swing Your Lady* got him seen and signed. He appeared in many all-but-forgotten programmers and married the leading lady from one of them, Adele Jergens. They appeared together in *Treasure of Monte Cristo*. The only film in which he appeared that continues to be shown is the one he made for Bert Gordon at AIP. AIP credits: *The Amazing Colossal Man, Outlaw Treasure*.

Lembeck, Harvey (1925). New York born, he was educated at the University of Alabama, was in the Armed Forces during World War II, and appeared on Broadway in a number of plays, *Mister Roberts* and *Stalag 17* included. He was a featured actor on "You'll Never Get Rich" which was a major network series in the early 50s. He came to AIP for their "Beach Party" series and created a character called Eric Von Zipper, a parody of Brando's Johnny in *The Wild One*. He doesn't appear to have done much acting since. AIP credits: *Beach Party, Muscle Beach Party, Operation Bikini, Bikini Beach, Beach Blanket Bingo, How to Stuff a Wild Bikini, Fireball 500*.

Lime, Yvonne (1936). Born in Glendale, Calif., finished Junior College there then enrolled at the Pasadena Playhouse. In a performance of "Ah, Wilderness" she caught somebody's attention and ended up in several television shows, in small roles, then made her feature debut in *The Rainmaker* at Paramount. Herman Cohen saw her and signed her for a juvenile delinquency horror film. She went on to other films — *Loving You, Untamed Youth* — but nothing ever really clicked for her. This is another lady I regret not having been able to contact. AIP credits: *I Was a Teenage Werewolf, High School Hellcats, Dragstrip Riot*.

Lorre, Peter (June 26, 1904–1964). Born Laszlo Lowenstein in Rosenberg, Hungary. His parents were strict so when he was 17 he ran away from his home in Vienna to join the theatre. When he couldn't land any parts he organized his own theatre and wrote the plays performed there. When that went bust he took a job as a bank clerk until he couldn't take it any longer and joined a repertory company in Breslau, Germany. He kept bouncing from stock company to stock company until Fritz Lang cast him as the child murderer in *M*. He came to Hollywood in 1935. He had a successful career at Fox, appearing in the "Mr. Moto" series, and moved on to Warners where he had featured roles in classic films like *Casablanca* and *The Maltese Falcon*. He was an incurable prankster and loved to ad lib. Oddly enough, because he could ad lib so outrageously in the pictures he made for AIP, they were more fun to watch than the bulk of his work the decade before. He was between takes on the set of one of those AIP films one day when a visitor, a young girl, saw a monster in one corner of the studio and asked her father if it was a good or bad monster. Peter leaned toward her and in an exaggerated whispered voice said: "It's bad. AIP has no good monsters." His death was the result of a heart seizure. AIP credits: *Tales of Terror, The Raven, Comedy of Terrors, Muscle Beach Party*.

Malone, Dorothy (Jan. 20, 1925). Born Dorothy Eloise Maloney in Chicago, daughter of a telephone company auditor. She modeled as a child and performed in a college play at Southern Methodist University where she was spotted and signed to an RKO contract. She was given bit parts in movies like *The Falcon and the Co-Eds* before being spotlighted in *The Big Sleep*. Although she was quite active in television and motion pictures when she consented to do a picture for Roger Corman, she still hadn't made a name for herself. After a few Corman films she was signed by U-I and won an Oscar for best supporting actress in the studio's *Written on the Wind*. By 1963 she was back at AIP again, then landed the lead in television's "Peyton Place." Nothing major has happened for her career-wise since. AIP credits: *The Fast and the Furious, Five Guns West, Beach Party*.

Marshall, William (Aug. 19, 1924). Born in Gary, Ind., educated at NYU, he worked in steel mills, was a commerical artist, a waiter and a soldier before entering the dramatic field. His first stage appearance was in "Carmen Jones" as a chorus singer. He was Captain Hook in "Peter Pan." He toured with a road company, performing in England, Ireland, France, Switzerland, Luxembourg, Belgium and the Netherlands. He returned to the U.S. in the fall of 1963 and got parts in television shows like "Mannix," "The Nurses" and "The Man from U.N.C.L.E.," as well as movies like *Spartacus* and *The Boston Strangler*. During the 70s, when black exploitation features came into vogue, William was quite active, possibly most famous for his role as Dracula's soul brother Blacula. During the filming of the picture a young woman, wearing a long black cape approached him and asked the actor if he was *the* man? "If I understand your question, yes, I am," he replied. "I've always wanted to be a vampire," she confided. "Why?" he asked. Without hesitation the woman replied, "Because vampires live forever. There's really no way to kill them. If you pull the stake out of their hearts, they revive. They can't really be hurt, no matter what happens." She helped William better understand his role. The man has a great deal of knowledge about black history and has one hell of a speaking voice. He ought to be a teacher. AIP credits: *Blacula, Scream Blacula Scream, Abby*.

McCormack, Patty (Aug. 21, 1947). Born in Brooklyn, N.Y., she worked as a model at the age of four. She was on Broadway when she was six in "Touchstone." At seven she was on television in a "Kraft Theatre" presentation. After that she was on a number of shows including "I Remember Mama," where she was seen for two years. Her most famous role was the child murderess of *The Bad Seed* which she did on Broadway and in the motion picture. She received an Academy Award nomination for that. She had her own television show after that, "Peck's Bad Girl," and appeared in motion pictures and other television shows until she decided that she wanted to be a rock singer. That didn't work out so she came back to movies. AIP credits: *Maryjane, Born Wild, Mini-Skirt Mob*.

McCrea, Jody (1935). Son of actor Joel McCrea and actress Frances Dee, his real name is Joel Dee McCrea. He was educated with the children of the ranchhands and later attended UCLA. After graduating he went to New York to become an actor and enrolled in Sanford Meisner's acting class. He became a regular in the "Beach Party" series but not much else. AIP credits: *Operation Bikini, Beach Party, Muscle Beach Party, Bikini Beach, Beach Blanket Bingo, How to Stuff a Wild Bikini, Pajama Party, The Glory Stompers*.

Melchior, Ib (Sept. 17, 1917). Son of Lauritz Melchior, the Wagnerian tenor, he was born in Copenhagen and educated at Denmark's Stenhus College.

He was an actor and a stage manager with English Players, got into radio for a while in the production end, was a set designer at the Radio City Music Hall, served in World War II in military intelligence, then directed over 500 shows, "Perry Como" one of the many. AIP credits: *The Angry Red Planet* (screenplay, director), *Journey to the Seventh Planet* and *Reptilicus* (screenplay), *The Time Travellers* (screenplay, director), *Planet of the Vampires* (screenplay).

Milland, Ray (Jan. 3, 1905). Son of a steel-mill superintendent, Ray attended public school, King's College at Cardiff, then was accepted into the Household Cavalry, King's Royal Guards. There he established himself as a champion boxer, marksman, and horseman. He turned to acting and with the help of actress Estelle Brody secured some extra's work. He was signed to a Paramount contract in 1934 and was nearly typed as the all-purpose suave lead in bedroom comedies until his dramatic role in *The Lost Weekend*, which won him the best actor award. When his career started to decline he turned to directing (*A Man Alone, Lisbon*) but his movies were generally unexceptional. He was on television in two series: "Meet Mr. McNulty" and "Markham." His real name is Reginald Truscott-Jones. So there. AIP credits: *The Premature Burial, Panic in the Year Zero, Frogs, The Thing with Two Heads, "X" — The Man with X-Ray Eyes.*

Miller, Dick (Dec. 25, 1928). Born in the Bronx, where he spent his first 22 years. He wanted to be a musician. He was singing at age eight, played the drums for a while, then turned to the guitar. One night, during a fight, Dick busted his guitar over somebody's head. When a friend suggested that he take up the trumpet Dick told the fellow he didn't dare. With a trumpet he could kill someone. He came to California in 1952 where his old friend Jonathan Haze took him to see Roger Corman who put Dick to work as an actor. Dick is quite proud of his reputation as "One-Take Miller," so-called because he always knows his lines. He's played a variety of roles but seems to work best in comedy. He's written a couple of screenplays and one of them was made into a movie titled *TNT Jackson*. He continues to work, often employed by Joe Dante, a young film fan who has earned a name for himself as a director of well-made horror films. Joe liked Dick in *Not of This Earth* and *A Bucket of Blood* too so he likes having Dick around. He can currently be seen as a sleazy motel clerk on "General Hospital." AIP credits: *Apache Woman, Oklahoma Woman, It Conquered the World, Naked Paradise, The Undead, A Bucket of Blood, Ski Party, The Terror, The Wild Angels, Rock All Night, Sorority Girl.*

Morris, Barboura (dates not known). Began her acting career as Barboura O'Neill. She majored in Theatre Arts at UCLA then joined the Stumptown stock group at the Russian River in Northern California. With them she appeared in presentations of "The Philadelphia Story" and "Come Back Little Sheba." She did a little television then studied acting with Jeff Corey where she caught the attention of Roger Corman who was taking the same class. He signed her for *Sorority Girl* and she continued to appear in his films, her roles ranging from star to bit depending on the calibre of the production, until her death in the early 70s. I always enjoyed seeing her. AIP credits: *Sorority Girl, Machine Gun Kelly, Viking Women and the Sea Serpent, A Bucket of Blood, The Haunted Palace, The Trip, Dunwich Horror.*

Dick Miller admires his new creation, 'Murdered Man' in "A Bucket of Blood."

Nader, George (Oct. 9, 1921). Born in Pasadena, Calif., and educated at Occidental College, where he earned a B.A. Attended the Pasadena Playhouse from 1946 to 1949, then did a four year stretch in the Navy. He was seen on television in "Chevron Theatre" and "Fireside Theatre" and made his film debut in *Monsoon* (1953). That same year he got the lead role in what has become a favorite among bad movie lovers, *Robot Monster*. U-I signed him to a contract and tried to make a star out of him but nothing ever happened. George had a television series, "The Man and the Challenge." AIP credits: *The Million Eyes of Su-Muru, House of 1,000 Dolls.*

Nelson, Ed(win) (1928). A prisoner in numerous low-budget features, he finally found a home on television, first in the series "Peyton Place" as Dr. Rossi, then later as a guest star on countless other shows like "Ironside" and "Barnaby Jones." His first acting jobs came from Roger Corman. Ed played a sailor in *Attack of the Crab Monsters*. After the character was killed off he played the giant crab. AIP credits: *Invasion of the Saucer-Men, Night of the Blood Beast, Teenage Caveman, The Brain Eaters* (also producer), *A Bucket of Blood.*

Nelson, Lori (Aug. 15, 1933). Born Dixie Kay Nelson in Santa Fe, N.M., she was a child actress and a model. *Ma and Pa Kettle at the Fair* (1952) marked her first screen appearance. She was given parts in many U-I programmers. No matter where she went—RKO, Warners—she couldn't seem to punch her way out of the programmers. She was a little on the shrill side but always seemed convincing enough to me. AIP credits: *The Day the World Ended, Hot Rod Girl.*

Nicholson, Jack (April 22, 1937). Born in Neptune, N.J. His father, an alcoholic, abandoned the family when Jack was very young, leaving Jack's mother, who owned a beauty parlor, to take care of things. Jack's first ambition was to be a newspaperman and it wasn't until he and his mother moved to Los Angeles that Jack became interested in becoming an actor. He went to work as an office boy in MGM's cartoon department and finally got the courage to ask Joe Pasternak for a job. The producer advised him to join the famous Players Ring, an acting class headed by Jeff Corey who was teaching others to act since the black-listing had made it impossible for him to act himself. It was during class that Jack met Roger Corman, which led to his being cast in the lead role in *Cry Baby Killer*. Jack was certain the film would make him a star but nothing happened afterwards, at least for a while. He continued to take bit parts in a number of low budget pictures and television shows. (He was seen on "The G.E. Theatre," "Hawaiian Eye," "Mr. Lucky," etc.) He married actress Sandra Knight. They starred together in *The Terror*. He continued to knock around in lackluster movies until his role in *Easy Rider*, a part originally intended for Rip Torn, brought him to the attention of the critics. He was nominated for an Academy Award, as he was a few years later for *The Last Detail* and *Chinatown*. He finally won it for *One Flew Over the Cuckoo's Nest* in 1975. Recalling his performances in some of his early films it's all pretty hard to believe. AIP credits: *The Raven, The Terror, Hell's Angels on Wheels, The Trip* (screenplay only), *Psych-Out.*

Paget, Debra (Aug. 19, 1933). Born Debralee Griffin in Denver, took her name from Lord and Lady Paget of England, her ancestors. At age 11 she studied dramatics with Queenie Smith of the New York Theatre Guild. She made her stage debut in "Merry Wives of Windsor." Her first films was *Cry of the City* (1948). She was signed to a contract at Fox where she played in many costume epics, most of them silly things like *Prince Valiant* and *Princess of the Nile*. Her career was looking shaky by 1958 when she took a role in a wheezing science fiction film, *From the Earth to the Moon*. It was downhill from there. She was married to Budd Boetticher for 22 days. AIP credits: *Why Must I Die?, Journey to the Lost City, Tales of Terror, The Haunted Palace.*

Persson, Gene (1937). Born in Long Beach, Calif., his family moved to Hollywood. He studied drama while in grade school and by the time he'd graduated from John Marshall High School he had appeared in over 50 features, appearing with people like James Stewart and Claudette Colbert. During his days with Los Angeles City College he devoted much of his time to Theatre Arts. After a year there he dropped out and went to New York where he found work in radio and television, including "Kraft Theatre," "Good Year Playhouse," "Studio One," "The Eddie Fisher Show," "United States Steel Hour," and many more. Then he was drafted into the Army, did his time, then returned to California and was seen on "The Jane Wyman Show" and "Dragnet." AIP credits: *Earth vs. the Spider*.

Quarry, Robert (1923). Made his film debut in *Shadow of a Doubt* in 1943, and was signed to a Universal contract which asked that he attend their juvenile actors' training school. He hated the experience and drifted toward the stage. His performance in the Margaret Webster production of "The Taming of the Shrew" brought him once again to the attention of Hollywood. In the early 60s he suffered a bout with cancer for two years, then returned to work. He kicked around in the movies for years but virtually went unnoticed until his appearance in horror movies during the early 70s. AIP credits: *Count Yorga, Vampire, The Return of Count Yorga, The Deathmaster, Madhouse, Dr. Phibes Rises Again, Sugar Hill*.

Rathbone, Basil (June 13, 1892–1967). Born in Johannesburg, South Africa, he was the son of a mining engineer. He was educated in England at Repton College where he made high grades in sports and low grades academically. (He won 15 gold cups in track.) His father wanted him to get involved with one of England's larger insurance companies so after Basil finished with the Liverpool Scottish Regiment during World War I he took a job with the London and Globe Insurance Company. That didn't last long. He began to embark on a career in acting, making his first appearance on stage in 1911 in "The Taming of the Shrew." He toured with Sir Frank Benson's No. 2 Company making his London debut in 1914 in "Sin of David," and made his New York debut in 1922 in a number of Shakesperean roles. *The Masked Bride* in 1925 marked his first screen appearance. He appeared in a number of costume dramas at MGM — *David Copperfield, Anna Karenina, A Tale of Two Cities* — but he is best known as Arthur Conan Doyle's Sherlock Holmes and his sword swinging villains. He was magnificent in the larger-than-life roles he played in swashbucklers like *Captain Blood, Robin Hood,* and *Mark of Zorro*. He was also wonderful in *The Court Jester*. But as he grew older, and the movies began looking for more realistic performers, Basil could rarely find work in anything but period horror films. *The Black Sleep* in 1956 was more or less the beginning of the end of his happier acting days. His full name was Philip St. John Basil Rathbone. AIP credits: *Tales of Terror, Comedy of Terrors, Queen of Blood, The Ghost in the Invisible Bikini, Voyage to a Prehistoric Planet*.

Roarke, Adam (Aug. 8, 19--). Grew up in the Bay Ridge section of Brooklyn; was taught early to steal and fight with a street gang. Became a semi-finalist in the 1954 Golden Gloves championship. He loved movies with Jimmy Cagney and Humphrey Bogart. Began to study acting with Brian Hutton. Adam's first role was that of a tough in an Alan Ladd movie and from there he went on to appear in films like *Ensign Pulver* and *Fluffy*, and more than 20 television shows. AIP credits: *Hell's Belles, Psych-Out, The Savage Seven*.

Saxon, John (Aug. 5, 1935). Born Carmen Orrico in Brooklyn, he studied acting with Stella Adler before signing with U-I in the mid-50s, where he played in a number of mild juvenile delinquency dramas (*The Unguarded Moment, The Restless Years*). He rarely played leads and when assignments dwindled he went abroad. He continues to be active both on television (he once had his own series, "The Doctors,") and movies and made one hell of a cold villain in *The Electric Horseman*. AIP credits: *The Evil Eye, Queen of Blood, Strange Shadows in an Empty Room*.

Shire, Talia (1947). Born in Lake Success, N.Y., sister of Francis Ford Coppola who introduced her to Roger Corman. She got an Academy Award nomination for her role in her brother's film, *The Godfather Part II* and scored another screen success with her performance in *Rocky*. She married composer David Shire. AIP credits: *The Wild Racers, The Dunwich Horror, Gas-s-s-s-s!*

Slate, Jeremy (1925). Born in Margate City, N.J., and raised in Bennington, Vermont, he served for three years aboard a destroyer during World War II. Following his discharge from the Navy he entered St. Lawrence University in Canton, N.Y., where he majored in English. He worked as a dairy hand, ship line publicist, writer, bullfighter, lifeguard, and a radio announcer before he began a career in television as an actor in the series "Malibu Run." Some of his other television credits include "Run for Your Life," "Gunsmoke," and "Alcoa Presents." In films he's been featured in *The Devil's Brigade, True Grit* and *The Sons of Katie Elder*. AIP credits: *Hell's Angels '69, Hell's Belles, Born Losers, Mini-Skirt Mob*.

Steele, Barbara (Dec. 29, 1938). Born in Trenton Wirrall, England, she was the last female starlet to be signed by Rank's acting school. Her first film appearance was in *Bachelor of Hearts* (1958). She appeared in one other film before Rank sold her contract to 20th Century–Fox. She sat around for two years waiting for a part but nothing ever happened. For a brief time it looked as if she'd be appearing with Elvis Presley in *Flaming Star* but someone decided she didn't look "American" enough and the part was given to Barbara Eden. She went to Italy and director Mario Bava signed her for the lead in his first movie, a horror film. Since that time, in spite of the fact that she has appeared in films like *8½* and *Pretty Baby*, she continues to be associated with horror films, a fact that she finds somewhat distressing. Speaking about movies like *The Horrible Dr. Hitchcock* the actress remarked: "I always used to think they'd end up only in Sicily. It's not so. They end up at the Marble Arch Odeon in London while the things you did for love and nothing end up in late-night showings at the Tokyo Film Festival." She was recently seen in *Piranha* and *La Cle sur la Porte*. AIP credits: *Black Sunday, The Pit and the Pendulum, The Crimson Cult*.

Stein, Ronald (1930). Attended Yale University among others. He was a professor of music at California State University and may still be there for all I know. He was one of the most prolific soundtrack composers ever yet his name is virtually unknown. All things considered, some of his scores are pretty good. AIP credits: *Apache Woman, The Day the World Ended, The Phantom from 10,000 Leagues, Gunslinger, The She-Creature, It Conquered the World, Oklahoma Woman, Naked Paradise, She-Gods of Shark Reef, Reform School Girl, Runaway Daughters, Sorority Girl, Dragstrip Girl, Hot Rod Gang, Flesh and*

Barbara Steele

the Spur, *Ghost of Dragstrip Hollow, Invasion of the Saucer-Men, The Undead,*
Suicide Battalion, Paratroop Command, Jet Attack, The Bonnie Parker Story,

Psych-Out, Dementia 13, The Premature Burial, The Haunted Palace, The Terror, Voyage to the Prehistoric Planet.

Strock, Herbert L. (Jan. 13, 1918). From Boston; was a professor of cinema at the University of Southern California while working as a film editor. He was working for Ivan Tors as an editor when he was asked to direct *The Magnetic Monster.* He directed another film for Tors, *Gog,* then moved into television. His early work on shows like *Highway Patrol* earned him the nickname "The Cop." He had to beg the folks at Warners to let him direct westerns. After spending years on shows like "Maverick" and "Cheyenne" he had to plead with the bosses to take him out of the horse manure (to use his own phrase). He continues to be active as a motion picture editor, and has recently directed several films that haven't been able to get released. AIP credits: *Blood of Dracula, I Was a Teenage Frankenstein, How to Make a Monster.*

Topper, Burt (1934). Born in Southern California, he was working on a roof in Beverly Hills when someone asked him if he was interested in being in the movies. He tried out for the role of Hiawatha but the part went to Vince Edwards. Burt was a contract actor for a while but he hated that and decided to make his own film, *Hell Squad,* for about $12,000, shot on weekends. "If I was going to gamble, I reckoned that I might as well gamble on myself." He was eventually put in charge of theatrical production at AIP. AIP credits: (producer, screenplay, director) *Hell Squad, Tank Commandos*; (producer, director) *Diary of a High School Bride, The Devil's 8*; (screenplay, director) *The Hard Ride*; (producer) *The Devil's Angels, Space Monster*; (executive producer) *Wild in the Streets,* (producer) *Thunder Alley.*

Tourneur, Jacques (Nov. 12, 1904–Dec. 19, 1977). Born in Paris, the son of Maurice Tourneur. Came to the U.S. in 1914 and became a U.S. citizen in 1919. Worked as an office boy at MGM in 1924, later was a stock actor and script clerk. He returned to Paris to become a film cutter with Pathé. Once he'd become a director he was back at MGM directing shorts, was second unit director on *A Tale of Two Cities.* After that he went to work at RKO. His best known films are the horror melodramas he directed for Val Lewton — *The Cat People, I Walked with a Zombie, The Leopard Man* —and later on, on his own, *The Night of the Demon.* But in this writer's opinion his best all around film was *Out of the Past.* AIP credits: *Journey to the Lost City, Comedy of Terrors, War-Gods of the Deep.*

Towers, Harry Alan (Oct. 19, 1920). Born in London, got into broadcasting in 1937. He was the supplier of programs to British Forces overseas, became a freelance script writer and formed Towers of London Ltd. in 1946 with offices in London, Sydney, Johannesburg, Toronto, and New York, a company that produced and distributed radio and television shows throughout the world. He became the British agent for ZIV television in the 50s, eventually became a motion picture producer. AIP credits: *Bang, Bang, You're Dead, House of 1,000 Dolls, Million Eyes of Su-Muru, Night of the Blood Monster, Venus in Furs.*

Townsend, Leo (May 11, 1908). Born in Faribault, Minn., educated at the university there, a writer for magazines and radio before collaborating on a

Yvette Vickers

screenplay in 1942, *It Started with Eve*. Wrote a series of undistinguished scenarios before coming to AIP where he continued to do so. AIP credits: *Bikini Beach, Beach Blanket Bingo, How to Stuff a Wild Bikini*.

Varsi, Diane (1937). Born in San Mateo, Calif., the product of a broken home. She was raised in various West Coast convents, married at 15 and again at 17. She took jobs as an apple picker, a waitress, and a factory worker before coming to Hollywood to try her hand at folksinging. After a while she enrolled in Jeff Corey's acting class and was signed to play Lana Turner's daughter in the film version of *Peyton Place*. She got an Oscar nomination right off the bat but walked out of her Fox contract stating that she was "running away from destruction." She stayed in Vermont for a while. When she was ready to resume her acting career only AIP was interested in hiring her. AIP credits: *Wild in the Streets, Killers Three, Bloody Mama*.

Vickers, Yvette (Aug. 26, 1936). Born in Kansas City, Mo., the daughter of Mr. and Mrs. Charles Vedder, Yvette was schooled at UCLA where she majored in motion picture and theatre arts. She was the "White Rain Girl" for a time and finally made her motion picture debut in *Short Cut to Hell* in 1957. Her career has been sporadic, mostly in low budget pictures or a bit in something like *Hud*. She was absolutely marvelous in *Attack of the Fifty Foot Woman* as the sensuous, scheming Honey Parker. In fact, as spouse bumper-offers, she and William Hudson were a better pair than Barbara Stanwyck and Fred MacMurray in *Double Indemnity*. Yvette played it sleazy to the hilt and no one could top her. I love you, Yvette, wherever you are. AIP credits: *Reform School Girl, Attack of the Giant Leeches*.

Winters, Shelley (Aug. 18, 1922). Born Shirley Schrift in St. Louis and raised in Brooklyn. Appeared in high school plays and worked as a store clerk and model to finance her dramatic studies. She became a chorus girl and made her Broadway debut in 1941. Columbia brought her to Hollywood two years later but it wasn't until 1948 that she gained some recognition after her appearance in *A Stolen Life*. She's been in several classic films—*A Place in the Sun, Night of the Hunter, Diary of Anne Frank*—but more often she was in routine programmers like *Johnny Stool Pigeon* at Universal. Age and weight forced her into matronly, off-beat roles; she recently wrote her autobiography. AIP credits: *Wild in the Streets, Bloody Mama, Who Slew Auntie Roo? Tentacles*.

Witney, William (May 15, 1910). Born in Lawton, Okla., was a messenger boy at Mascot Studios and Republic. At the latter he worked his way up to script supervision and then director. He worked on westerns and serials, joined the Marines, then came back. AIP credits: *The Cool and the Crazy, The Bonnie Parker Story, Paratroop Command, Master of the World*.

Yates, George Worthington (Oct. 14, 1900–197?). Born in New York, he was educated at Dartmouth, Brown and Princeton universities. He became a writer in 1922 and scripted a number of forgettable action pictures, such as *Man from Frisco* and *Sinbad the Sailor*. He wrote the original treatment for *Them!* Because of the success of that movie Yates was given a second wind scripting science fiction films in the 50s. He died sometime in the early 70s. AIP credits: *Attack of the Puppet People, War of the Colossal Beast, Earth vs. the Spider*.

Filmography

This is not a complete list of the motion pictures released by the American Releasing Corporation and American International Pictures. Deliberately omitted are a number of foreign features that had already been in release (La Dolce Vita, The Pawnbroker, etc.) before AIP had purchased them. Also absent are a number of the releases acquired from companies like Hallmark and Commonwealth in 1969. Abbreviations used are: C Color, Dir Director, Mus Music, Pro Producer, Sp Screenplay.

Abby. 1974, C 91 min. *Mus* Robert O. Ragland. *Pro* William Girdley, Mike Henry, Gordon C. Layne. *Sp* Gordon C. Layne. *Dir* William Girdley. *Cast:* William Marshall, Terry Carter, Austin Stoker, Carol Speed, Juanita Moore.

Abominable Doctor Phibes, The. 1971, C 94 min. *Mus* Basil Kirchin. *Pro* Louis M. Heyward, Ronald S. Dunas. *Sp* James Whiton, William Goldstein. *Dir* Robert Fuest. *Cast:* Vincent Price, Joseph Cotton, Virginia North, Terry-Thomas, Hugh Griffith.

Alakazam the Great. 1961, C 78 min. *Pro* Hiroshi Okawa (U.S. Lou Rusoff). *Sp* O. Tezeuka, Keinosuke Uekusa (U.S. Lee Kresel). *Dir* Teiji Tabushita, Osama Tezuka, Daisaku Shiakawa. *Mus* (U.S.) Les Baxter. *Voices*: Frankie Avalon, Dodie Stevens, Jonathan Winters, Arnold Stang, Sterling Holloway.

Amazing Colossal Man, The. 1957, 80 min. *Mus* Albert Glasser. *Sp* Mark Hanna, Bert I. Gordon. *Pro-Dir* Bert I. Gordon. *Cast:* Glenn Langan, Cathy Downs, William Hudson, Larry Thor, James Seay.

Amazing Transparent Man, The. 1960, 56 min. *Mus* Darrell Calker. *Pro* Lester D. Guthrie. *Sp* Jack Lewis. *Dir* Edgar G. Ulmer. *Cast:* Marguerite Chapman, Douglas Kennedy, James Griffith, Ivan Triesault.

Amityville Horror, The. 1979, C 117 min. *Mus* Lalo Schifrin. *Pro* Ronald Saland, Elliot Geisinger. *Sp* Sandor Stern. *Dir* Stuart Rosenberg. *Cast:* James Brolin, Margot Kidder, Rod Steiger, Don Stroud.

Angel, Angel, Down We Go (Cult of the Damned). 1969, C 103 min. *Pro* Jerome F. Katzman. *Sp-Dir* Robert Thom. *Cast:* Jennifer Jones, Jordon Christopher, Holly Near, Roddy McDowell, Lou Rawls.

Angel Unchained. 1970, C 90 min. *Mus* Randy Sparks. *Sp* Jeffrey Alladin. *Pro-Dir.* Lee Madden. *Cast:* Don Stroud, Luke Askew, Larry Bishop, Tyne Daly, Aldo Ray.

Angels from Hell. 1968, C 86 min. *Mus* Stu Phillips. *Pro* Kurt Neumann. *Sp* Jerome Wish. *Dir* Bruce Kessler. *Cast:* Tom Stern, Arlene Martel, Ted Markland, Stephen Oliver, Paul Bertoya.

Angry Red Planet, The. 1959, *C* 94 min. *Mus* Paul Dunlap. *Pro* Sid Pink, Norman Maurer. *Sp* Sid Pink, Ib Melchior. *Dir* Ib Melchior. *Cast:* Gerald Mohr, Nora Hayden, Les Tremayne, Jack Kruschen, Paul Hahn.

Apache Woman. 1955, *C* 69 min. *Mus* Ronald Stein. *Sp* Lou Rusoff. *Pro-Dir* Roger Corman. *Cast:* Lloyd Bridges, Joan Taylor, Lance Fuller, Morgan Jones, Paul Birch.

Assignment Outer Space. 1960, *C* 73 min. *Mus* J.K. Broady. *Sp* Vassily Petrov. *Dir* Antonio Margheriti. **English Language Version:** *Pro* Hugo Grimaldi. *Cast:* Rik Von Nutter, Gaby Farinon, David Montressor, Archie Savage, Alain Dijon.

Astounding She-Monster, The. 1950, 60 min. *Mus* Guenther Kauer. *Sp* Frank Hall. *Pro-Dir* Ronnie Ashcroft. *Cast:* Robert Clarke, Kenne Duncan, Marilyn Harvey, Jeanne Tatum, Shirley Kilpatrick.

At the Earth's Core. 1976, *C* 90 min. *Pro* John Dark. *Sp* Milton Subotsky. *Dir* Kevin Connor. *Cast:* Doug McClure, Peter Cushing, Caroline Munro, Cy Grant, Godfrey James.

Atragon. 1963, *C* 79 min. *Mus* Akira Ifukube. *Sp* Shinichi Sekizawa. *Dir* Inoshiro Honda. *Cast:* Tadao Takshima, Yoko Fujiyama, Yu Fujiki, Hiroshi Koizumi, Ken Vehrar.

Attack of the Giant Leeches. 1959, Starring Ken Clark, Yvette Vickers, Jan Shepard, Michael Emmet, Tyler Monvey. *Mus* Alexander Laszlo. *Sp* Leo Gordon. *Pro* Gene Corman. *Dir* Bernard Kowalski.

Attack of the Monsters. 1969, *C*. *Pro* Hidemasa Nagata. *Sp* Fumi Takahashi. *Dir* Noriaki Yuasa. *Cast:* Nobuhiro Najima, Miyuki Akiyama, Christopher Murphy, Yuko Hamada, Eiji Fanakoshi.

Attack of the Mushroom People. 1963, *C* 89 min. *Sp* Takeshi Kimura. *Dir* Inoshiro Honda, Eiji Tsuburaya. *Cast:* Akiro Kubo, Yoshio Tsuchiya, Hiroshi Koizumi, Hiroshi Tachikawa, Kumi Mizuno.

Attack of the Puppet People (Fantastic Puppet People, Six Inches Tall). 1958, 79 min. *Mus* Albert Glasser. *Sp* George Worthington Yates. *Pro-Dir* Bert I. Gordon. *Cast:* John Agar, June Kenney, John Hoyt, Michael Mark, Mariene Willis.

Bamboo Gods and Iron Men. 1974, *C* 96 min. *Mus* Tito Sotto. *Pro* Cirio H. Santiago. *Sp* Kenneth Metcalfe. *Dir* Cesar Gallardo. *Cast:* James Iglehart, Shirley Washington, Chiquito, Marissa Delgado.

Bang, Bang, You're Dead (Our Man in Marrakesh). 1966, *C* 92 min. *Mus* Malcolm Lockyer. *Pro* Harry Alan Towers. *Sp* Peter Yeldham. *Dir* Don Sharp. *Cast:* Tony Randall, Senta Berger, Herbert Lom, Wilfred Hyde-White, Terry-Thomas.

Baron Blood. 1972, *C* 90 min. *Mus* (U.S.) Lex Baxter. *Sp* Vincent Fotre, William A. Bairn. *Dir* Mario Bava. *Cast:* Joseph Cotton, Elke Sommer, Massimo Girotti, Antonio Cantafora, Alan Collins.

Bat People, The (It Lives By Night). 1974, *C* 95 min. *Mus* Artie Kane. *Pro-Sp* Lou Shaw. *Dir* Jerry Jameson. *Cast:* Stewart Moss, Marianne McAndrew, Michael Pataki, Paul Carr, Arthur Space.

Battle Beyond the Sun. 1963, *C* 75 min. *Mus* Yu Meytus. *Sp* A. Sazonov, Ye Pomeshchikov (U.S. Nicholas Colbert, Edwin Palmer, Francis Ford Coppola). *Dir* A Kozyr (U.S. Thomas Colchart). *Cast:* Ivan Pereverzev (U.S. Edd Perry), A. Shvorin (U.S. Arla Powell), K. Bartashevich (U.S. Andy Stewart), G. Tonunts (U.S. Bruce Hunter), V. Chernyak (U.S. Gene Tonner).

Battle of Neretva. 1971, *C* 102 min. *Mus* Bernard Herrmann. *Pro* Steve Previn. *Sp* Ugo Pirro. *Dir* Veliko Bulajic. *Cast:* Yul Brynner, Sergei Bondarcuk, Curt Jurgens, Silva Koscina, Hardy Kruger.

Beach Blanket Bingo. 1965, *C* 98 min. *Mus* Les Baxter. *Pro* James H. Nicholson, Samuel Z. Arkoff. *Sp* William Asher, Leo Townsend. *Dir* William Asher. *Cast:* Frankie Avalon, Annette Funicello, Deborah Walley, Harvey Lembeck, John Ashley.

Beach Party. 1963, *C* 101 min. *Mus* Les Baxter. *Pro* James H. Nicholson, Samuel Z. Arkoff. *Sp* Lou Rusoff. *Dir* William Asher. *Cast:* Frankie Avalon, Annette Funicello, Harvey Lembeck, Jody McCrea, John Ashley.

Beast with 1,000,000 Eyes, The. 1955, 78 min. *Mus* John Bickford. *Sp* Tom Filer. *Pro-Dir* David Kramarksy. *Cast:* Paul Birch, Lorna Thayer, Chester Conklin, Donna Cole, Richard Sargent.

Beyond the Time Barrier. 1960, 75 min. *Mus* Darrell Calker. *Pro* Robert Clarke. *Sp* Arthur C. Pierce. *Dir* Edgar G. Ulmer. *Cast:* Robert Clarke, Darlene Tompkins, Arianne Arden, Vladimir Sokoloff, John Van Dreelan.

Beware of Children (No Kidding). 1961, 87 min. *Mus* Bruce Montgomery. *Pro* Peter Rogers. *Sp* Norman Hudis, Robin Estridge. *Dir* Gerald Thomas. *Cast:* Leslie Phillips, Geraldine McEwan, Julia Lockwood, Noel Purcell, Irene Hand.

Big T.N.T. Show, The (This Could Be the Night). 1966, 93 min. *Pro* Phil Spector. *Dir* Larry Peerce. *Cast:* David McCallum, Roger Miller, Ray Charles, Joan Baez, Donovan.

Bikini Beach. 1964, *C* 100 min. *Mus* Les Baxter. *Pro* James H. Nicholson, Samuel Z. Arkoff. *Sp* William Asher, Leo Townsend, Robert Dillon. *Dir* William Asher. *Cast:* Frankie Avalon, Annette Funicello, Martha Hyer, Harvey Lembeck, Don Rickles.

Black Caesar. 1973, *C* 92 min. *Mus* James Brown. *Pro-Sp-Dir* Larry Cohen. *Cast:* Fred Williamson, Gloria Hendry, Philip Raye, Art Lund, Minnie Gentry.

Black Jack (Wild in the Sky). 1974, *C* 87 min. *Mus* Jerry Styner. *Pro* William T. Naud, Dick Gautier. *Sp* Dick Gautier. *Dir* William T. Naud. *Cast:* George Standford Brown, Brandon de Wilde, Keenan Wynn, Tim O' Connor, Dick Gautier.

Black Mama, White Mama. 1974, *C* 87 min. *Pro* John Ashley, Eddie Romero. *Sp* H.R. Christian. *Dir* Eddie Romero. *Cast:* Pam Grier, Margaret Markov, Sid Haig, Lynn Borden, Zaldy Zshornack.

Black Sabbath. 1964, *C* 99 min. *Mus* Roberto Nicolosi (U.S. Les Baxter. *Sp* Marello Fondato. *Dir* Mario Bava. *Cast:* Boris Karloff, Susy Anderson, Mark Damon, Michele Mercer, Lidia Alfonis.

Black Sunday. 1960, 84 min. *Mus* Roberto Nicolosi (U.S. Les Baxter. *Pro* Massimo De Rita (U.S.) Lou Rusoff. *Sp* Ennio de Concini, Mario Bava, Marcello Coscia, Mario Serandre. *Dir* Mario Bava (U.S. Lee Kresel).

Blacula. 1972, *C* 92 min. *Pro* Joseph T. Naar. *Sp* Joan Torres, Raymond Koenig. *Dir* William Crain. *Cast:* William Marshall, Denise Nichols, Vonetta McGee, Gordon Pinset, Thalmus Rasulala.

Blood and Lace. 1971, *C* 87 min. *Pro* Ed Carlin, Gil Lasky. *Sp* Gil Lasky. *Dir* Philip Gilbert. *Cast:* Gloria Grahame, Melody Paterson, Milton Selzer, Len Lesser, Vic Tayback.

Blood Bath (Track of the Vampire). 1966, 80 min. *Mus* Mark Lowry. *Pro* Jack Hill. *Sp-Dir* Jack Hill, Stephanie Rothman. *Cast:* William Campbell, Marissa Mathes, Lori Sanders, Sandra Knight.

Blood from the Mummy's Tomb. 1971, *C* 94 min. *Mus* Tristram Cary. *Pro* Howard Brandy. *Sp* Christopher Wicking. *Dir* Seth Holt, Michael Carreras. *Cast:* Andrew Keir, Valarie Leon, James Villiers, Mark Edwards, George Coulouris.

Blood of Dracula (Blood Is My Heritage). 1957, 69 min. *Mus* Paul Dunlap. *Pro* Herman Cohen. *Sp* Ralph Thornton. *Dir* Herbert L. Strock. *Cast:* Sandra Harrison, Louise Lewis, Gail Ganley, Jerry Blaine, Thomas B. Henry.

Bloody Mama. 1970, *C* 90 min. *Mus. Don Randi. Sp* Robert Thom. *Pro-Dir* Roger Corman. *Cast:* Shelley Winters, Pat Hingle, Don Stroud, Diane Varsi, Bruce Dern.

Bonnie Parker Story. 1958, 79 min. *Mus* Ronald Stein. *Pro-Sp* Stan Shpetner. *Dir* William Witney. *Cast:* Dorothy Provine, Jack Hogan, Richard Bakalyan, Joseph Turkel, William Stevens.

Bora Bora. 1970, *C* 90 min. *Mus* Les Baxter. *Pro* Alfredo Bini. *Sp-Dir* Ugo Liberatore. *Cast:* Haydee Politoff, Corrado Pani, Doris Kunstmann, Rosine Copie, Antoine Coco Puputauki.

Born Losers. 1967, *C* 112 min. *Mus* Mike Curb. *Pro* Donald Henderson. *Sp* E. James Lloyd. *Dir* T.C. Frank. *Cast:* Tom Laughlin, Elizabeth James, Jane Russell, Jeremy Slate, William Wellman Jr.

Born Wild (The Young Animals). 1968, *C* 100 min. *Mus* Les Baxter. *Sp* James Bordon White. *Pro-Dir* Maury Dexter. *Cast:* Tom Nardini, Patty McCormack, David Macklin, Joanna Frank, "The American Revolution."

Boxcar Bertha. 1972, *C* 92 min. *Pro* Roger Corman. *Sp* Joyce H. and William Corrington. *Dir* Martin Scorsese. *Cast:* Barbara Hershey, David Carradine, Barry Primus, Bernie Casey, John Carradine.

Brain Eaters, The. 1958, 60 min. *Pro* Edwin Nelson. *Sp* Gordon Urquhart. *Dir* Bruno Ve Sota. *Cast:* Edwin Nelson, Alan Frost, Jack Hill, Jody Fair, Joanna Lee.

Brain That Wouldn't Die, The (The Black Door, The Head That Wouldn't Die). 1959, (1962), 81 min. *Mus* Abe Baker, Tony Restaino. *Pro* Rex Carlton. *Sp-Dir* Joseph Green. *Cast:* Virginia Leith, Herb Evers, Adele Lamont, Bruce Brighton, Doris Brent.

Breaker, Breaker. 1977, *C* 85 min. *Mus* Don Hulette. *Sp* Terry Chambers. *Pro-Dir* Don Hulette. *Cast:* Chuck Norris, George Murdock, Terry O'Connor, Don Gentry, John DiFusco.

Brute and the Beast. 1968, *C* 87 min. *Mus* Lallo Gori. *Sp* Fernando DiLeo. *Dir* Lucio Fulci. *Cast:* Franco Nero, George Hilton, Nino Castelnuovo, Lyn Shayne, John M. Douglas.

Bucket of Blood, A. 1959, Starring Dick Miller, Barboura Morris, Antony Carbone, Julian Burton, Ed Nelson. *Sp* Charles B. Griffith. *Mus* Fred Katz. *Pro-Dir* Roger Corman.

Bucktown. 1975, *C* 94 min. *Mus* Johnny Pate. *Pro* Bernard Schwartz. *Sp* Bob Ellison. *Dir* Arthur Marks. *Cast:* Fred Williamson, Pam Grier, Thalmus Rasulala, Tony King, Bernie Hamilton.

Bullet for Pretty Boy, A. 1970, *C* 88 min. *Mus* Harley Hatcher. *Sp* Henry Rosenbaum. *Pro-Dir* Larry Buchanan. *Cast:* Fabian Forte, Jocelyn Lane, Astrid Warner, Michael Haynes, Adam Roarke.

Bunny O'Hare (The Bunny O'Hare Mob). 1972, *C* 92 min. *Mus* Billy Strange. *Sp* Stanley Z. Cherry, Coslough Johnson. *Pro-Dir* Gerd Oswald. *Cast:* Bette Davis, Ernest Borgnine, Jack Cassidy, Joan Delaney, Jay Robinson.

Burn Witch, Burn (Night of the Eagle). 1961, 86 min. *Mus* Muir Matheson, William Alwyn. *Pro* Albert Fennell. *Sp* Charles Beaumont, Richard Matheson. *Dir* Sidney Hayers. *Cast:* Janet Blair, Peter Wyngarde, Margaret Johnston, Anthony Nicholls, Colin Gordon.

Cannibal Girls. 1974, C 84 min. *Mus* Doug Riley. *Pro* Daniel Goldberd. *Sp* Robert Sandler. *Dir* Ivan Reitman. *Cast:* Eugene Levy, Andrea Martin, Ronald Ulrich, Randell Carpenter, Bonnie Nelson.

Carry On Camping. 1972, C 88 min. *Pro* Petter Rogers. *Sp* Talbot Rothwell. *Dir* Gerald Thomas. *Cast:* Bernard Bresslaw, Terry Scott, Barbara Windsor, Hattie Jacques, Peter Butterworth.

Carry on Doctor. 1972, C 95 min. *Mus* Eric Rogers. *Pro* Peter Rogers. *Sp* Talbot Rothwell. *Dir* Gerald Thomas. *Cast:* Frankie Howerd, Sidney James, Kenneth Williams, Charles Hawtrey, Jim Dale.

Carry on Henry VIII. 1972, C 0; min. *Mus* Eric Rogers. *Pro* Peter Rogers. *Sp* Talbot Rothwell. *Dir* Gerald Thomas. *Cast:* Sidney Williams, Kenneth Williams, Joan Sims, Charles Hawtrey, Terry Scott.

Cat Girl, The. 1957, 75 min. *Pro* Lou Rusoff, Herbert Smith. *Sp* Lou Rusoff. *Dir* Alfred Shaughnessy. *Cast:* Barbara Shelley, Robert Ayres, Kay Callard, Paddy Webster, Ernest Miton.

Chastity. 1969, C 85 min. *Mus-Sp-Pro* Sonny Bono. *Dir* Alessio de Paola. *Cast:* Cher, Barbara London, Stephen Whittaker, Tom Nolan, Danny Zapien.

Chatterbox. 1977, C 73 min. *Mus* Fred Karger. *Pro* Bruch Cohn Curtis. *Sp* Mark Rosin, Norman Yonemoto. *Dir* Tom De Simone. *Cast:* Candice Rialson, Larry Gelman, Jane Kean, Perry Bullington, Arlene Martell.

Chosen, The. 1979, C 102 min. *Mus* Ennio Morricone. *Pro* Edmondo Amati. *Sp* Sergio Donati, Aldo De Martino, Michael Robson. *Dir* Alberto De Martino. *Cast:* Kirk Douglas, Agostine Belli, Simon Ward, Anthony Quayle, Virginia McKenna.

Chrome and Hot Leather. 1971, C 91 min. *Mus* Porter Jordon. *Pro* Wes Bishop. *Sp* Michael Allen Haynes, David Neibel, Don Tair. *Dir* Lee Frost. *Cast:* William Smith, Tony Young, Michael Haynes, Peter Brown, Marvin Gaye.

Circus of Horrors. 1960, C 91 min. *Mus* Franz Taizenstein. *Pro* Julian Wintle, Leslie Parkyn. *Sp* George Baxt. *Dir* Sidney Hayers. *Cast:* Anton Diffring, Erika Remberg, Yvonne Monlaur, Donald Pleasance, Jane Hylton.

Cobra, The. 1967, C 93 min. *Mus* Anton Garcia Abril. *Pro* Fulvio Lucisano. *Sp* Gumersindo Mollo. *Dir* Mario Sequi. *Cast:* Dana Andrews, Peter Martell, Anita Ekberg, Elisa Montes, Jesus Puente.

Coffy. 1973, C 91 min. *Pro* Robert A. Papazian. *Sp-Dir* Jack Hill. *Cast:* Pam Grier, Brooker Bradshaw, Robert Doquio, William Elliot, Allan Ambus.

Comedy of Terrors, The (The Graveside Story). 1963. C 88 min. *Mus* Les Baxter. *Pro* James H. Nicholson, Samuel Z. Arkoff. *Sp* Richard Matheson. *Dir* Jacques Tourneur. *Cast:* Vincent Price, Peter Lorre, Boris Karloff, Basil Rathbone, Joyce Jameson.

Commando. 1964, 98 min. *Sp* Arturo Tofanelli. *Dir* Frank Wisbar. *Cast:* Stewart Granger, Dorian Grey, Carlos Casaravilla, Fausto Tozzi, Hans Von Borsody.

Conquered City (The Captive City). 1962, 91 min. *Dir* Joseph Anthony. *Cast:* David Niven, Ben Gazzara, Michael Craig, Martin Balsam, Lea Massari.

Conqueror Worm, The (The Witchfinder General). 1968, C 87 min. *Mus* Paul Ferris. *Pro* Arnold L. Miller, Louis M. Heyward. *Sp* Michael Reeves, Tom

Baker. *Dir* Michael Reeves. *Cast:* Vincent Price, Ian Ogilvy, Hilary Dwyer, Rupert Davies, Patrick Wymark.

Cool and the Crazy, The. 1958, 78 min. *Mus* Raoul Kraushaar. *Pro* E.C. Rhoden Jr., *Sp* Richard C. Sarafian. *Dir* William Witney. *Cast:* Scott Marlowe, Gigi Perreau, Dick Bakalyan, Dick Jones, Shelby Storck.

Cooley High. 1975, *C* 107 min. *Mus* Freddie Perrin. *Pro* Steve Krantz. *Sp* Eric Monte. *Dir* Michael Schultz. *Cast:* Glynn Turman, Lawrence-Hilton Jacobs, Garrett Morris, Cynthia Davis, Corin Rogers.

Cornbread, Earl, and Me. 1975, *C* 95 min. *Sp* Leonard Lamensdorf. *Pro-Dir* Joe Manduke. *Cast:* Moses Gunn, Rosalind Cash, Bernie Casey, Made Sinclair, Keith Wilkes.

Count Yorga, Vampire. 1970, *C* 91 min. *Mus* William Marx. *Pro* Michael Macready. *Sp-Dir* Bob Kelljan. *Cast:* Robert Quarry, Roger Perry, Michael Murphy, Michael Macready, Donna Anders.

Cracking Up. 1977, *C* 69 min. *Mus* Ward Jewel, The Tubes. *Pro* C.D. Taylor, Rick Murray. *Dir* Rowby Goren, Chuck Staley. *Cast:* Phil Proctor, Peter Bergman, Michael Mislove, Fred Willard, Paul Zeglar.

Creature of Destruction. 1967, *C* 80 min. *Sp* Enrique Toucada. *Pro-Dir* Larry Buchana. *Cast:* Les Tremayne, Aron Kincaid, Pat Delaney, Neil Fletcher, Scotty McKay.

Crime and Passion. 1976, *C* 92 min. *Pro* Robert L. Abrams. *Sp* Jesse Lasky, Jr., Pat Silver. *Dir* Ivan Passer. *Cast:* Omar Sharif, Karen Black, Joseph Bottoms, Bernard Wicki.

Crimson Cult, The. 1968, *C* 89 min. *Mus* Peter Knight. *Pro* Louis M. Heyward. *Sp* Mervyn Haisman, Henry Lincoln, Gerry Levy. *Dir* Vernon Sewell. *Cast:* Boris Karloff, Christopher Lee, Mark Eden, Virginia Wetherell, Barbara Steele.

Cry of the Banshee. 1970, *C* 87 min. *Mus* Les Baxter. *Pro* James H. Nicholson, Samuel Z. Arkoff. *Sp* Tim Kelly, Christopher Wicking. *Dir* Gordon Hessler. *Cast:* Vincent Price, Elisabeth Bernger, Essy Persson, Hugh Griffith, Patrick Mower.

Curse of Nostradamus, The. 1960, 77 min. *Pro* Victor Para. *Sp* Charles Toboada, Alfred Tuanova. *Dir* Frederick Curiel. **English Language Version:** *Pro* K. Gordon Murray. *Dir* Stim Segar. *Cast:* German Robles, Julio Aleman, Domingo Soler.

Curse of the Aztec Mummy, The. 1959, (1965), 85 min. *Mus* Antonio Diaz Conde. *Pro* William Calderon Stell. *Sp* Alfredo Salazar. *Dir* Rafael Portello. *Cast:* Ramon Gay, Rosita Arenas, Crox Alvaradao, Lobo Negro, Mucielago Valazquez.

Curse of the Crying Woman, The. 1961, 74 min. *Mus* Gustavo Cesar Carrion. *Pro* Abel Salazar. *Sp* Raphael Baleson, F. Galiana. *Dir* Raphael Baleson. *Cast:* Rosita Arenas, Abel Salazar, Rita Macedo, Domingo Soler, Carlos Montezuma.

Curse of the Doll People, The. 1960. *Mus* A.D. Conde. *Pro* William Calderon Stell. *Sp* Alfred Salazar. *Dir* Benito Alazarki. *Cast:* Elvira Quintana, Ramon Gay, Robert G. Rivera, Jorge Mondragon.

Curse of the Swamp Creature. 1966, *C* 80 min. *Sp* Tony Huston. *Pro-Dir* Larry Buchanan. *Cast:* John Agar, Francine York, Shirley McLine, Bill Thurman, Jeff Alexander.

Cycle Savages. 1970, *C* 82 min. *Pro* Maurice Smith. *Sp-Dir* Bill Brame. *Cast:* Bruce Dern, Chris Robinson, Melody Patterson, Karen Ciral, Scott Brady.

Daddy 'O'. 1959, 71 min. *Mus* John Williams. *Pro* Elmer Rhoden, Jr., *Sp* David Moessinger. *Dir* Lou Place. *Cast:* Dick Contino, Sandra Giles, Bruno Ve Sota, Gloria Victor, Ron McNeil.

Day the Earth Froze, The. 1959, (1962), *C* 69 min. *Mus* Igor Morozov (U.S.) Otto Strode. *Pro* (U.S.) Julius Standberg. *Sp* Viktor Vitkovich, Grigoriy Yagdfeld. *Dir* Aleksandr Ptushko (U.S.) Gregg Sebelious. *Cast:* Urho Somersalmi (Nina Anderson), A. Orochko (Jon Powers), I. Voronov (Peter Sorenson), Andris Oshin (Ingrid Elhart).

Day That Shook the World, The. 1977, *C* 111 min. *Mus* Juan Carlos Calderon, Libus Fiser. *Sp* Paul Jarrico. *Dir* Veljko Bulajic. *Cast:* Christopher Plummer, Florinda Bolkan, Maximilian Schell, Irfan Mensur.

Day the World Ended, The. 1956, 81 min. *Mus* Ronald Stein. *Sp* Lou Rusoff. *Pro-Dir* Roger Corman. *Cast:* Richard Denning, Lori Nelson, Adele Jergens, Touch Connors, Paul Birch.

Deathmaster, The. 1972 *C* 88 min. *Mus* Bill Marx. *Pro* Fred Sadoff. *Sp* R.L. Grove. *Dir* Ray Danton. *Cast:* Robert Quarry, Bill Eging, Brenda Dickson, John Fiedler, Betty Ann Rees.

Deep Thrust. 1974 *C* 88 min. *Pro* Raymond Chow. *Dir* Heang Feng. *Cast:* Angelo Mao, Chang Yi, Pai Ying, June Wu, Annie Liu.

Defiance. 1980, *C* 103 min. *Mus* Gerard McMahon. *Pro* William S. Gilmore Jr., Jerry Bruckheimer. *Sp* Thomas Michael Donnelly. *Dir* John Flynn. *Cast:* Jan Michael Vincent, Theresa Saldana, Art Carney, Rudy Ramos, Joe Campanella.

Dementia 13. 1963, 81 min. *Mus* Ronald Stein. *Pro* Roger Corman. *Sp-Dir* Francis Ford Coppola. *Cast:* William Campbell, Luana Anders, Bart Patton, Mary Mitchell, Patrick Magee.

De Sade. 1969, *C* 72 min. *Mus* Billy Strange. *Pro* James H. Nicholson, Samuel Z. Arkoff. *Sp* Richard Matheson. *Dir* Cy Endfield. *Cast:* Keir Dullea, Senta Berger, Lilly Palmer, Anna Massey, John Huston.

Deranged. 1974, *C* 83 min. *Mus* Carl Zittrer. *Pro* Tom Karr. *Sp* Alan Ormsby. *Dir* Jeff Gillen, Alan Ormsby. *Cast:* Robert Blossom, Cosette Lee, Leslie Carlson, Robert Warner, Marcia Diamond.

Destroy All Monsters. 1968, *C* 88 min. *Mus* Akira Ifukube. *Pro* Tomoyuki Tanaka. *Sp* Kaoru Mabuchi. *Dir* Inoshiro Honda. *Cast:* Akira Kubo, Jun Tazaki, Toshio Tsuchiua, Kyoko Ai, Yukiko Kobayashi.

Destroy All Planets. 1968, *C* 75 min. *Pro* Hidemasa Nagata. *Sp* Fumi Takahashi. *Dir* Noriaki Yuasa. *Cast:* Kajiro Hongo, Toru Takatsuka, Peter Williams, Carl Clay, Michiko Yaegaki.

Destructors, The. 1974, *C* 89 min. *Mus* Roy Budd. *Pro-Sp* Judd Bernard. *Dir* Robert Parrish. *Cast:* Michael Caine, Anthony Quinn, James Mason, Maureen Kerwin, Marcel Bozzuff.

Devil's Angels. 1967, *C* 84 min. *Mus* Mike Curb. *Pro* Burt Topper. *Sp* Charles Griffith. *Dir* Daniel Haller. *Cast:* John Cassavetes, Beverly Adams, Mimsy Farmer, Maurice McEndree, Salli Sachse.

Devil's 8, The. 1969, *C* 98 min. *Mus* Mike Curb. *Sp* James Gordon White. *Pro-Dir* Burt Topper. *Cast:* Christopher George, Ralph Meeker, Fabian, Tom Nardini, Leslie Parish.

Devil's Widow, The. 1973, *C* 107 min. *Mus* The Pentangle. *Pro* Alan Ladd, Jr., Stanley Mann. *Sp* William Spier. *Dir* Roddy McDowall. *Cast:* Ava Gardner, Ian McShane, Stephanie Beacham, Cyril Cusack, Richard Wattis.

Die Monster, Die! 1965, *C* 80 min. *Mus* Don Banks. *Pro* Pat Green. *Sp* Jerry Sohl. *Dir* Daniel Haller. *Cast:* Boris Karloff, Nick Adams, Freda Jackson, Suzan Farmer, Terence de Marney.

Dillinger. 1973, *C* 96 min. *Mus* Barry Devorzon. *Pro* Buzz Feitshans. *Sp-Dir* John Milius. *Cast:* Warren Oates, Ben Johnson, Cloris Leachman, Michelle Phillips, Harry Dean Stanton.

Dirt Gang, The. 1972, *C* 89 min. *Pro* Jopseph E. Bishop, Art Jacobs. *Sp* William Mercer, Michael C. Healy. *Dir* Jerry Jameson. *Cast:* Paul Carr, Michael Forest, Ben Archibeck, Michael Pataki, Nancy Harris.

Dirty Game, The. 1966, 91 min. *Mus* Robert Mellin. *Sp* Jo Eisinger. *Dir* Terence Young, Christian-Jacque, Carlo Lizzani. *Cast:* Henry Fonda, Robert Ryan, Vittorio Gassman, Annie Girardot, Bourvil.

Dirty O'Neil. 1974, *C* 89 min. *Mus* Raoul Kraushaar. *Pro* John C. Broderick. *Sp* Howard Freen. *Dir* Howard Freen, Lewis Teague. *Cast:* Morgan Paull, Art Metrano, Pat Anderson, Jean Manson, Katie Saylor.

Dr. Goldfoot and the Bikini Machine. 1965, *C* 88 min. *Mus* Les Baxter. *Pro* James H. Nicholson, Samuel Z. Arkoff. *Sp* Elwood Ullman, Robert Kaufman. *Dir* Norman Taurog. *Cast:* Vincent Price, Frankie Avalon, Dwayne Hickman, Susan Hart, Jack Mullaney.

Dr. Goldfoot and the Girl Bombs. 1966, *C* 85 min. *Mus* Les Baxter. *Pro* Louis M. Heyward, Fulvio Luciano. *Sp* Louis M. Heyward, Robert Kaufman, Castellano Pipolo. *Dir* Mario Bava. *Cast:* Vincent Price, Fabian, Franco Franchi, Ciccio Ingrassia, Laura Antonelli.

Dr. Jekyll and Sister Hyde. 1971, *C* 97 min. *Mus* David Whittaker. *Pro* Albert Fennell, Brian Clemens. *Sp* Brian Clemens. *Dir* Roy Ward Baker. *Cast:* Ralph Bates, Martine Beswick, Susan Brodrick, Lewis Fiander, Gerald Sim.

Dr. Orloff's Monster. 1964, 88 min. *Sp* Jesus Franco, Nick Frank. *Dir* Jesus Franco. *Cast:* Jose Rubio, Agnes Spaak, Perla Cristal, Pastor Serrador, Hugo Blanco.

Dr. Phibes Rises Again. 1972, *C* 88 min. *Mus* John Gale. *Pro* Louis M. Heyward. *Sp* Robert Fuest, Robert Blees. *Dir* Robert Fuest. *Cast:* Vincent Price, Robert Quarry, Valli Kemp, Hugh Griffith, Peter Jeffrey.

Door to Door Maniac. 1966. *Mus* Gene Kauer. *Pro* James Ellsworth. *Sp* M.K. Forester. *Dir* Bill Karn. *Cast:* Johnny Cash, Donald Woods, Kay Forester, Pamela Mason, Midge War.

Dragonfly. 1976, *C* 95 min. *Mus* Stephen Lawrence. *Sp* N. Richard Nash. *Pro-Dir* Gilbert Cates. *Cast:* Beau Bridges, Susan Sarandon, Mildred Donnock, Ann Wedgeworth.

Dragstrip Girl. 1957, 69 min. *Mus* Ronald Stein. *Pro* Alex Gordon. *Sp* Lou Rusoff. *Dir* Edward L. Cahn. *Cast:* Fay Spain, Steve Terrell, John Ashley, Frank Gorshin, Russ Bender.

Dragstrip Riot. 1958, 68 min. *Mus* Nicholas Carras. *Pro* Dale Ireland. *Sp* George Hidgins. *Dir* David Bradley. *Cast:* Yvonne Lime, Gary Clark, Fay Wray, Connie Stevens, Gabe Delutri.

Dunwich Horror, The. 1969, *C* 90 min. *Mus* Les Baxter. *Pro* James H. Nicholson, Samuel Z. Arkoff. *Sp* Curtis Lee Hanson, Henry Rosenbaum, Ronald Silkosky. *Dir* Daniel Haller. *Cast:* Sandra Dee, Dean Stockwell, Ed Begley, Sam Jaffe, Lloyd Bochner.

Earth vs. the Spider, The (The Spider). 1958, 73 min. *Mus* Albert Glasser. *Sp* Laszlo Gorog, George Worthington Yates. *Pro-Dir* Bert I. Gordon. *Cast:* Ed Kemmer, June Kenney, Gene Persson, Gene Roth, Sally Fraser.

Empire of the Ants. 1977, C 89 min. *Mus* Dana Kaproff. *Sp* Jack Turley. *Pro-Dir* Bert I. Gordon. *Cast:* Joan Collins, Robert Lansing, John David Carson, Albert Salmi, Jacqueline Scott.

Erik, the Conqueror. 1961, C 81 min. *Mus* Roberto Nicolossi. *Sp* Mario Bava, Oreste Biancoli, Pieru Pierotti. *Dir* Mario Bava. *Cast:* Cameron Mitchell, Giorgio Ardisson, Andrea Checchi, Francoise Christopher, Helen Kessler.

Evictors, The. 1979, C 92 min. *Mus* Jaime Mendoza-Nava. *Pro-Sp-Dir* Charles B. Pierce. *Cast:* Vic Morrow, Michael Parks, Jessica Harper, Sue Anne Langdon, Dennis Femple.

Evil Eye, The. 1962, 92 min. *Mus* Roberto Nicolosi (U.S.) Les Baxter. *Pro* Franco Prosperi. *Sp* Sergio Corbucci, Mino Guerrini, Mario Bava. *Dir* Mario Bava. *Cast:* Leticia Roman, John Saxon, Valentina Cortese, Dante Di Paolo, Robert Buchanan.

Explosion. 1970, C 96 min. *Mus* Sol Kaplan. *Pro* Julian Roffman. *Sp* Alene and Jules Bricken. *Dir* Jules Bricken. *Cast:* Don Stroud, Gordon Thomson, Michele Chicoine, Cecil Linder, Robin Ward.

Eye Creatures, The. 1965, C 80 min. *Pro-Dir* Larry Buchanan. *Cast:* John Ashley, Cynthia Hull, Warren Hammack, Chet Davis.

F.T.A. 1972, C 94 min. *Pro* Francine Parker, Jane Fonda, Donald Sutherland. *Sp* Robin Menken, Michael Alimo, Rita Martinson, Holly Near, Len Chandler, Pamela Donegan, Jane Fonda, Donald Sutherland, Dalton Trumbo. *Dir* Francine Parker.

Fast and the Furious, The. 1954, 65 min. *Mus* Alexander Gerens. *Pro* Roger Corman. *Sp* Jerome Odlum, Jean Howell. *Dir* Edwards Sampson, John Ireland. *Cast:* John Ireland, Dorothy Malone, Bruce Carlisle, Jean Howell, Marshal Brandford.

Fireball 500. 1966, C 91 min. *Mus* Les Baxter. *Pro* James H. Nicholson, Samuel Z. Arkoff. *Sp* William Asher, Leo Townsend. *Dir* William Asher. *Cast:* Frankie Avalon, Annette Funicello, Fabian, Chill Wills, Harvey Lembeck.

Five Guns West. 1955, C 73 min. *Mus* Buddy Bregman. *Sp* R. Wright Campbell. *Pro-Dir* Roger Corman. *Cast:* John Lund, Dorothy Malone, Touch Connors, Paul Birch, James Stone.

Flesh and the Spur. 1956, C 80 min. *Mus* Ronald Stein. *Pro* Alex Gordon. *Sp* Mark Hanna, Charles B. Griffith. *Dir* Edward L. Cahn. *Cast:* John Agar, Marla English, Touch Connors, Maria Monay, Joyce Meadows.

Food of the Gods, The. 1976, C 88 min. *Mus* Elliot Kaplan. *Pro-Sp-Dir* Bert I. Gordon. *Cast:* Marjoe Gortner, Pamela Franklin, Ralph Meeker, Ida Lupino, Jon Cypher.

Force 10 from Navarone. 1979, C 118 min. *Mus* Ron Goodwin. *Pro* Oliver A. Unger. *Sp* Robin Chapman. *Dir* Guy Hamilton. *Cast:* Robert Shaw, Harrison Ford, Edward Fox, Barbara Bach, Franco Nero.

Foxy Brown. 1974, C 94 min. *Mus* Willie Hutch. *Pro* Buzz Feitshans. *Sp-Dir* Jack Hill. *Cast:* Pam Grier, Antonio Fargas, Peter Brown, Terry Carter, Kathryn Loder.

Frankenstein Conquers the World. 1964, C 87 min. *Mus* Akira Ifukube. *Pro* Tomoyuki Tanaka. *Sp* Kaoru Mabuchi. *Dir* Inoshiro Honda. *Cast:* Nick Adams, Tadao Takashima, Kumi Mizuno, Toshio Tsuchiya, Takeshi Shimura.

Free, White and 21. 1964, 102 min. *Mus* Joe Johnson. *Sp* Hal Dwain, Larry Buchanan, Cliff Pope. *Pro-Dir* Larry Buchanan. *Cast:* Frederick O'Neal, Annalena Lund, George Edgely, Johnny Hicks.

Friday Foster. 1975, *C* 89 min. *Mus* Luchi De Jesus. *Sp* Orville H. Hampton. *Pro-Dir* Arthur Marks. *Cast:* Pam Grier, Yaphet Kotto, Godfrey Cambridge, Thalmus Rasulala, Eartha Kitt.

Frogs. 1971, *C* 90 min. *Mus* Les Baxter. *Pro* Peter Thomas, George Edwards. *Sp* Robert Hutchison, Robert Blees. *Dir* George McCowan. *Cast:* Ray Milland, Sam Elliot, Joan Van Ark, Adam Roarke, Judy Pace.

Futureworld. 1975, *C* 104 min. *Pro* Paul N. Lazarus, III, James T. Aubrey Jr. *Sp* Mayo Simon, George Schenchk. *Dir* Richard Heffron. *Cast:* Peter Fonda, Blythe Danner, Arthur Hill, Yul Brynner, Stuart Margolin.

Gamera vs. Monster X. 1970, *C* 83 min. *Mus* Shunsuke Kikuche. *Sp* Fumi Takahashi. *Dir* Noriaki Yuasa. *Cast:* Tsutomu Takakuwa, Kelly Varis, Katherine Murphy, Kon Omura, Junko Yashiro.

Gas-s-s...Or It Became Necessary to Destroy the World in Order to Save It. 1970, *C* 80 min. *Sp* George Armitage. *Pro-Dir* Roger Corman. *Cast:* Robert Gorf, Elaine Giptos, Pat Patterson, George Armitage, Alex Wilson.

Ghost in the Invisible Bikini. 1966, *C* 82 min. *Mus* Les Baxter. *Pro* James H. Nicholson, Samuel Z. Arkoff. *Sp* Louis M. Heyward, Elwood Ullman. *Dir* Don Weis. *Cast:* Tommy Kirk, Deborah Walley, Aron Kincaid, Quinn O'Hara, Jesse White.

Ghost of Dragstrip to Hollow. 1959, 65 min. *Mus* Ronald Stein. *Sp-Pro* Lou Rusoff. *Dir* William Hole Jr. *Cast:* Jody Fair, Martin Braddock, Russ Bender, Paul Blaisdell.

Giant Leeches, The (Attack of the Giant Leeches). 1959, 62 min. *Mus* Alexander Laszlo. *Pro* Gene Corman. *Sp* Leo Gordon. *Dir* Bernard L. Kowalski. *Cast:* Ken Clark, Yvette Vickers, Michael Emmet, Bruno Ve Sota, Jan Shepard.

Girl-Getters, The. 1966, *C* 79 min. *Mus* Stanley Black. *Pro* Kenneth Shipman. *Sp* Peter Draper. *Dir* Michael Winner. *Cast:* Oliver Reed, Jan Morrow, Barbara Ferris, Julia Foster, Harry Andrews.

Glass Sphinx, The. 1968, *C* 91 min. *Mus* Roberto Pregadio (U.S.) Les Baxter. *Pro* Fulvio Lucisano. *Sp* Adalberto Albertino, Camas Gil, Jose A. Cascales (U.S.) Louis M. Heyward, Adriano Bolzoni. *Dir* Luigi Scattini. *Cast:* Robert Taylor, Anita Ekberg, Gianna Serra, Giacomo Rossi-Stuart, Angel Del Pozo.

Glory Stompers, The. 1968, *C* 85 min. *Pro* John Lawrence. *Sp* James Gordon White, John Lawrence. *Dir* Anthony Lanza. *Cast:* Dennis Hopper, Jody McCrea, Chris Noel, Jock Mahoney.

Go Go Mania. 1965, *C* 70 min. *Pro* Harry Field. *Sp* Roger Dunton. *Dir* Frederic Goode. *Cast:* The Beatles, The Animals, Matt Monro, the Nashville Teens, Susan Maughan.

Godzilla vs. the Smog Monster. 1971, *C* 97 min. *Mus* Riichiro Manabe. *Sp* Kaoru Mabuchi, Y. Banno. *Dir* Yoshimitsu Banno. *Cast:* Akira Yamauchi, Toshie Kimura, Hiroshi Koisumi, Emi Ito, Yumi Ito.

Godzilla vs. the Thing. 1964, *C* 94 min. *Mus* Akira Ifkube. *Pro* Tomoyuki Tanaka. *Sp* Shinichi Sekizawa. *Cir* Inoshiro Honda. *Cast:* Akira Takarada, Yuriko Hoshi, Hiroshi Koisumi, Emi Ito, Yumi Ito.

Golden Needles. 1974, *C* 95 min. *Mus* Lalo Schifrin. *Pro* Fred Weintraub, Paul Heller. *Sp* S. Lee Pogostin, Sylvia Schneble. *Dir* Robert Clouse. *Cast:* Joe Don Baker, Elizabeth Ashley, Ann Southern, Burgess Meredith, Jim Kelly.

Goliath and the Dragon. 1960, *C* 90 min. *Mus* (U.S.) Les Baxter. *Pro* Achille Piazzi, Gianni Fuchs. *Pro* Mario Piccolo, Archibald Zounds Jr., *Dir* Vittorio Cottafavi. *Cast:* Mark Forest, Broderick Crawford, Eleanora Ruffo, Gaby Andre, Phillipe Hersent.

Goliath and the Sins of Babylon. 1963, *C* 80 min. *Mus* Francesco De Masi. *Pro* Elio Scardamaglia. *Sp* Roberto Gianviti, Francesco S. Ardamaglia, Lionello de Felice. *Dir* Michele Lupo. *Cast:* Mark Forest, Eleanora Bianchi, Scillas Gabel, John Chevron, Jose Greci.

Goliath and the Vampires. 1961, *C* 92 min. *Mus* Angelo Francesco Lavagnino. *Pro* Paolo Moffa. *Sp* Sergio Corbucci, Duccio Tessari. *Dir* Giacomo Gentilomo, Sergio Corbucci. *Cast:* Gordon Scott, Jacques Sernas, Gianna Maria Canale, Eleanora Ruffo, Annabella Incontrera.

Grayeagle. 1977, *C* 90 min. *Mus* Jaime Mendoza-Nava. *Pro-Sp-Dir* Charles B. Pierce. *Cast:* Ben Johnson, Iron Eyes Cody, Lana Wood, Jack Elam, Paul Fix.

Great Scout and Cathouse Thursday, The. 1974, *C* 102 min. *Mus* John Cameron. *Pro* Jules Buck, David Korda. *Sp* Richard Shapiro. *Dir* Don Taylor. *Cast:* Lee Marvin, Oliver Reed, Robert Culp, Elizabeth Ashley, Kay Lenz.

Great Spy Chase, The. 1966, *C* 84 min. *Mus* Michel Magne. *Sp* Michel Audiard, Albert Simonin. *Pro-Dir* Georges Lautner. *Cast:* Lino Ventura, Bernard Blier, Francis Blanche, Mireille Darc, Charles Millot.

Guns of the Black Witch. 1961, *C* 83 min. *Mus* Michele Cozzoli. *Sp* Luciano Martino, Ugo Guerra. *Pro-Dir* Domencio Paolella. *Cast:* Don Megowan, Emma Danieli, Silvana Pampanini, Livo Lorenzon.

Gunslinger. 1956, *C* 71 min. *Mus* Ronald Stein. *Sp* Charles B. Griffith, Mark Hanna. *Pro-Dir* Roger Corman. *Cast:* John Ireland, Beverly Garland, Allison Hayes, Martin Kingsley, Jonathan Haze.

Hand, The. 1961, 60 min. *Pro* Bill Luckwell. *Sp* Ray Cooney, Tony Hilton. *Dir* Henry Cass. *Cast:* Derek Bond, Ronald Leigh Hunt, Reed De Roven, Ray Cooney, Bryan Coleman.

Hard Ride, The. 1971, *C* 93 min. *Mus* Harley Hatcher. *Pro* Charles Hanawalt. *Sp-Dir* Burt Topper. *Cast:* Robert Fuller, Sherry Bain, Tony Russell.

Haunted Palace (Haunted Village). 1963, *C* 85 min. *Mus* Ronald Stein. *Sp* Charles Beaumont. *Pro-Dir* Roger Corman. *Cast:* Vincent Price, Debra Paget, Lon Chaney Jr. John Dierkes, Leo Gordon.

Headless Ghost, The. 1959, 63 min. *Mus* Gerard Schumann. *Pro* Herman Cohen. *Sp* Kenneth Langtry. *Dir* Peter Scott. *Cast:* Richard Lyon, Lillianne Scottane, David Rose, Clive Revill, Jack Allen.

Heavy Traffic. 1974 *C* 77 min. *Mus* Ray Shanklin. *Pro* Steve Krantz. *Sp-Dir* Ralph Bakshi. *Voices:* Joseph Kaufman, Beverly Hope Atkinson, Frank DeKova, Terri Haven, Mary Dean Lauria.

Helga. 1968, *C* 84 min. *Mus* Kurt Graunke. *Pro* Karl-Ludwig Ruppel (U.S.) *Vers* Salvatore Billitteri. *Sp-Dir* Erich F. Bender (U.S.) Terry Van Tell. *Cast:* Ruth Gassmann, Eberhard Mondry, Asgard Hummell, Ilse Zielstrorff.

Hell's Angels on Wheels. 1967, *C* 95 min. *Mus* Stu Phillips. *Pro* Joe Solomon. *Sp* R. Wright Campbell. *Dir* Richard Rush. *Cast:* Adam Roarke, Jack Nicholson, Sabrina Scharf, Jana Taylor, Joan Garwood.

Hell's Angels '69. 1969, *C* 97 min. *Mus* Tony Bruno. *Pro* Tom Stern. *Sp* Don Tait. *Dir* Lee Madden. *Cast:* Tom Stern, Jeremy Slate, Conny Van Dyke, Steve Sandor, Sonny Barger.

Hell's Belles. 1969, *C* 98 min. *Mus* Les Baxter. *Sp* James Gordon White, R.G. McMullen. *Pro-Dir* Maury Dexter. *Cast:* Jeremy Slate, Adam Roarke, Jocelyn Lane, Angelique Pettyjohn, Michael Waler.

Hell Squad. 1958, 64 min. *Mus* James Richardson. *Pro-Sp-Dir* Burt Topper. *Cast:* Wally Campo, Brandon Carrol, Fred Gavlin, Greg Stuart, Cecil Addis.

Hell Up in Harlem. 1974, *C* 96 min. *Mus* Freddie Perren. *Pro-Sp-Dir* Larry Cohen. *Cast:* Fred Williamson, Julius W. Harris, Gloria Hendry, Margaret Avery, D'Urville Martin.

Hennessy. 1975, *C* 103 min. *Mus* John Scott. *Pro* Peter Snell. *Sp* John Gay. *Dir* Don Sharp. *Cast:* Rod Steiger, Lee Remick, Richard Johnson, Eric Porter, Trevor Howard.

Hercules, Prisoner of Evil. 1964, *C* 80 min. *Pro* Adelpho Ambrosiand. *Dir* Antonio Margheriti. *Cast:* Reg Park, Mireille Granelli, Ettore Manni, Maria Teresa Orsini, Furio Meniconi.

Here Come the Tigers. 1979, *C* 90 min. *Pro-Dir* Sean Cunningham. *Cast:* Richard Lincoln, James Zvanut, Samantha Grey, Manny Lieberman, William Cadwell.

High-Ballin'. 1979, *C* 100 min. *Pro* John Slan. *Sp* Paul Edward. *Dir* Peter Carter. *Cast:* Peter Fonda, Jerry Reed, Helen Shaver, Chris Wiggins, David Ferry.

High School Hellcats. 1958, 68 min. *Pro* Charles "Buddy" Rogers. *Sp* Mark and Jan Lowell. *Dir* Edward Bernds. *Cast:* Yvonne Lime, Brett Halsey, Jana Lund, Suzanne Sidney, Heather Ames.

Horror House. 1969, *C* 92 min. *Mus* Reg Tilsely. *Pro* Tony Tenser. *Sp* Michael Armstrong, Peter. Marcus. *Dir* Michael Armstrong. *Cast:* Frankie Avalon, Jill Haworth, Dennis Price, Mark Wynter, Julian Barnes.

Horrors of the Black Musuem. 1959, *C* 95 min. *Mus* Gerard Schumann. *Pro* Herman Cohen. *Sp* Aben Kandel, Herman Cohen. *Dir* Arthur Crabtree. *Cast:* Michael Gough, June Cunningham, Graham Curnow, Shirley Ann Field, Geoffrey Keen.

Hot Rod Gang. 1958, 72 min. *Mus* Ronald Stein. *Sp-Pro* Lou Rusoff. *Dir* Lew Landers. *Cast:* John Ashley, Jody Fair, Gene Vincent, Steve Drexel, Henry McCann.

Hot Rod Girl. 1956, 75 min. *Pro* Norman Herman. *Sp* John McGreevey. *Dir* Leslie Martinson. *Cast:* Lori Nelson, John Smith, Chuck Connors, Roxanne Arlen, Mark Andrews.

House by the Lake, The. 1977, *C* 89 min. *Pro* Ivan Reitman. *Sp-Dir* William Fruet. *Cast:* Brenda Vaccaro, Don Stroud, Chuck Shamata, Richard Ayres, Kyle Richards.

House of Fright. 1961, *C* 89 min. *Mus* Monty Norman, David Heneker. *Pro* Michael Carreras. *Sp* Wolf Mankowitz. *Dir* Terence Fisher. *Cast:* Paul Massie, Dawn Addams, Christopher Lee, David Kossoff, Francis De Wolff.

House of 1,000 Dolls. 1967, *C* 83 min. *Mus* Charles Camilleri. *Pro* Harry Alan Towers. *Sp* Peter Welbeck, Carman M. Roman. *Dir* Jeremy Summers. *Cast:* Vincent Price, Martha Hyer, George Nader, Anne Smyrner, Wolfgang Kieling.

House of Usher. 1960, *C* 80 min. *Mus* Les Baxter. *Sp* Richard Matheson. *Pro-Dir* Roger Corman. *Cast:* Vincent Price, Mark Damon. Myrna Fahey, Harry Ellerby.

House of Whipcord, The. 1975, *C* 94 min. *Sp* David McGillivray. *Pro-Dir* Pete Walker. *Cast:* Barbara Markham, Patrick Barr, Roy Brooks, Ann Michelle, Penny Irving.

House That Screamed, The. 1969, *C* 104 min. *Mus* Waldo de los Rios. *Pro* Arturo Gonzalez. *Sp* Luis Verna Penafiel. *Dir* Narciso Ibanez Serrador. *Cast:* Lilly Palmer, Cristina Galbo, John Moulder Brown, Mary Maude, Candida Losada.

How to Make a Monster. 1958, *C seq.* 73 min. *Mus* Paul Dunlap. *Pro* Herman Cohen. *Sp* Kenneth Langtry. *Dir* Herbert L. Strock. *Cast:* Robert H. Harris, Paul Brinegar, Gary Conway, Gary Clarke, Walter Reed.

How to Stuff a Wild Bikini. 1965, *C* 90 min. *Mus* Les Baxter. *Pro* James H. Nicholson, Samuel Z. Arkoff. *Sp* William Asher, Leo Townsend. *Dir* William Asher. *Cast:* Annette Funicello, Dwayne Hickman, Brian Donlevy, Harvey Lembeck, Beverly Adams.

I Was a Teenage Frankenstein. 1957, *C seq.* 74 min. *Mus* Paul Dunlap. *Pro* Herman Cohen. *Sp* Kenneth Langry. *Dir* Herbert L. Strock. *Cast:* Whit Bissell, Phyllis Coates, Robert Burton, Gary Conway, George Lynn.

I Was a Teenage Werewolf. 1957, 76 min. *Mus* Paul Dunlap. *Pro* Herman Cohen. *Sp* Ralph Thornton. *Dir* Gene Fowler Jr. *Cast:* Michael Landon, Yvonne Lime, Whit Bissell, Guy Williams, Robert Griffiin.

In the Year 2889. 1966, *C* 80 min. *Sp* Harold Huffman. *Pro-Dir* Larry Buchanan. *Cast:* Paul Peterson, Quinn O'Hara, Charla Doherty, Neil Fletcher, Billy Thurman.

Incredible Melting Man, The. 1977, *C* 86 min. *Mus* Arlon Ober. *Pro* Samuel W. Gelfman. *Sp-Dir* William Sachs. *Cast:* Alex Rebar, Burr DeBenning, Myron Healey, Michael Alldredge, Ann Sweeny.

Incredible Two-Headed Transplant, The. 1970, *C* 87 min. *Mus* John Barber. *Pro* John Lawrence. *Sp* James Gordon White, John Lawrence. *Dir* Anthony Lanza. *Cast:* Bruce Dern, Pat Priest, Casey Kasem, Berry Kroeger, Albert Cole.

Invasion of the Saucer-Men. 1957, 68 min. *Mus* Ronald Stein. *Pro* James H. Nicholson, Robert Gurney Jr. *Sp* Robert Gurney Jr., Al Martin. *Dir* Edward L. Cahn. *Cast:* Steve Terrell, Gloria Castillo, Frank Gorshin, Raymond Hatton, Lynn Osborn.

Invasion of the Star Creatures. 1962, 81 min. *Mus* Jack Cookerly. *Pro* Berj Hagopian. *Sp* Jonathan Haze. *Dir* Bruno Ve Sota. *Cast:* Bob Ball, Frankie Ray, Gloria Victor, Dolores Reed, Mark Ferris.

Invisible Creature, The. 1960, 70 min. *Mus* John Veale. *Pro-Sp* Maurice J. Wilson. *Dir* Montgomery Tully. *Cast:* Tony Wright, Patricia Dainton, Sandra Dorne, Derek Aylward, Sam Kydd.

Island of Dr. Moreau, The, 1977, *C* 98 min. *Mus* Laurence Rosenthal. *Pro* John Temple-Smith. *Sp* John Herman Shaner, Al Ramrus. *Dir* Don Taylor. *Cast:* Burt Lancaster, Michael York, Nigel Davenport, Barbara Carrera, Richard Basehart.

It Conquered the World. 1956, 71 min. *Mus* Ronald Stein. *Sp* Lou Rusoff. *Pro-Dir* Roger Corman. *Cast:* Peter Graves, Beverly Garland, Lee Van Cleef, Sally Fraser, Charles Griffith.

J.D.'s Revenge. 1974, *C* 95 min. *Mus* Robert Prince. *Sp* Jaison Starkes. *Pro-Dir* Arthur Marks. *Cast:* Glynn Turman, Lou Gossett, Joan Pringle, Carl Crudup, James Louis Watkins.

Jaguar Lives. 1979, *C* 100 min. *Mus* Robert O. Ragland. *Pro* Derek Gibson. *Sp* Yabo Yablonsky. *Dir* Ernest Pintoff. *Cast:* Joe Lewis, Christopher Lee, Donald Pleasance, Barbara Bach, Capucine.

Jailbreakers. 1959, 65 min. *Mus* Andre Brummer. *Pro-Sp-Dir* Alexander Grasshoff. *Cast:* Robert Hutton, Mary Castle, Michael O'Connell, Gabe Delutri, Anton Van Stralen.

Jennifer. 1978, *C* 90 min. *Pro* Steve Krantz. *Sp* Kay Cousins Johnson. *Dir* Brice Mack. *Cast:* Lisa Pelikan, Bert Convy, Nina Foch, Amy Johnston, John Gavin.

Jet Attack. 1958, 68 min. *Mus* Ronald Stein. *Pro* Alex Gordon. *Sp* Lou Rusoff. *Dir* Edward L. Cahn. *Cast:* John Agar, Audrey Totter, Gregory Walcott, James Dobson, Leonard Strong.

Journey to the Seventh Planet. 1961, *C* 83 min. *Mus* Ib Glindemann. *Sp* Ib Melchior, Sid Pink. *Pro-Dir* Sid Pink. *Cast:* John Agar, Greta Thyssen, Ann Smyrner, Mimi Heinrich, Carl Ottosen.

Joyride. 1977, *C* 92 min. *Mus* Jimmie Haskell. *Pro* Bruce Cohn Curtis. *Sp-Dir* Joseph Rubin. *Cast:* Desi Arnez Jr., Robert Carradine, Melanie Griffith, Anne Lockhart, Tom Ligon.

Julius Caesar. 1971, *C* 117 min. *Mus* Michael Lewis. *Pro* Peter Snell. *Sp* Robert Furnival. *Dir* Stuart Burge. *Cast:* Charlton Heston, Jason Robards, John Gielgud, Richard Johnson, Robert Vaughn.

Kidnapped. 1971, *C* 107 min. *Mus* Roy Budd. *Pro* Frederick H. Brogger. *Sp* Jack Pulman. *Dir* Delbert Mann. *Cast:* Michael Caine, Trevor Howard, Jack Hawkins, Donald Pleasance, Lawrence Douglas.

Killer Force, The (The Diamond Mercenaries). 1975, *C* 100 min. *Mus* George Garvaventz. *Pro* Nat and Patrick Wachsberger. *Dir* Val Guest. *Cast:* Telly Savalas, Peter Fonda, Hugh O'Brian, O.J. Simpson, Maud Adams.

Killers Three. 1969, *C* 88 min. *Mus* Mike Curb, Harley Hatcher, Jerry Styner. *Pro* Dick Clark. *Sp* Michael Fisher. *Dir* Bruce Kessler. *Cast:* Robert Walker, Diane Varsi, Dick Clark, Norman Alden, Maureen Arthur.

Konga. 1960, *C* 90 min. *Mus* Gerard Schumann. *Pro* Herman Cohen. *Sp* Aben Kandel, Herman Cohen. *Dir* John Lemont. *Cast:* Michael Gough, Margo Johns, Jess Conrad, Claire Gordon, Austin Trevor.

Land that Time Forgot, The. 1975, *C* 90 min. *Mus* Douglas Gamley. *Pro* John Dark. *Sp* James Cawthorn, Michael Moorcock. *Dir* Kevin Connor. *Cast:* Doug McClure, John McEnery, Susan Penhaligon, Keith Baron, Anthony Ainly.

Last Man on Earth, The. 1963, 86 min. *Mus* Paul Sawtell, Bert Shefter. *Pro* Robert L. Lippert. *Sp* Logan Swanson, William P. Leicester. *Dir* Sidney Salkow. *Cast:* Vincent Price, Franca Bettoia, Emma Danieli, Giacomo Rossi-Stuart, Umberto Rau.

Last Survivor, The, 1969, *C* 88 min. *Pro* Giorgio Carlo Rossi. *Sp* Tito Cardi Giafranco Clerici, Renzo Genta. *Dir* Ruggero Deodato. *Cast:* Massimo Foschi, Me-Me Lai, Ivan Rassimow, Sheik Renal Shker, Judy Rosly.

Little Cigars. 1974, *C* 92 min. *Pro* Albert Band. *Sp* Louis Garfinkle, Frank Ray Perilli. *Dir* Chris Christenberry. *Cast:* Angela Tompkins, Billy Curtis, Jerry Maren, Frank Delfino, Emory Souza.

Little Girl Who Lives Down the Lane, The. 1977, *C* 94 min. *Mus* Christian Gaubert. *Pro* Zev Braun. *Sp* Laird Koenig. *Dir* Nicolas Gessner. *Cast:* Jodie Foster, Martin Sheen, Alexis Smith, Mort Shuman, Scott Jacoby.

Live a Little, Steal a Lot (Murph the Surf). 1975, *C* 101 min. *Mus* Philip Lambro. *Pro* J. Skeet Wilson, Chuck Courtney. *Sp* E. Arthur Kean. *Dir* Marvin Chomsky. *Cast:* Robert Conrad, Don Stroud, Donna Mills, Robyn Millan, Luther Adler.

Lizard in a Woman's Skin. 1974, C 96 min. *Mus* Ennio Morricone. *Dir* Lucio Fulci. *Cast:* Florina Bolkan, Stanley Baker, Jean Sorel, Alberto De Mondoza, Leo Genn.

Lola. 1974, C 88 min. *Pro* Clive Sharp. *Dir* Richard Donner. *Cast:* Charles Bronson, Susan George, Trevor Howard, Honor Blackman, Michael Rigg.

Love at First Bite (Dracula Sucks Again). 1979, C 93 min. *Mus* Charles Bernstein. *Pro* Joel Freeman. *Sp* Robert Kaufman. *Dir* Stan Dragoti. *Cast:* George Hamilton, Susan Saint James, Richard Benjamin, Dick Shawn, Arte Johnson.

Lost Battalion. 1961, 83 min. *Sp* Cesar Amigo, Eddie Romero. *Pro-Dir* Eddie Romero. *Cast:* Leopold Salcedo, Diane Jergens, Johnny Monteiro, Jennings Sturgeon, Bruce Baxter.

Lost World of Sinbad, The (Samurai Pirate). 1963, C 94 min. *Mus* Masura Sato. *Pro* Yuko Tanaka. *Sp* Takeshi Kimura. *Dir* Senkichi Taniguchi. *Cast:* Toshiro Mifune, Makoto Satoh, Jun Fanado, Ichiro Arishima.

Machine Gun Kelly. 1958, 84 min. *Mus* Gerald Fried. *Sp* R. Wright Campbell. *Pro-Dir* Roger Corman. *Cast:* Charles Bronson, Susan Cabot, Morey Amsterdam, Jack Lambert, Wally Campo.

Macon County Line. 1974, C 89 min. *Mus* Stu Phillips. *Pro* Max Baer. *Sp* Max Baer. Richard Compton, *Dir* Richard Compton. *Cast:* Alan Vint, Cheryl Waters, Max Baer, Geoffrey Lewis, Joan Blackman.

Madhouse. 1973, C 89 min. *Mus* Douglas Gamley. *Pro* Max J. Rosenberg, Milton Subotsky. *Sp* Greg Morrison. *Dir* James Clark. *Cast:* Vincent Price, Robert Quarry, Peter Cushing, Natasha Pyne, Adrienne Corri.

Mad Max. 1980, C 93 min. *Mus* Brian May. *Pro* Byron Kennedy. *Sp* James McCausland. *Dir* George Miller. *Cast:* Mel Gibson, Joanne Samuel, Hugh Heays-Byrne, Steve Bisley, Tim Burns.

Manson. 1976, C 83 min. *Sp* Joan Huntington. *Pro-Dir* Laurence Merrick. *Cast:* Charles Manson, Vincent Bugliosi, Patricia Krenwinkle, Leslie Van Houten, Tex Watson.

Marco Polo. 1962, C 95 min. *Mus* Les Baxter. *Pro* Ermanno Donati, Luigi Carpentier. *Sp* Oreste Biancoli, Duccio Tessari, Piero Pierotti, Antoinette Pellevant. *Dir* Hugo Fregonese. *Cast:* Rory Calhoun, Yoko Tani, Robert Hunder, Camillo Pilotto, Pierre Cressov.

Mars Needs Women. 1966, C 80 min. *Pro-Sp-Dir* Larry Buchanon. *Cast:* Tommy Kirk, Yvonne Craig, Byron Lord, Roger Ready, Warren Hammack.

Maryjane. 1968, C 95 min. *Mus* Mike Curb. *Sp* Richard Gautier, Peter J. Marshall. *Pro-Dir* Maury Dexter. *Cast:* Fabian, Diane McBain, Kevin Coughlin, Michael Margotta, Patty McCormack.

Masque of the Red Death, The. 1964, C 89 min. *Mus* David Lee. *Pro* George Willoughby. *Sp* Charles Beaumont, R. Wright Campbell. *Dir* Roger Corman. *Cast:* Vincent Price, Hazel Court, Jane Asher, David Weston, Patrick Magee.

Master of the World. 1961, C 104 min. *Mus* Les Baxter. *Pro* James H. Nicholson. *Sp* Richard Matheson. *Dir* William Witney. *Cast:* Vincent Price, Charles Bronson, Henry Hull, Mary Webster. David Frankham.

Matilda. 1978, C 105 min. *Pro* Timothy Galfas, Albert S. Ruddy. *Sp* Timothy Galfas. *Dir* Daniel Mann. *Cast:* Elliot Gould, Robert Mithcum, Harry Guardino, Clive Revill, Karen Carlson.

Matter of Time, A. 1977, *C* 97 min. *Mus* Nino Oliviero. *Pro* Jack H. Skirball, J. Edmund Grainger. *Sp* John Gay. *Dir* Vincent Minnelli. *Cast:* Liza Minnelli, Ingrid Bergman, Charles Boyer, Shiros Andros, Tina Aumont.

McCullochs, The. 1975, *C* 93 min. *Mus* Ernest Gold. *Pro-Sp-Dir* Max Baer. *Cast:* Forrest Tucker, Max Baer, Julie Adams, Janice Heiden, Dennis Redfield.

Mean Dog Blues. 1979, *C* 108 min. *Pro* Charles A. Pratt, George Lefferts. *Sp* George Lefferts. *Dir* Mel Stuart. *Cast:* George Kennedy, Kay Lenz, Scatman Crothers, Tina Louise, Felton Perry.

Meteor. 1979, *C* 107 min. *Mus* Laurence Rosenthal. *Pro* Arnold Orgolini, Theodore Paruin. *Sp* Stanley Mann, Edmund H. North. *Dir* Ronald Neame. *Cast:* Sean Connery, Natalie Wood, Brian Keith, Martin Landau, Trevor Howard.

Michael and Helga. 1969, *C* 87 min. *Mus* Karl Barthel. *Pro* Roland Cammerer. *Sp-Dir* Erich F. Bender. *Cast:* Ruth Gassmann, Felix Franchy, Hildegard Linden, Elfi Rueter, Christian Margulies.

Million Eyes of Su-Muru. 1967, *C* 95 min. *Mus* Johnny Scott. *Pro* Harry Alan Towers. *Sp* Kevin Kavanaugh. *Dir* Lindsay Shonteff. *Cast:* Frankie Avalon, George Nader, Shirley Eaton, Wilfred Hyde-White, Klaus Kinski.

Mind Benders, The. 1963, 113 min. *Mus* Georges Auric. *Pro* Michael Relph. *Sp* James Kennaway. *Dir* Basil Dearden. *Cast:* Dirk Bogarde, Mary Ure, John Clements, Michael Bryant, Wendy Craig.

Mini-Shirt Mob. 1968, *C* 82 min. *Mus* Les Baxter. *Sp* James Gordon White. *Pro-Dir* Maury Dexter. *Cast:* Jeremy Slate, Diane McBain, Sherry Jackson, Patty McCormack, Ross Hagen.

Monkey Hustle, The. 1974, *C* 90 min. *Mus* Jack Conrad. *Sp* Charles Johnson. *Pro-Dir* Arthur Marx. *Cast:* Yaphet Kotto, Rudy Ray Moore, Rosalind Cash, Randy Brooks, Debbi Morgan.

Monster from a Prehistoric Planet. 1967, *C* 90 min. *Mus* Seitaro Omori. *Pro* Hideo Koi. *Sp* Iawao Yamazak. *Dir* Haruyasu Noguchi. *Cast:* Tamio Kawaji, Yoko Yamaoto, Tatsuya Fugi, Koji Wada, Yuji Odaka.

Motorcycle Gang. 1957, 78 min. *Mus* Albert Glasser. *Pro* Alex Gordon. *Sp* Lou Rusoff. *Dir* Edward l. Cahn. *Cast:* Anne Neyland, Steve Terrell, John Ashley, Carl Switzer, Raymond Hatton.

Murders in the Rue Morgue. 1971, *C* 87 min. *Pro* Louis M. Heyward. *Sp* Christopher Wicking, Henry Selsar. *Dir* Gordon Hessler. *Cast:* Jason Robards, Christine Kaufmann, Herbert Lom, Adolfo Celi, Michael Dunn.

Muscle Beach Party. 1964, *C* 94 min. *Mus* Les Baxter. *Pro* James H. Nicholson, Samuel Z. Arkoff. *Sp* William Asher, Robert Dillon. *Dir* William Asher. *Cast:* Frankie Avalon, Annette Funicello, Morey Amsterdam, Buddy Hackett, Luciana Paluzzi.

Naked Africa. 1957, *C* 71 min. *Photographed by Ray Phoenix. Pro-Dir* Cedric Worth. Narrator Quentin Reynolds.

Naked Paradise. 1956, *C* 68 min. *Mus* Ronald Stein. *Sp* Charles B. Griffith, Mark Hanna. *Pro-Dir* Roger Corman. *Cast:* Richard Denning, Beverly Garland, Lisa Montell, Leslie Bradley, Richard Miller.

Navajo Run. 1966, 83 min. *Mus* William Loose. *Sp* Jo Heims. *Pro-Dir* Johnny Seven. *Cast:* Johnny Seven, Warren Kemmerling, Virginia Vincent, Ron Soble.

Night of the Blood Beast. 1958, 65 min. *Mus* Alexander Laszlo. *Pro* Gene Corman. *Sp* Martin Varno. *Dir* Bernard Kowalski. *Cast:* Michael Emmet, Angela Greene, John Baer, Ed Nelson, Tyler McVey.

Night of the Blood Monster. 1970, *C* 96 min. *Mus* Bruno Nicolai. *Pro* Harry Alan Towers, Anthony Scott Veitch. *Sp* Jesus Franco, E. Colombo. *Dir* Jesus Franco. *Cast:* Christopher Lee, Maria Schell, Leo Genn, Maria Rohm, Margaret Lee.

Night Tide. 1961, 84 min. *Mus* David Raskin. *Pro* Aram Kantarian. *Sp-Dir* Curtis Harrington. *Cast:* Dennis Hopper, Linda Lawson, Gavin Muir, Luana Anders, Marjorie Eaton.

Nine Lives of Fritz the Cat, The. 1974, *C* 76 min. *Pro* Steve Krantz. *Sp* Robert Taylor, Fred Halliday, Eric Monte. *Dir* Robert Taylor. *Voices:* Skip Hinnant, Reva Rose, Bob Holt, Robert Ridgley, Fred Smoot.

Norseman, The. 1979, *C* 90 min. *Pro-Sp-Dir* Charles B. Pierce. *Cast:* Lee Majors, Cornel Wilde, Mel Ferrer, Jack Elam, Chris Connelly.

Nothing Personal. 1980, 97 min. *Pro* David M. Perlmutter. *Sp* Robert Kaufman. *Dir* George Bloomfield. *Cast:* Donald Sutherland, Suzanne Sommers, Lawrence Dane, Roscoe Lee Brown, Dabney Coleman.

Oblong Box, The. 1969, *C* 91 min. *Mus* Harry Robinson. *Sp* Lawrence Huntington, Christopher Wicking. *Pro-Dir* Gordon Hessler. *Cast:* Vincent Price, Christopher Lee, Alastair Williamson, Hilary Dwyer, Peter Arne.

Oklahoma Woman. 1955, 73 min. *Mus* Ronald Stein. *Sp* Lou Rusoff. *Pro-Dir* Roger Corman. *Cast:* Richard Denning, Peggie Castle, Cathy Downs, Tudor Owen, Martin Kingsley.

Old Dracula. 1974, *C* 89 min. *Mus* David Whitaker. *Pro* Jack H. Wiener. *Sp* Jeremy Lloyd. *Dir* Clive Donner. *Cast:* David Niven, Teresa Graves, Jennie Linden, Nicky Henson, Peter Bayliss.

1,000 Convicts and a Woman. 1971, *C* 94 min. *Mus* Peter J. Elliot. *Pro* Philip N. Krasne. *SP* Oscar Brodney. *Dir* Ray Austin. *Cast:* Alexandra Hay, Sandor Eles, Harry Baird.

Operation Bikini (The Seafighters). 1963, *C seq.* 84 min. *Mus* Les Baxter. *Pro* James H. Nicholson, Lou Rusoff. *Sp* John Tomerlin. *Dir* Anthony Carras. *Cast:* Tab Hunter, Frankie Avalon, Scott Brady, Jim Backus, Eva Six.

Operation Camel. 1961, 74 min. *Mus* Ib Glindemann. *Pro* Henrik Sanberg. *Sp* Bob Ramsing. *Dir* Sven Methling. *Cast:* Nora Hayden, Louis Renard, Paul Hagen, Ebbe Langberg, Preben Kaas.

Operation Dames. 1959, 74 min. *Mus* Richard Markowitz. *Pro* Stanley Kallis. *Sp* Ed Lakso. *Dir* Louis Clyde Stoumen. *Cast:* Eve Meyer. Chuck Henderson, Don Devlin, Ed Craig, Cindy Girard.

Operation Malaya. 1955, 65 min. *Photography* Geoffrey Faithful, Arthur Graham. *Sp* John Croydon, David MacDonald. *Pro* John Croydon, Peter Crane. *Dir* David MacDonald. *Narrated:* John Humphry, Winford Vaughn, Thomas John Slater, Chips Rafferty.

Operation Snafu (On the Fiddle, Operation Warhead). 1961, 97 min. *Dir* Cyril Frankel. *Cast:* Sean Connery, Alfred Lynch, Cecil Parker, Stanley Holloway, Alan King.

Our Winning Season. 1978, *C* 92 min. *Mus* Charles Fox. *Pro* Joe Roth. *Sp* Nick Niciphor. *Dir* Joseph Ruben. *Cast:* Scott Jacoby, Deborah Benson, Dennis Quaid, Randy Herman, Joe Penny.

Pacific Vibrations. 1971, *C* 92 min. *Mus* Paul Bever, Bernie Krause, Sky Oats, Leo Kottke, Wolfgang, Little Walter, Colorado Purple Gang, Steve Miller,

Hard Meat, Cream, Ashish Khan, Pranesh Khan, Zakir Hussain, Darby and
Tarlton, Ry Cooder. *Pro-Sp-Dir* John Severson. *Cast:* Jock Sutherland, Rolf
Aurness, Corky Carroll, Tom Stone, Mike Tabeling.

Pajama Party. 1964, C 85 min. *Mus* Les Baxter. *Pro* James H. Nicholson,
Samuel Z. Arkoff. *Sp* Louis M. Heyward. *Dir* Don Weis. *Cast:* Tommy Kirk,
Annette Funicello, Elsa Lanchester, Harvey Lembeck, Jesse White.

Panic in Year Zero. 1962, 92 min. *Mus* Les Baxter. *Pro* Arnold Hough-
land, Lou Rusoff. *Sp* Jay Simms, John Morton. *Dir* Ray Milland. *Cast:* Ray
Milland, Jean Hagen, Frankie Avalon, Mary Mitchell, Joan Freeman.

Paratroop Command. 1958, 83 min. *Mus* Ronald Stein. *Pro* Stan Shpetner.
Dir William Witney. *Cast:* Richard Bakalyan, Ken Lynch, Jack Hogan, Jimmy
Murphy, Jeff Morris.

Part 2 Walking Tall. 1975, C 109 min. *Mus* Walter Scharf. *Pro* Charles A.
Pratt. *Sp* Howard B. Kreitsek. *Dir* Earl Bellamy. *Cast:* Bo Svenson, Luke Askew,
Noah Berry, John Chandler, Robert Dogui.

People That Time Forgot, The. 1977, C 90 min. *Mus* John Scott. *Pro* John
Dark. *Sp* Patrick Tilley. *Dir* Kevin Connor. *Cast:* Patrick Wayne, Doug McClure,
Sarah Douglas, Dana Gillespie, Thorley Walters.

Phantom from 10,000 Leagues. 1956, 81 min. *Mus* Ronald Stein. *Pro* Jack
and Dan Milner. *Sp* Lou Rusoff. *Dir* Dan Milner. *Cast:* Kent Taylor, Cathy
Downs, Michael Whalen, Rodney Bell, Helene Stanton.

Phantom Planet, The. 1961, 82 min. *Mus* Hayes Pagel. *Pro* Fred Gebhardt.
Sp William Teleak, Fred De Gorter, Fred Gebhardt. *Dir* William Marshall. *Cast:*
Dean Fredericks, Coleen Gray, Dolores Faith, Anthony Dexter, Francis X. Bush-
man.

Pickup on 101. 1972, C 93 min. *Mus* Stu Phillips. *Pro* Christian Whittaker, Ed Garner. *Sp* Anthony Blake. *Dir* John Florea. *Cast:* Jack Albertson,
Lesley Warren, Martin Sheen, Michael Ontakean. Hal Baylor.

Pit and the Pendulum, The. 1961, C 85 min. *Mus* Les Baxter. *Sp* Richard
Matheson. *Pro-Dir* Roger Corman. *Cast:* Vincent Price, John Kerr, Barbara
Steele, Luana Anders, Antony Carbone.

Planet of the Vampires. 1965, C 86 min. *Mus* Gino Marinuzzi. *Pro* Fulvio
Lucisano. *Sp* Castillo Cosulich, Antonio Roman, Alberto Bevilacqua, Mario
Bava, Rafael J. Salvia. (English language version: Ib Melchior, Lewis M. Hey-
ward). *Dir* Mario Vava. *Cast:* Barry Sullivan, Norma Bengell, Angel Aranda, Evi
Morandi, Marlo Marales.

Premature Burial, The. 1961, C 81 min. *Mus* Ronald Stein. *Sp* Charles
Beaumont, Ray Russell. *Pro-Dir* Roger Corman. *Cast:* Ray Milland, Hazel Court,
Richard Ney, Heather Angel, Alan Napier.

Prison Girls. 1973, (C-3D) 84 min. *Mus* Christopher Huston. *Pro* Nicholas
J. Grippo, Burton C. Gerschfield. *Sp* Lee Walters. *Dir* Thomas De Simone. *Cast:*
Robin Whitting, Angie Monet, Tracy Handfuss, Maria Arnold, Liz Wolfe.

Prisoner in the Iron Mask. 1962, C 80 min. *Mus* Carlo Innocenzi. *Pro*
Francesco Thellung. *Sp* Silvio Amadio, Ruggero Jacobbi, Francesco De Feo. *Dir*
Francesco De Feo (U.S.) Lee Kresel. *Cast:* Michael Lemoine, Wandisa Guida,
Andrea Bosic, Jany Clair, Giovanni Materassi.

Private Files of J. Edgar Hoover. 1979, C 112 min. *Mus* Miklos Rozsa. *Pro-
Sp-Dir* Larry Cohen. *Cast:* Broderick Crawford, Jose Ferrer, Michael Parks,
Ronee Blakley, Celeste Holm.

Psych-Out. 1968, *C* 101 min. *Mus* Ronald Stein. *Pro* Dick Clark. *Sp* E. Hunter Willett, Betty Ulius. *Dir* Richard Rush. *Cast:* Susan Strasberg, Dean Stockwell, Jack Nicholson, Bruce Dern.

Pyro. 1964, *C* 99 min. *Mus* Jose Sola. *Pro* Sidney W. Pink, Richard C. Meyer. *Sp* Luis de los Arcos, Sidney W. Pink. *Dir* Julio Coll. *Cast:* Barry Sullivan, Martha Hyer, Sherry Moreland, Soledad Miranda, Luis Prendes.

Queen of Blood (Planet of Blood). 1966, *C* 81 min. *Mus* Leonard Morand. *Pro* George Edwards. *Sp-Dir* Curtis Harrington. *Cast:* John Saxon, Basil Rathbone, Judi Meredith, Dennis Hopper, Florence Marly.

Raven, The. 1962, *C* 86 min. *Mus* Les Baxter. *Sp* Richard Matheson. *Pro-Dir* Roger Corman. *Cast:* Vincent Price, Peter Lorre, Boris Karloff, Hazel Court, Jack Nicholson.

Raw Meat. 1974, *C* 88 min. *Mus* Jeremy Rose, Wil Malone. *Pro* Paul Maslansky. *Sp* Ceri Jones. *Dir* Gary Sherman. *Cast:* Donald Pleasance, Norman Rossington, Christopher Lee, David Ladd, Sharon Gurney.

Record City. 1979, *C* 90 min. *Mus* Freddie Perren. *Pro* James T. Aubray, Joe Burne. *Sp* Ron Friedman. *Dir* Dennis Steinmetz. *Cast:* Leonard Barr, Ed Begley Jr., Sorrell Booke, Dennis Bowen, Ruth Buzzi.

Reform School Girl. 1957, 71 min. *Mus* Ronald Stein. *Pro* Robert J. Gurney, Samuel Z. Arkoff. *Sp-Dir* Edward Bernds. *Cast:* Gloria Castillo, Ross Ford, Edward Byrnes, Ralph Reed, Jan Englund.

Reincarnation of Peter Proud, The. 1975, *C* 104 min. *Mus* Jerry Goldsmith. *Pro* Frank P. Rosenberg. *Sp* Max Ehrlich. *Dir* J. Lee Thompson. *Cast:* Michael Sarrazin, Jennifer O'Neill, Margot Kidder, Cornelia Sharpe, Paul Hecht.

Reptilicus. 1962, *C* 90 min. *Mus* Sven Gyldmark. *Sp* Ib Melchior, Sidney Pink. *Pro-Dir* Poul Bang, Sidney Pink. *Cast:* Carl Ottosen, Ann Smyrner, Mimi Heinrich, Asjorn Andersen, Marla Behrens.

Return of Count Yorga. 1971, *C* 97 min. *Mus* Bill Marx. *Pro* Michael Macready. *Sp* Bob Kelljan, Yvonne Wilder. *Dir* Bob Kelljan. *Cast:* Robert Quarry, Mariette Hartley, Roger Perry, Yvonne Wilder, Edward Walsh.

Return of the Giant Monsters, The. 1967, *C* 87 min. *Mus* Tadashi Yamaguchi. *Pro* Hidemasa Nagata. *Sp* Fumi Takahashi. *Dir* Noriaki Yuasa. *Cast:* Kojiro Hongo, Kichijiro Ueda, Hisayuki Abe, Reiko Kasahara, Taro Marui.

Return to Macon County. 1975, *C* 90 min. *Mus* Robert O. Ragland. *Pro* Elliot Schick. *Sp-Dir* Richard Compton. *Cast:* Nick Nolte, Don Johnson, Robin Mattson, Robert Viharo, Eugene Daniels.

Riot on Sunset Strip. 1967, *C* 83 min. *Mus* Karger. *Pro* Sam Katzman. *Sp* Orville H. Hampton. *Dir* Arthur Dreifuss. *Cast:* Aldo Ray, Mimsy Farmer, Michael Evans, Laurie Mock, Tim Rooney.

Road Hustlers, The. 1968, *C* 94 min. *Mus* Michael Colicchio. *Pro* Robert M. Newson. *Sp* Robert Baron. *Dir* Larry E. Jackson. *Cast:* Jim Davis, Scott Brady, Bruce Yarnell, Bob Dix, Victoria Carroll.

Road Racers. 1958, 73 min. *Pro* Stanley Kallis. *Sp* Ed Lakso, Stanley Kallis. *Dir* Arthur Swerdloff. *Cast:* Sally Fraser, Alan Dinehart Jr., Skip Ward, Joel Lawrence, Marian Collier.

Robot vs. the Aztec Mummy, The. 1959, 65 min. *Mus* Antonio Diaz Conde. *Pro* William C. Stell. *Sp* Alfred Salazar. *Dir* Rafael Protillo. *Cast:* Ramon Gay, Rosita Arenas, Crox Alvarado, Luis Acevas Castaneda, Emma Roldan.

Rock Around the World (The Tommy Steele Story). 1957, 71 min. *Pro* Peter Rogers, Herbert Smith. *Dir* Gerard Bryant. *Cast:* Tommy Steele, Nancy Whiskey, Hunter Hancock, The Steelman, Humphrey Lyttleson and His Band.

Rolling Thunder. 1977, C 99 min. *Mus* Barry DeVorzon. *Pro* Norman T. Herman. *Sp* Paul Schrader, Heywood Gould. *Dir* John Flynn. *Cast:* William Devane, Tommy Lee Jones, Linda Haynes, Lisa Richards, Dabney Coleman.

Runaway Daughters. 1956, 90 min. *Mus* Ronald Stein. *Pro* Alex Gordon. *Sp* Lou Rusoff. *Dir* Edward L. Cahn. *Cast:* Marla English, Gloria Castillo, Mary Ellen Kaye, Anna Sten, John Litel.

Saga of the Viking Women and Their Voyage to the Waters of the Great Sea Serpent (Viking Women and the Sea Serpent). 1957, 70 min. *Mus* Albert Glasser. *Sp* Lawrence Louis Goldman. *Pro-Dir* Roger Corman. *Cast:* Abby Dalton, Susan Cabot, Betsy Jones-Moreland, Brad Jackson, Richard Devon.

Samson and the 7 Miracles of the World. 1961, C 95 min. *Mus* Carlo Innocenzi (U.S.) Les Baxter. *Pro* Ermanno Donati, Luigi Carpenter. *Sp* Oreste Biancoli, Duccio Tessari. *Dir* Riccardo Freda. *Cast:* Gordon Scott, Yoko Tani, Dante Di Paolo, Gabriele Antonini, Leonardo Severini.

Samson and the Slave Queen. 1963, C 92 min. *Mus* Francesco Lavagnino. *Pro* Fortunato Misiano. *Sp* Guido Malatesta. *Dir* Ymberto Lenzi. *Cast:* Pierre Brice, Sergio Cianai, Moria Orfei, Marla Grazia Spina, Andrea Aureli.

Samson in the Wax Museum. 1963, 90 min. *Pro* Alberto Lopez. *Sp* Fernando Galiana, Julio Porter. *Dir* Alfonso Corona Blake. *Cast:* Santo, Claudio Brook, Ruben Rojo, Norma Mora, Roxana Bellini.

Samson vs. the Vampire Women. 1961. *Mus* Raul Lavista. *Pro* Luis Garcia DeLeon. *Sp-Dir* Alfonso Corona Blake. *Cast:* Santo, Lorena Valazquez, Jaime Fernandez, Orfelia Montesco, Maria Duval.

Savage Seven. 1968, C 97 min. *Mus* Mike Curb, Jerry Styner. *Pro* Dick Clark. *Sp* Michael Fisher. *Dir* Richard Rush. *Cast:* Robert Walker, Larry Bishop, Joanna Frank, Adam Roarke, John Garwood.

Savage Sisters. 1974, C 89 min. *Pro* John Ashley, Eddie Romero. *Sp* H. Franco Moon, Harry Corner. *Dir* Eddie Romero. *Cast:* Gloria Hendry, Cheri Caffaro, Rosanna Ortiz, John Ashley, Eddie Garcia.

Savage Wild, The. 1970, C 103 min. *Mus* Jaime Mendoza-Nova. *Pro-Sp-Dir* Gordon Eastman. *Cast:* Gordon Eastman, Carl Spore, Maria Eastman, Arlo Curtis, Jim Timiaough.

School for Unclaimed Girls. 1973, C 95 min. *Mus* Bobby Richards. *Pro* Peter Newbrook. *Sp* John Peacock. *Dir* Robert Hartford-Davis. *Cast:* Madeline Hinde, Renee Asherson, Dennis Watterman, Patrick Mower, Faith Brook.

Scorchy. 1974, C 99 min. *Pro-Sp-Dir* Hickmet Avedis. *Cast:* Connie Stevens, Cesare Danova, Marlene Schmidt, William Smith, Normann Burton.

Scream and Scream Again. 1969, C 94 min. *Mus* David Whittaker. *Pro* Max J. Rosenberg, Milton Subotsky. *Sp* Christopher Wicking. *Dir* Gordon Hessler. *Cast:* Vincent Price, Christopher Lee, Peter Cushing, Alfred Marks, Anthony Newlands.

Scream Blacula Scream. 1973, C 95 min. *Mus* Bill Marx. *Pro* Joseph T. Naar. *Sp* Joan Torres, Raymond Koenig, Maurice Jules. *Dir* Bob Kelljan. *Cast:* William Marshall, Pam Grier, Don Mitchell, Michael Conrad, Richard Lawson.

Screaming Skull, The. 1958, 68 min. *Mus* Ernest Gold. *Pro-Sp* John Kneubuhl. *Dir* Alex Nicol. *Cast:* Alex Nicol, Peggy Webber, John Hudson, Russ Conway, Tony Johnson.

Secret Agent Fireball. 1965, C 95 min. *Mus* Carlo Savina. *Pro* Mino Loy, Luciano Martino. *Sp* Sergio Martino. *Dir* Mario Donen. *Cast:* Richard Harrison, Dominque Boschero, Wanda Guida, Alcide Borik, Jim Clay.

Secret of Dorian Gray, The. 1970, C 98 min. *Mus* Peppino De Luca, Carlos Pes. *Pro* Harry Alan Towers. *Sp* Marcello Coascia. *Dir* Massimo Dallamano. *Cast:* Helmut Berger, Richard Todd, Herbert Lom, Marie Lijedahl, Margaret Lee.

Sergeant Deadhead (Sergeant Deadhead, the Astronaut). 1965, C 89 min. *Mus* Les Baxter. *Pro* James H. Nicholson, Samuel Z. Arkoff. *Sp* Louis M. Heyward. *Dir* Norman Taurog. *Cast:* Frankie Avalon, Deborah Walley, Cesar Romero, Fred Clark, Gale Gordon.

Seven. 1979, C 100 min. *Sp* William Driskill, Robert Baird. *Pro-Dir* Andy Sidaris. *Cast:* William Smith, Barbara Leigh, Guich Koock, Art Metrano, Martin Kove.

Shake, Rattle, and Rock. 1956, 74 min. *Pro* James H. Nicholson. *Sp* Lou Rusoff. *Dir* Edward L. Cahn. *Cast:* "Touch" Connors, Lisa Gaye, Sterling Holloway, Fats Domino, Big Joe Turner.

Sheba Baby. 1975, C 90 min. *Mus* Monk Higgins, Alex Brown. *Pro* David Sheldon. *Sp-Dir* William Gurdler. *Cast:* Pam Grier, Austin Stocker, D'Urville Martin, Rudy Challenger, Dick Merrifield.

She-Creature, The. 1956, 77 min. *Mus* Ronald Stein. *Pro* Alex Gordon. *Sp* Lou Rusoff. *Dir* Edward L. Cahn. *Cast:* Chester Morris, Marla English, Tom Conway, Cathy Downs, Lance Fuller.

She Gods of Shark Reef. 1956, C 63 min. *Mus* Ronald Stein. *Pro* Ludwig H. Gerber. *Sp* Robert Hill, Victor Stoloff. *Dir* Roger Corman. *Cast:* Don Durant, Bill Cord, Lisa Montell, Jeanne Gerson, Carol Lundsay.

Shout at the Devil. 1974, C 128 min. *Mus* Maurice Jarre. *Pro* Michael Klinger. *Sp* Wilbur Smith, Alistair Reid. *Dir* Peter Hunt. *Cast:* Lee Marvin, Roger Moore, Barbara Parkins, Rene Killdehoff, Ian Holm.

Sign of the Gladiator. 1959, C 80 min. *Mus* A. Francesco La Vagnino. *Pro* Guido Brignone. *Sp* G. Mangione, G. Brigone. *Dir* Vittorio Musy Glori. *Cast:* Anita Ekberg, George Marshall, Folco Lulli, Chelo Alonso, Jacque Sernas.

Sisters. 1973, C 92 min. *Mus* Bernard Herrmann. *Pro* Edward R. Pressman. *Sp* Brian De Palma, Louisa Rose. *Dir* Brian De Palma. *Cast:* Margot Kidder, Jennifer Salt, Charles Durning, Barnard Hughes, Lisle Wilson.

Slaughter. 1972, C 92 min. *Mus* Luchi De Jesus. *Pro* Monroe Sachson. *Sp* Mark Hanna, Don Williams. *Dir* Jack Starret. *Cast:* Jim Brown, Stella Stevens, Rip Torn, Don Gordon, Cameron Mitchell.

Slaughter's Big Rip-Off. 1974, c 94 min. *Mus* James Brown. *Pro* Monroe Sachson. *Sp* Charles Johnson. *Dir* Gordon Douglas. *Cast:* Jim Brown, Ed McMahon, Brock Peters Don Stroud, Gloria Hendry.

Small Town in Texas, A. 1974, C 95 min. *Mus* Charles Bernstein. *Pro* Joe Solomon. *Sp* William Norton. *Dir* Jack Starret. *Cast:* Timothy Bottoms, Susan George, Bo Hopkins, Art Hindle, John Karlen.

Some of My Best Friends Are... 1971, C 94 min. *Mus* Gordon Rose. *Pro* Marty Richards, John Lauricella. *Sp-Dir* Mervyn Nelson. *Cast:* Tom Bade, Carleton Carpenter, David Baker, Paul Blake, Gary Campbell.

Some People. 1962, C 93 min. *Mus* Ron Grainer. *Pro* James Archibald, *Sp* John Eldridge. *Dir* Clive Donner. *Cast:* Kenneth More, Ray Brooks, Annika Wills, David Andrews, Angela Douglas.

Sorority Girl (Confessions of a Sorority Girl). 1957, 60 min. *Mus* Ronald Stein. *Sp* Ed Walters, Leo Lieberman. *Pro-Dir* Roger Corman. *Cast:* Susan Cabot, Dick Miller, Barboura O'Neill, June Kenney, Barbara Crane.

Space Monster. 1965, *C* 80 min. *Mus* Marlin Skiles. *Pro* Burt Topper. *Sp-Dir* Leonard Katzman. *Cast:* Russ Bender, Francine York, James Brown, Baynes Barron.

Spirits of the Dead. 1967, *C* 123 min. *Mus* Jean Prodromides, Diego Masson, Nino Rota. *Sp* Roger Vadim, Pascal Cousin, Louis Malle, Frederico Fellini, Bernardino Zapponi. *Dir* Roger Vadim, Louis Malle, Frederico Fellini. *Cast:* Jane Fonda. Brigitte Bardot, Peter Fonda, Alain Delon, Terence Stamp.

Spy in Your Eye. 1965, *C* 88 min. *Mus* Riz Ortolani. *Pro* Fulvio Lucisano, Lucio Marcuzzo. *Sp* Romano Ferrea, Adriano Baracco, Adrano Bolzoni, Lucio Marcuzzo. *Dir* Vittorio Sala. *Cast:* Brett Halsey, Pier Angeli, Dana Andrews, Gaston Moschin, Tania Beryl.

Squirm. 1974, *C* 92 min. *Mus* Robert Prince. *Pro* George Manasse. *Sp-Dir* Jeff Lieberman. *Cast:* Don Scardion, Patricia Pearcy, R.A. Dow, Jean Sullivan, Peter MacLean.

Strange Shadows in an Empty Room. 1977, *C* 99 min. *Mus* Armando Trovajoli. *Pro* Admondo Amati. *Sp* Vincent Mann, Frank Clark. *Dir* Martin Herbert. *Cast:* Stuart Whitman, John Saxon, Martin Landau, Tisa Farrow, Carole Laure.

Street People. 1974, *C* 92 min. *Mus* Luis Enriquez. *Sp* Ernest Tidyman, Randall Kleiser. *Dir* Maurice Lucidi. *Cast:* Roger Moore, Stacy Keach, Ivo Garrani, Entore Manni, Ennio Balbo.

Submarine Seahawk. 1958, 83 min. *Mus* Alexander Laszlo. *Pro* Alex Gordon. *Sp* Lou Rusoff, Owen Harris. *Dir* Spencer Gordon Bennett. *Cast:* John Bentley, Brett Halsey, Wayne Heffley, Steve Mitchell, Henry McCann.

Succubus. 1968, *C* 83 min. *Mus* Friedrich Gulda, Jerry Van Rooyen. *Pro* Adrian Hoven. *Sp* Pier A. Caminneci. *Dir* Jesus Franco. *Cast:* Janine Reynaud, Jack Taylor, Howard Vernon, Michel Lemoine, Nathalie Nord.

Suga: Hill. 1974, *C* 90 min. *Mus* Nick Zesses, Dino Ferakis. *Pro* Elliot Schick. *Sp* Tim Kelly. *Dir* Paul Maslansky. *Cast:* Marki Bey, Robert Quarry, Don Pedro Colley, Richard Lawson, Betty Ann Rees.

Suicide Battalion. 1958, 79 min. *Mus* Ronald Stein. *Pro-Sp* Lou Rusoff. *Dir* Edward L. Cahn. *Cast:* Michael Connors, John Ashley, Russ Bender, Jewell Lain, Bing Russell.

Sunday in the Country. 1975, *C.* *Mus* Paul Hoffert. *Pro* David Perlmutter. *Dir* John Trent. *Cast:* Ernest Borgnine, Michael J. Pollard, Hollis McLaren, Louis Carich, Cec Linder.

Sunnyside. 1979, *C* 100 min. *Mus* Alan Douglas, Harold Wheeler. *Pro* Robert L. Schaffel. *Sp* Timothy Galfas, Jeff King. *Dir* Timothy Galfas. *Cast:* Joey Travolta, John Lansing, Stacey Pickren, Andrew Rubin, Michael Tucci.

Swedish Fly Girls (Christa). 1971, *C* 100 min. *Mus* Manfred Mann. *Pro-Sp-Dir* Jack O'Connell. *Cast:* Birte Tove, Clinton Greyn, Baard Ove, Daniel Gelin, Gastone Rosilli.

Swinger's Paradise. 1965, *C* 83 min. *Pro* Kenneth Harper. *Sp* Peter Myers, Ronald Cass. *Dir* Sidney J. Furie. *Cast:* Cliff Richard, Walter Slezak, Susan Hampshire, Hank B. Marvin, Richard O'Sullivan.

Taboos of the World. 1965, *C* 86 min. *Mus* Francesco Lavagnino, Armando Trovajoli. *Pro* Guido Giambartolomei. *Sp* Romolo Marcellini, Ugo Guerra. *Dir* Romolo Marcellini. *Narrator:* Vincent Price.

Tales of Terror. 1961, *C* 90 min. *Mus* Les Baxter. *Sp* Richard Matheson. *Pro-Dir* Roger Corman. *Cast:* Vincent Price, Peter Lorre, Basil Rathbone, Debra Paget, Joyce Jameson.

T.A.M.I. Show, The. 1964, 113 min. *Pro* Lee Savin. *Dir* Steve Binder. *Cast:* The Beach Boys, Chuck Berry, Marvin Gaye, Lesley Gore, The Rolling Stones.

Tank Battalion. 1958, 80 min. *Mus* Dick La Salle. *Pro* Richard Bernstein. *Sp* Richard Bernstein, George W. Waters. *Dir* Sherman A. Rose. *Cast:* Don Kelly, Marjorie Hellen, Edward G. Robinson Jr., Frank Gorshin, Regina Gleason.

Tank Commanos. 1958, 79 min. *Pro-Sp-Dir* Burt Topper. *Cast:* Robert Barron, Maggie Lawrence, Wally Campo, Donato Faretta, Leo V. Metranga.

Tarzan and the Valley of Gold. 1966, *C* 90 min. *Mus* Van Alexander. *Pro* Sy Weintraub. *Sp* Clair Huffaker. *Dir* Robert Day. *Cast:* Mike Henry, Nancy Kovac, David Opatashu, Manuel Padilla Jr., Don Megowan.

Teenage Caveman (Prehistoric World). 1958, 65 min. *Mus* Albert Glasser. *Sp* R. Wright Campbell. *Pro-Dir* roger Corman. *Cast:* Robert Vaughn, Leslie Bradley, Darrah Marshall, Jonathan Haze, Robert Shayne.

Tentacles. 1977, *C* 90 min. *Mus* S.W. Cipriani. *Pro* Enzo Doria. *Sp* Jerome Max, Tito Carpi. *Dir* Oliver Hellman. *Cast:* John Huston, Shelley Winters, Bo Hopkins, Henry Fonda, Cesare Danova.

Terror, The (Lady in the Shadows). 1963, *C* 81 min. *Mus* Ronald Stein. *Sp* Leo Gordon, Jack Hill. *Pro-Dir* Roger Corman. *Cast:* Boris Karloff, Jack Nicholson, Sandra Knight, Dick Miller, Dorothy Neuman.

Terror from the Year 5,000 (The Girl from 5,000 A.D., Cage of Doom). 1958, 74 min. *Pro-Sp-Dir* Robert Gurney Jr. *Cast:* Ward Costello, Joyce Holden, John Stratton, Frederic Downs, Fred Herrick.

They Call Her One Eye. 1974, *C* 89 min. *Pro* Bo A. Vibenius. *Sp-Dir* Alex Fridolinski. *Cast:* Christina Lindberg, Heinz Hopf.

Thing with Two Heads, The. 1982, *C* 90 min. *Mus* Robert O. Ragland. *Pro* Wes Bishop. *Sp* Lee Frost, Wes Bishop, James Gordon White. *Dir* Lee Frost. *Cast:* Ray Milland, Rosey Grier, Don Marshall, Roger Perry, Kathy Baumann.

Those Fantastic Flying Fools (Blast Off). 1967, *C* 101 min. *Mus* Patrick John Scott. *Pro* Harry Alan Towers. *Sp* Dave Freeman. *Dir* Don Sharp. *Cast:* Burl Ives, Troy Donahue, Gert Frobe, Daliah Lavi, Terry-Thomas.

3 in the Attic. 1968, *C* 92 min. *Mus* Chad Stuart. *Sp* Stephen Yafa. *Pro-Dir* Richard Wilson. *Cast:* Yvette Mimieux, Christopher Jones, Judy Pace, Maggie Thrett, Nan Martin.

Thunder Alley. 1967, *C* 90 min. *Pro* Burt Topper. *Sp* Sy Salkowitz. *Dir* Richard Rush. *Cast:* Annette Funicello, Fabian, Diane McBain, Warren Berlinger, Jan Murray.

Time Travellers (Time Trap). 1964, *C* 84 min. *Mus* Richard La Salle. *Pro* William Redlin. *Sp-Dir* Ib Melchior. *Cast:* Preston Foster, Philip Carey, Merry Anders, John Hoyt, Dennis Patrick.

Tomb of Ligeia. 1964, *C* 81 min. *Mus* Kenneth V. Jones. *Pro* Roger Corman, Pat Green. *Sp* Robert Towne. *Dir* Roger Corman. *Cast:* Elizabeth Shepherd, Vincent Price, John Westbrook, Derek Francis, Oliver Johnston.

Torpedo Bay. 1964, 95 min. *Sp* Charles Frend. *Pro-Dir* Bruno Vailati. *Cast:* James Mason, Lilli Palmer, Goeffrey Keen, Andrea Checci, Alberto Lupo.

Town That Dreaded Sundown, The. 1977, *C* 90 min. *Mus* Jaime Mendoza-Nava. *Sp* Earl E. Smith. *Pro-Dir* Charles B. Pierce. *Cast:* Ben Johnson, Andrew Prine, Dawn Wells, Jimmy Clem, Charles B. Pierce.

Trip, The. 1967, *C* 85 min. *Mus* The American String Band. *Sp* Jack Nicholson. *Pro-Dir* Roger Corman. *Cast:* Peter Fonda, Susan Strasberg, Bruce Dern, Dennis Hopper, Salli Sacshe.

Truck Turner. 1974, *C* 91 min. *Mus* Isaac Hayes. *Pro* Fred Weintraub, Paul Heller. *Sp* Oscar Williams. *Dir* Jonathan Kaplan. *Cast:* Isaac Hayes, Yaphet Kotto, Alan Weeks, Annazette Chase, Nichelle Nichols.

Twist All Night (The Continental Twist). 1962, 82 min. *Pro* Maurice Duke. *Sp* Berni Gould. *Dir* William Hole Jr., *Cast:* Louis Prima, June Wilkinson, Sam Butera, The Witnesses, Gertrude Michael.

Two Gentlemen Sharing. 1969, *C* 112 min. *Mus* Stanley Myrers. *Pro* J. Barry Kulick. *Sp* Evan Jones. *Dir* Ted Kotcheff. *Cast:* Robin Phillips, Judy Geeson, Hal Frederick, Esther Anderson, Norman Rossington.

Undead, The. 1956, 71 min. *Mus* Ronald Stein. *Sp* Charles B. Griffith, Mark Hanna. *Pro-Dir* Roger Corman. *Cast:* Pamela Duncan, Richard Garland, Allison Hayes, Val Dofour, Dorothy Neumann.

Under Age. 1964, 90 min. *Pro* Harold Hoffman. *Sp* Larry Buchanan, Harold Hoffman. *Dir* Larry Buchanan. *Cast:* Anne MacAdams, Judy Adler, Roland Royter, George Russell, John Hicks.

Unearthly Stranger. 1963, 74 min. *Mus* Edward Williams. *Pro* Albert Fennell. *Sp* Rex Carlton. *Dir* John Krish. *Cast:* John Neville, Gabriella Lucudi, Philip Stone, Patrick Newell, Jean Marsh.

Unholy Rollers. 1973, *C* 89 min. *Mus* Bobby Hart. *Pro* John Prizer, Jack Bohrer. *Sp* Howard R. Cohen. *Dir* Vernon Zimmerman. *Cast:* Claudia Jennings, Louis Quinn, Betty Ann Rees, Roberta Collins.

Up in the Cellar. 1970 *C* 92 min. *Mus* Don Randi. *Pro* Samuel Z. Arkoff, James H. Nicholson. *Sp-Dir* Theodore J. Flicker. *Cast:* Wes Stern, Joan Collins, Larry Hagman, Judy Pace, David Arkin.

Vampire, The. 1957, 95 min. *Mus* Gustavo C. Carrion. *Pro* Abel Salazar. *Sp* Henrich Rodriguez. Ramon Obon. *Dir* Fernando Mendez. *Cast:* Abel Salazar, Carmen Montejo, German Robles, Jose Luis Jimenez, July Danery.

Vampire Lovers, The. 1970, *C* 91 min. *Mus* Harry Robinson. *Pro* Harry Fine. *Sp* Tudor Gates. *Dir* Roy Ward Baker. *Cast:* Ingrid Pitt, George Cole, Kate O'Mara, Peter Cushing, Dawn Addams.

Vampire's Coffin, The. 1957, 86 min. *Mus* Gustavo C. Carrion. *Pro* Abel Salazar. *Sp* Ramon Obon, Javier Mateos. *Dir* Fernando Mendez. *Cast:* German Robles, Abel Salazar, Ariadne Welter, Yeire Beirute, Alicia Montoya.

Venus in Furs. 1970, *C* 86 min. *Mus* Manfred Mann, Mike Hugg. *Pro* Harry Alan Towers. *Sp* Marvin Wald, Jess Franco, Bruno Leder. *Dir* Jess Franco. *Cast:* James Darren, Barbara McNair, Maria Rohm, Klaus Kinski, Dennis Price.

Voodoo Woman. 1956, 77 min. *Mus* Darrell Calker. *Pro* Alex Gordon. *Sp* Russell Bender, V.I. Voss. *Dir* Edward L. Cahn. *Cast:* Marla English, Tom Conway, "Touch" Connors, Mary Ellen Kaye, Lance Fuller.

Voyage to the End of the Universe. 1963, *C* 81 min. *Mus* Danny List (Zdenek Liska), *Pro* Rudolph Wolf (Rudolph Wohl). *Sp* Jack Pollack (Jindrich Polak), Pavel Juracek. *Dir* Jack Pollack. *Cast:* Dennis Stephans (Zdenek Stepanek), Francis Smolen (Frantisek Smolik), Dana Meredith (Dana Medricka), Irene Kova (Irene Kacirkova), Rodney Lucas (Radovan Lukavsky).

Voyage to the Planet of Prehistoric Women. 1968, *C* 78 min. *Pro* Norman D. Wells. *Sp* Henry Ney. *Dir* Peter Bogdanovich. *Cast:* Mamie Van Doren, Mary Mark, Paige Lee.

Voyage to the Prehistoric Planet. 1965, *C*. *Mus* Ronald Stein. *Pro* George Edwards. *Sp-Dir* John Sebastian. *Cast:* Basil Rathbone, Faith Domergue, Marc Shannon, Christopher Brand, John Bix.

Walking Tall see Part 2 **Walking Tall.**

War Goddess. 1975, *C* 89 min. *Mus* Riz Ortolani. *Pro* Nino Krisman. *Sp* Richard Aubrey. *Dir* Terence Young. *Cast:* Alean Johnston, Sabine Sun, Luciana Paluzzi, Angelo Infanti, Malissa Longo.

War-Gods of the Deep (Warlords of the Deep, City in the Sea). 1965, *C* 84 min. *Mus* Stanley Black. *Pro* Daniel Haller. *Sp* Charles Bennett, Louis M. Heyward. *Dir* Jacques Tourneur. *Cast:* Vincent Price, David Tomlinson, Tab Hunter, Susan Hart, John Le Mesurier.

War Italian Style. 1967, *C* 74 min. *Mus* Piero Umiliani. *Pro* Fulvio Lucisano. *Sp* Franco Castellano. *Dir* Luigi Scattini. *Cast:* Buster Keaton, Franco Franchi, Ciccio Ingrassia, Martha Hyer, Fred Clark.

War of the Colossal Beast. 1958, *C seq.* 68 min. *Mus* Albert Glasser. *Sp* George Worthington Yates. *Pro-Dir* Bert I. Gordon. *Cast:* Sally Fraser, Roger Pace, Dean Parkin, Russ Bender, Charles Stewart.

War of the Zombies (Night Star, the Goddess Electra). 1963, *C* 105 min. *Mus* Roberto Nicolosi. *Sp* Piero Pierotti, Marcello Sartarelli. *Dir* Guiseppe Vari. *Cast:* John Drew Barrymore, Susi Andersen, Ettore Manni, Ida Galli, Phillippe Hersent.

Warriors 5. 1962, 84 min. *Mus* Armando Trovajoli. *Pro* Fulvio Lucisano. *Sp* Gino De Santis, Ugo Pirro, Leopoldo Savana. *Dir* Leopoldo Savona. *Cast:* Jack Palance, Giovanna Ralli, Serge Reggiani, Folco Lulli, Venantino Venantini.

What's Up Tiger Lily? 1966, *C* 80 min. *Mus* The Lovin' Spoonful. *Pro* James H. Nicholson, Samuel Z. Arkoff. *Sp* Woody Allen (Re-edited version of *Key of Keys*) *Dir* Senkichi Tanigzuchi. *Cast:* Tatsuya Mihashi, Mie Hana, Akiko Wakayabayashi, Tadao Nakamaru, Susumu Kurobe.

White Huntress. 1957. *Mus* Philip Green. *Pro* John Croydon, Peter Crane. *Sp* Dermot Quin. *Dir* George Breakston. *Cast:* Susan Stephan, John Bently, Robert Urquhart.

White Slave Ship (The Mutiny). 1962, *C* 103 min. *Mus* Angelo Lavagnino. *Pro* Giorgio Agliani, Rodolphe Solmsen. *Sp* Sandro Contineza. *Dir* Silvio Amadio. *Cast:* Pier Angeli, Edmund Purdom, Ivan Desny, Armand Mestral, Michele Girardon.

Who Slew Auntie Roo? 1971, *C* 91 min. *Mus* Kenneth V. Jones. *Pro* Samuel Z. Arkoff, James H. Nicholson. *Sp* Jimmy Sangster, Robert Blees, Gavin Lambert. *Dir* Curtis Harrington. *Cast:* Shelley Winters, Mark Lester, Ralph Richardson, Judy Cornwell, Michael Gothard.

Why Must I Die? 1960, 86 min. *Mus* Dick LaSalle. *Pro* Richard Bernstein. *Sp* George W. Waters, Richard Bernstein. *Dir* Roy Del Ruth. *Cast:* Terry Moore, Debra Paget, Bert Freed, Julie Reding, Lionel Ames.

Wild Angels, The. 1966, *C* 90 min. *Mus* Mike Curb. *Sp* Charles B. Griffith. *Pro-Dir* Roger Corman. *Cast:* Peter Fonda, Nancy Sinatra, Bruce Dern, Diane Ladd, Lou Procopio.

Wild Pack, The. 1972, *C* 102 min. *Mus* Louis Oliveira. *Pro-Sp-Dir* Hal Barlett. *Cast:* Kent Lane, Tisha Sterling, John Rubinstein, Butch Patrick, Mark de Vries.

Wild Racers, The. 1968, *C* 79 min. *Pro-Sp* Joel Rapp. *Dir* Dan Haller. *Cast:* Fabian, Mimsy Farmer, Judy Cornwall, David Landers.
Wild in the Streets. 1968, *C* 97 min. *Mus* Les Baxter. *Pro* James H. Nicholson, Samuel Z. Arkoff. *Sp* Robert Thom. *Dir* Barry Shear. *Cast:* Shelley Winters, Christopher Jones, Diane Varsi, Hal Holbrook, Millie Perkins.
Wild Party, The. 1976, *C* 90 min. *Mus* Laurence Rosenthal. *Pro* Ishmail Merchant. *Sp* Walter Marks. *Dir* James Ivory. *Cast:* James Coco, Raquel Welch, Perry King, Tiffany Bolling, Royal Dano.
World of the Vampires, The. 1960. *Mus* Gustavo Cesar Carrion. *Pro* Abel Salazar. *Sp* Ramon Obon. *Dir* Alfonso Corona Blake. *Cast:* Mauricio Garces, Silvia Fournier, Erna Martha Bauman, Guillermo Murray, Jose Baviera.
Wrestling Women vs. the Aztec Mummy, The. 1964, 88 min. *Mus* Antonio Conde. *Pro* William C. Stell. *Sp* Alfredo Salazar. *Dir* Rene Cardona. *Cast:* Lorena Velazquez, Armando Silvestre, Elizabeth Campbell, Maria Eugenia San Martin.
Wuthering Heights. 1970, *C* 104 min. *Mus* Michel Legrand. *Pro* Samuel Z. Arkoff, James H. Nicholson. *Sp* Patrick Tilley. *Dir* Robert Fuest. *Cast:* Anna Calder-Marshall, Timothy Dalton, Harry Andrews, Hugh Griffith, Ian Ogilvy.
"X"-The Man with X-Ray Eyes. 1963, *C* 88 min. *Mus* Les Baxter. *Sp* Robert Dillon, Ray Russell. *Pro-Dir* Roger Corman. *Cast:* Ray Milland, Diane Van Der Vlis, John Hoyt, Don Rickles, John Dierkes.
Year of the Cannibals, The. 1971, *C* 95 min. *Mus* Ennio Morricone. *Pro* Enzo Doris. *Sp-Dir* Liliana Cavani. *Cast:* Britt Ekland, Pierre Clementti, Delia Boccardo, Tomas Milian, Francesco Leonetti.
Yog—Monster from Space. 1970, *C* 84 min. *Mus* Akira Ifukube. *Pro* Tomoyuki Tanaka, Fumio Tanaka. *Sp* Ei Ogawa. *Dir* Inoshiro Honda. *Cast:* Akira Kubo, Atsuko Takahashi, Yoshio Tsuchiua, Kenji Sahara, Noritake Saito.
Youngblood. 1978, *C* 92 min. *Mus* War. *Pro* Nick Grillo, Alan Riche. *Sp* Paul Carter Harrison. *Dir* Noel Nosseck. *Cast:* Lawrence-Hilton Jacobs, Bryan O'Dell, Ren Woods, Tony Allen, Vince Cannon, Art Evans.
Young, the Evil, and the Savage, The. 1968, *C* 82 min. *Mus* Carlo Savina. *Pro* Lawrence Woolner, G. De Blasio. *Sp* Frank Bottar, Antonio Margheriti. *Dir* Antonio Margheriti. *Cast:* Michael Rennie, Mark Damon, Eleonora Brown, Sally Smith, Pat Valturri.
Young Racers, The. 1963, *C* 82 min. *Mus* Les Baxter. *Sp* R. Wright Campbell. *Pro-Dir* Roger Corman. *Cast:* Mark Damon, William Campbell, Luana Anders, Robert Campbell, Patrick Magee.
Zontar, the Thing from Venus. 1966, *C* 80 min. *Sp* Larry Buchanon, H. Taylor. *Pro-Dir* Larry Buchanon. *Cast:* John Agar, Susan Bjurman, Anthony Houston, Patricia De Laney, Warren Hammack.

Index

Page numbers in boldface refer to photographs